ETHNICITY, GENDER AND SOCIAL CHANGE

Also by Rohit Barot

RELIGION AND ETHNICITY: Minorities and Social Change in the Metropolis

THE RACISM PROBLEMATIC: Contemporary Sociological Debates on Race and Ethnicity

Also by Harriet Bradley

MEN'S WORK, WOMEN'S WORK

FRACTURED IDENTITIES

GENDER AND POWER IN THE WORKPLACE: Analysing the Impact of Economic Change (*forthcoming*)

Also by Steve Fenton

DURKHEIM AND MODERN SOCIOLOGY

ETHNICITY: Social Structure, Culture, Identity (*forthcoming*)

Ethnicity, Gender and Social Change

Edited by

Rohit Barot
Lecturer in Sociology
Department of Sociology
University of Bristol

Harriet Bradley
Senior Lecturer in Sociology
Department of Sociology
University of Bristol

and

Steve Fenton
Senior Lecturer in Sociology
Department of Sociology
University of Bristol

First published in Great Britain 1999 by
MACMILLAN PRESS LTD
Houndmills, Basingstoke, Hampshire RG21 6XS and London
Companies and representatives throughout the world

A catalogue record for this book is available from the British Library.

ISBN 0–333–71111–4 hardcover
ISBN 0–333–71112–2 paperback

First published in the United States of America 1999 by
ST. MARTIN'S PRESS, INC.,
Scholarly and Reference Division,
175 Fifth Avenue, New York, N.Y. 10010

ISBN 0–312–21763–3

Library of Congress Cataloging-in-Publication Data
Ethnicity, gender, and social change / edited by Rohit Barot, Harriet
Bradley, and Steve Fenton.
p.   cm.
Includes bibliographical references and index.
ISBN 0–312–21763–3 (alk. paper)
1. Minority women—Social conditions.   2. Minority women—Great
Britain—Social conditions.   3. Women immigrants—Social conditions.
4. Women immigrants—Great Britain—Social conditions.
5. Ethnicity.   6. Sex role.   I. Barot, Rohit.   II. Bradley,
Harriet.   III. Fenton, Steve, 1942–   .
HQ1161.E74   1998
305.3—dc21   98–19163
                                                   CIP

This book is printed on paper suitable for recycling and made from fully managed and
sustained forest sources.

10   9   8   7   6   5   4   3   2
08   07   06   05   04   03   02   01

Printed & bound by Antony Rowe Ltd, Eastbourne

Contents

Acknowledgements

On behalf of the Centre for the Study of Minorities and Social Change, Department of Sociology, University of Bristol, we would like to extend our thanks to all the participants and contributors to our biannual conference which, in September 1995, centred on Gender, Ethnicity and Social Change. We would like to extend warmest thanks to those contributors who agreed to offer their papers for publication in this book. Their research on the conference theme provides new insights into the link between gender, ethnicity and social change.

Our Departmental Conference Co-ordinator Cheryl Miller deserves special thanks for her efficient and successful running of our proceedings and for all her help in the preparation of this book. We are also grateful to the University of Bristol Burwalls Hall for Continuing Education for the excellent facilities and support which helped to make the conference a stimulating and enjoyable event. We are also grateful to Katherine Cole for her editorial assistance with the preparation of the manuscript for publication. For their support in production of this volume, we are grateful to Macmillan, our publishers.

Finally, we are grateful to all our colleagues in the Department of Sociology for their continuing support for the activities of the Centre for the Study of Minorities and Social Change.

Rohit Barot, Harriet Bradley and Steve Fenton
Department of Sociology
University of Bristol

Notes on Contributors

Rohit Barot is Lecturer in Sociology at the University of Bristol. He has carried out fieldwork studying the Swaminarayan movement and migrations and group formation among South Asians in Bristol. His most recent publication is *The Racism Problematic: Contemporary Sociological Debates on Race and Ethnicity* (1996).

Kalwant Bhopal is a Research Officer at the Thomas Coram Research Unit (Institute of Education, University of London). Her research interests include 'race'/ethnicity, gender/feminism and the use of different research methodologies. Her book *Gender, 'Race' and Patriarchy: A Study of South Asian Women* was published by Avebury in December 1997.

Hannah Bradby is a researcher at the Medical Research Council, Medical Sociology Unit, at Glasgow University where she studies ethnicity, religion, gender and health. Her publications include 'Health, heating and heart attack: Glaswegian Punjabi women's thinking about everyday food', in *The Cultural Construction of Food*, edited by Pat Caplan, Routledge, 1997, and 'Ethnicity: Not a Black and White Issue', in *Sociology of Health and Illness*, 17 (3), 405–17, 1995.

Harriet Bradley is Senior Lecturer in the Department of Sociology at the University of Bristol. She has written extensively on women's work and has an interest in studying the interaction of gender with class and ethnicity. Her publications include *Fractured Identities*, Polity, 1996, and a forthcoming book about gender and trade unions, *Gender and Power in the Workplace*, Macmillan.

Charlotte Butler is currently completing her PhD at the Centre for Research into Ethnic Relations at Warwick University, looking at the significance of religion, culture and ethnicity in relation to second-generation British Muslims.

John Carter has recently completed his PhD at the University of Bristol and is teaching at the University of the West of England. He has taught sociology at a variety of levels. His research interests include equal opportunities, ethnic relations, the sociology of labour markets and the NHS.

Steve Fenton has researched and published in the general field of ethnicity and health and with specific reference to minorities, culture and mental health. He is currently part of a team engaged on an ESRC-funded project on ethnicity, socio-economic position and health under the Health Variations Programme. He is the author of *Ethnicity: Racism, Modernity, Culture, Structure* for Macmillan. He is Senior Lecturer and Head of Department at the University of Bristol, Department of Sociology.

Shirley Firth was born and educated in India. She had a social work background before turning to the study of Indian religions. She has taught at several universities in England and the United States. Her book, *Dying, Death and Bereavement in a British Hindu Community* (Peeters), is based on her doctoral research at SOAS. Currently she runs seminars and workshops on multicultural aspects of death and bereavement at hospices and on postgraduate nursing courses.

Jayne Ifekwunigwe is a Lecturer in Sociology at the University of East London. She has a joint PhD from the University of California, Berkeley/San Francisco based on her fieldwork in Bristol studying the sense of belonging among children with European mothers and African or African-Caribbean fathers. She has research interests in the African diaspora, 'race', nationalism and identity.

Helen Kanitkar teaches in the Department of Anthropology and Sociology, School of Oriental and African Studies, University of London. Her main research interests are Hindu communities in Britain, the Indo-Anglian novel and juvenile imperialist literature.

Werner Menski is Senior Lecturer at the School of Oriental and African Studies, where he teaches family and constitutional laws of South Asia, a course on ethnic minorities and the law in Britain and immigration law. He has published widely on South Asian laws and on immigration-related issues.

Annie Phizacklea is Professor of Sociology at Leicester University, having formerly lectured at the Universities of Bristol and Warwick. She is the author of numerous articles and books on ethnicity, gender and race relations and is currently working on her book *Gender, Migration and Globalization*.

Vieda Skultans is a Senior Lecturer at the University of Bristol. She has worked on the history of insanity and her publications include *English Madness* and *Madness and Morals*. She has conducted fieldwork in India and Nepal on trance and healing and, most recently, on memory and narrative in Latvia.

Ineke Van Wetering teaches anthropology at the Amsterdam School for Social Science Research, and has published on African Surinamese cultures, on witchcraft, religious movements and migrant women's rituals.

Rethinking Ethnicity and Gender
Rohit Barot, Harriet Bradley and Steve Fenton

One of the most notable recent developments in sociology has been the increased attention to ethnicity and gender as key aspects of social relations. The study of these two dimensions has developed separately, as two distinct sub-disciplines; but in the past ten years there has been an emerging awareness that in concrete social contexts ethnicity and gender are intimately involved. The experience of ethnicity is gendered and gender relations are ethnically distinct. The exploration of exactly *how* ethnicity and gender intersect in particular situations has become a popular topic for new research, especially among younger researchers. It is fitting, then, that in 1995 the Bristol University Centre for the Study of Minorities and Social Change chose for its annual conference the theme of 'ethnicity, gender and social change'.

The chapters in this book, which derive from some of the papers given at the conference, are in the main devoted to presenting some findings from this type of new research, exploring the interplay of ethnicity and gender in very specific social settings and dealing with specific ethnic populations. This reflects our belief that the best sociological insights derive from close and careful empirical study, and that conceptual work must be grounded in such study. However, in this introduction we seek to locate the research findings against a background of broader theoretical and conceptual developments.

The discussion reflects our varied interests and intellectual starting points, as a social anthropologist interested in cultures and ethnicity, a sociologist of gender and a sociologist of ethnic relations. We start with a short sketch of the growing interest in ethnicity as a concept and then consider how best to utilize the concept. Next we consider the coming together of ethnicity and gender as topics of study. How does ethnicity influence gender relations? How is the experience of ethnicity shaped by gender? Finally, we give some brief consideration to the methodological implications of these conceptual developments and conclude with some reflections on processes of change.

THE SHIFT TO ETHNICITY

Over several decades ethnicity has been emerging as a key term in social sciences, superceding the use of tribe and race as important concepts in social anthropology and sociology. As decolonization brought independence to African nations, the anthropological concept of 'tribalism' became unacceptable to the African elites. In colonial anthropology, the word tribe had acquired negative associations of primitive backwardness that applied to simple, pre-literate and technologically less advanced groups in Black Africa. In studying the social structure of African societies, anthropologists turned to the concept of ethnicity which was seen as being more neutral than the word tribe. From the 1950s onwards it became a common anthropological practice to reconceptualize 'tribes' as 'ethnic groups' with distinctive cultures and organization. The period of decolonization in Africa and Asia coincided with two critical junctures of civil rights struggle in the USA: the 1954 Supreme Court decision and the de-segregation process; and the emergence of powerful civil rights and Black Power movements. First integrationist and nationalist Black leaders, then in subsequent decades Chicanos, women and gay people, began to campaign for their cultural and political rights. As these populations and groups organized themselves politically, social scientists began to apply the concept of ethnicity to describe the process of group formation and the use of cultural symbolism as a source of identity for groups and individuals.

In Britain, Abner Cohen's influential 1969 text about the relationship between the Yorubas and Hausas, *Custom and Politics in Urban Africa* became an important focus for the study of what Cohen described as 'political ethnicity'. Cohen not only influenced other anthropologists to research the 'ethnic phenomenon' but also encouraged them to apply the concept of ethnicity to metropolitan situations. He himself undertook a study of the Notting Hill Festival in London, arguing that the festival had come to symbolize Caribbean identity in Britain, and explored the relevance of ethnicity to the culture of British stockbrokers. In the USA, publication of Glazer and Moynihan's *Ethnicity: Theory and Experience* (1975), was one mark of American interest in ethnicity; James Watson's introduction to *Between Two Cultures: Migrants and Minorities in Britain* (1977), took up Glazer and Moynihan's proposition that ethnicity is a more fundamental source of stratification than property-based class relations, a theme that has been developed in subsequent exploration of the relationship between class and ethnicity (Gilroy,

1987). As the use of the term ethnicity and ethnic group gained ground, debates about the very nature of ethnicity began to centre upon the concept of primordialism, and the notion of 'situational' and 'instrumental' ethnicity (for a discussion see Eriksen 1993, Chapter 3). The concept of primordialism had its origins in Shils's (1957) distinction between primordial and civic ties, applied by Geertz in a seminal essay on the newly independent nations of Asia and Africa (Geertz, 1993). While 'primordiality' stressed the given-ness of social ties and identifications, the concepts of 'situational' and 'instrumental' ethnicity stressed the shifting relevance of ethnicity according to social context and the interest base of ethnic identifications. Ethnic groups themselves often present a primordial argument about their existence but a systematic historical examination of the group in question may show that a particular set of economic and political circumstances determine ethnic identities. Roger Ballard's work (1993), provides an excellent example of the processes promoting the crystallization of ethnic identity among the Sikhs in the Punjab.

When Fredrik Barth published *Ethnic Groups and Boundaries: The Social Organization of Cultural Difference* in 1969, theories of stratification and inequality were much more influential and the question of equality and welfare a more common concern than is the case in the 1990s. But the 1990s provided a new impetus to the study of ethnicity, one source being the re-ordering of the political map of Europe. With the end of communism and disintegration of the Soviet Empire, the apparent new interest in religious and linguistic identifications among former Soviet populations (Tishkov, 1997) has led many social scientists and historians to speak of a resurgence of ethnicity in modern politics.

Just as the anthropologists had used tribe and tribalism in Africa to explain the formation of social groups, American and British social scientists had used the now challenged concept of 'race' to explain what came to be known as 'race relations' in the USA and Britain and other English speaking countries such as Australia and New Zealand. A series of UNESCO conferences had questioned the notion of race as a biological entity which could influence the mental and social make up of a population through genetic inheritance (UNESCO, 1975). However, scholars in the USA and the UK continued to use 'race relations' as a formal designation as the British contributions of Michael Banton (1967, 1983) illustrate. Robert Miles developed a comprehensive analysis and criticism of the approach which he termed the 'race relations problematic' (Miles, 1982). His central argument was that race was not a scientific concept and therefore it was a methodological error to treat it as a sociological reality of the same kind as class. What really mattered was not the question of race but racism – an ideology of innate superiority that brought about discrimination, exclusion and marginalizing of particular categories of individuals. In the context of this debate in the 1980s, many scholars chose to talk about racism rather than 'race' which is put into quotation marks to signal its unacceptability as a sociological fact. Fenton speaks of sociology undergoing an 'emancipation from the concept of race' (Fenton, 1996, p. 141). The demise of 'race' as an analytic term does not, of course, mean its disappearance from popular and political discourses and in the USA the term 'race' also retains a central position in academic discourse.

None the less, with the growing use of the term 'ethnicity' both in social anthropology and sociology, social scientists had a choice of using ethnicity and ethnic relations or 'race' and 'race' relations for their field of inquiry. In the UK, one of the earliest organizations concerned with research in race relations was the Institute of Race Relations, a designation that still bears the mark of the earlier history. The Economic and Social Science Research Centre established at Bristol University in 1971 (subsequently transferred to Aston and then to Warwick), was called the Research Unit in Ethnic Relations, later renamed the Centre for Research in Ethnic Relations. To some extent, social scientists and policy makers were making a transition from 'race' to 'ethnicity' and from 'race' relations to ethnic relations – a transition that the contributions to this book reflect.

However, as we indicated above, it was not a simple case of replacement of race by ethnicity. What happened was that ethnicity as a concept began to gain currency in conferences and academic institutions. Courses with the title of Ethnic Relations began to appear at institutions of higher education. One of the issues that sociologists and anthropologists took up was the question of the connection and relationship between race and ethnicity. Influenced by Barth's concept of boundary maintenance, Michael Lyon constructed a scheme to explain the connection between race and ethnicity with reference to boundaries (Lyon, 1973). He argued that race was a boundary of exclusion and ethnicity was a boundary of inclusion. The dominant majority imposed the boundary of exclusion while the minorities created a boundary of inclusion. He illustrated this scheme with two examples. According to him African Caribbeans provided a case of a boundary of exclusion, being denied their rights and full participation in the White society and having been stripped of their original African culture, while he saw Gujaratis as providing a boundary of inclusion, which they created through their own language, religion and aspects of their social organization. The scheme was not without its problems. It assumed that African Caribbeans did not have a culture of their own and implied that British Gujaratis were not subject to a boundary of exclusion. None the less, Lyon's contribution introduced a clear distinction between race and ethnicity of a kind that had not existed hitherto in literature.

Subsequently, a notion of race related to biology and ethnicity related to the question of culture was deployed in the literature. However, these distinctions have not necessarily brought about consistent use of race and ethnicity in the literature in the USA or the UK. Academics, politicians and commentators use ethnicity to mean different things at different times. In addition, race and ethnicity appear conflated, if not confused, in many discussions which are not entirely free from the earlier legacy of writing on race and culture. Most recently, ethnicity has emerged in a parallel fashion to the concept of community in sociological theory as a dynamic term that embodies many different meanings. As Abner Cohen (1974) has argued, ethnicity may best be used as a signal of the relationship between the symbolism of identity and its deployment in political mobilization and the political process.

Moreover, as some contributions to this book show, in the study of any group or category where an attribute of ethnicity is an important dimension, it is unsatisfactory to treat ethnicity purely in its own terms. It is conceptually important that the research examines whatever is 'ethnic' in the context of a wider set of concepts such as class, racism and gender. More recent writing on the topic appears to address itself to such multidimensional concerns. For instance, Anthias and Yuval-Davis go some way towards addressing the question of ethnicity, 'race' and racism in terms of nation, gender, colour and class (1992). Some of the contemporary writing identified as the 'new sociology of ethnicities' (Hall, 1992; Bradley, 1996) tends to focus on a multiplicity of factors and complex dynamics that influence the position of ethnic minority populations in any particular European location.

RECONCEPTUALIZING ETHNICITY

Thus, concern with ethnicity and concern with gender intrude upon sociology in two forms: first, as a set of *specific* concerns (ethnic relations, gender relations) and second as the infusion of *general* sociological understandings (for example, of class, power, inequalities) with a belated awareness of the ways in which all or most social relations have ethnic and gender implications and dimensions. It is difficult empirically and even more difficult theoretically to embrace this whole set of questions simultaneously; yet most sociologists have now become aware that a too exclusive focus on class relations is a way of *not* seeing. In such circumstances, how may we begin to reconceptualize ethnicity and its intersection with gender? We wish here to highlight three trends: the social constructionist approach to ethnicity; the rethinking of the erroneous category of race in terms of a discourse of racism; and the view of ethnicity as operating in specific contexts.

We begin with a recognition of one of the principal developments in the field of ethnicity in the last two decades: the growing awareness that earlier studies of 'ethnic groups' bestowed an undue concreteness on this phrase, implicated not so much in the term 'ethnic' as in the term 'group'. The notion that people belonged to easily identifiable groups and that these groups were properly called ethnic (rather than being 'races') allowed the possibility of a study called ethnic relations, which concerned relations between groups or between individuals of different groups. The existence of groups was itself seen as relatively unproblematic, these being groups differentiated along the lines of ancestry (kin, region, country of origin), shared culture and language.

The shift of emphasis comes in the recognition that the boundaries of groups, the very definition of groups as socially constituted in a concrete sense, and the way in which people represent themselves as bearers of culture and as having a shared ancestry, are all problematic and subject to change, whether the change is long and slow or short and dramatic. Groups or identities are socially constructed, shaped and re-shaped, and their content (the 'cultural stuff' as Barth (1969) described it) is subject to constant revision. Indeed the shift is in part away from an unduly concrete notion of groups towards a conceptualization of ethnicity as a dimension of social relations, relations which are simultaneously structured around principles other than ethnicity. Thus as Eriksen summarizes, 'ethnicity is not an attribute of groups, it is a dimension of relationships' (Eriksen, 1993, p. 12).

This does not mean that we have to abandon utterly the term 'groups' although there will be occasions where other phrases are preferable. The relative stability of some definitions of the boundaries of populations, both by those inside and outside the boundary, gives sufficient permanence to make the idea of groups plausible. The boundaries of White and Black in the USA were sufficiently stable for three centuries for us to speak credibly of the USA's White and the USA's Black population. In the 1990s it remains possible to speak of White and Black populations but the USA's system of ethnic classification is now much more complex and the cultural content immeasurably more contested.

A further sense in which the term 'group' or equivalents (for example, network, association, community) have a basis in social life (and not just as a system of classification), is when they refer to a substratum of ties and obligations that are primarily or partly ethnically defined. Among migrant populations in the urban centres of their new country, obligations and reciprocities are sustained in the daily lives of the migrant workers. At the same time a certain collective identity takes shape in the new setting which has its origins both in the internal processes of mutuality and daily life of the migrant population, and at the boundary of their intersection with the indigenous population. That is to say ethnicity is a socially reproduced system of classification, but not *merely* a system of classification.

As we indicated in the previous section, the second *bouleversement* in the study of ethnicity, or what is still sometimes called 'race' and ethnicity, is the recognition that 'race', being in its historical contours a discredited term, cannot form part of the analytic language of sociology. This naturally entails the conclusion that equally the term 'race relations' is either so imprecise or so confounded by its reliance on a term of scientific error that it can no longer serve any useful purpose. None of this means that racism is not real; it is in part constituted by the persistence in political and popular consciousness, of the discredited conception of race. The sharpness and force with which racism persists is the principle reason why we cannot simply substitute for a discourse of race and racism a discourse of ethnicity, even though there is much to be said for Wallman's dictum that 'phenotype is [but] one element in the repertoire of boundary markers' (Wallman, 1986, p. 229). The historical association of the term 'race' with colour or appearance and the fact that colour and appearance continue to function as socially constructed dimensions of group definition and ideology seem to be the reasons why people still speak of 'race' and certainly of racism. The two discourses (of race/racism and of ethnicity) appear destined to co-exist with respective differences of emphasis but a wide terrain of overlap. Certainly the logic of Wallman's argument is that racism could be subsumed under the general heading of ethnicity and ethnic boundary making. There is, however, more to it than that.

It is possible to draw up a list of the dimensions of group boundary definition or, to put it another way, of the way in which systems of classification are socially reproduced. One dimension is represented by the answer to the question 'who is doing the classifying?'; a second and related question is, 'are the categories of group definition chosen or imposed?'; a third asks, 'what are the bases of group classification – alternatively (or of course in variously weighted combinations), appearance type, culture, religion and ancestry?' Finally we can raise the question, 'are the definitions rooted in experience as against blanket categories of classification?'

With respect to social systems of oppression based on racism the answers – in the discourse of race and racism – would be: a dominant group creates and implements the classification; the categories are imposed on subordinated populations; the bases of the system of classification are principally colour and appearance type, and they are blanket systems of classification not, at least in the first instance, rooted in the experience of the classified populations.

By and large in the context of the discourse of ethnicity the answers would be: a population or group creates its own system of classification, albeit unmistakably by dint of relations with others; the categories are, therefore, chosen rather than imposed; the bases of classification are principally culture, religion, language and ancestry; and equally they are related to collective and individual memories and current lives, in the system of obligations and mutual ties which are daily sustained – they are rooted in experience.

This set of distinctions is based upon conventions and practices in much of the current literature. Despite the apparent neatness, it is important to acknowledge that there are many complexities and contradictions when we begin to apply the models to specific examples of boundary construction. It is rare, for example, that a system of classification is exclusively based on appearance, even though the USA and South Africa represent outstanding examples of binary Black/White systems. None the less, this approach is useful, we suggest, to begin to distinguish discourses of racism and ethnicity.

A third development we wish to endorse is that ethnicity, as a socially reproduced system of classification and as a set of social ties, takes place within wider contexts, the most important of which are political and economic. These political and economic contexts may be conceptualized as macro-social (structural), meso-social (institutional) and micro-social (face-to-face, 'private') spheres.

In the macro-political sphere we are interested in the disposition of ethnicity in nation-states, in regions and at a global level. Ethnically identified groups are found as minorities both dominant (Afrikaaners and English speaking Whites in apartheid South Africa) and non-dominant (French Canadian in Canada, Catalans in Spain) within nation-states. In many nation-states there is a majority population which is ethnically defined and in some cases the majority ethnicity is identified with the nation; there is a political claim that equates the nation and the majority ethnicity. In countries such as Germany this ethnic identity is expressed also in immigration laws and in the granting of citizenship so that there is a presumption in favour of ethnic Germans (*ius sanguini*) over persons in-migrating and even born in Germany of non-German parents (*ius soli*). Citizenship and immigration controls are commonly the site for the definition and sustaining of ethnic and national identities at this macro level. Ethnicity is commonly contextualised within the economic system in the form of an ethnicized division of labour and class structure. The ever widening circles of an internationalized migration of workers means that new diasporas are in constant formation. In many but not all circumstances these migrant worker groups take on an ethnic minority status in their new country. Chapter 1 by Annie Phizacklea also illustrates the salience of gender in these evolving patterns of migration.

Indeed, there are many points of contact between the conceptualization of ethnicity set out above and the understanding of gender. Both ethnicity and gender may, at least in part, be understood as social constructions subject to shifts in social definitions which may respond to social and economic changes or reflect the cultural politics of classification. The hopeful aspect of this is that – for those who cannot rest contented with current definitions – what has been constructed can always be deconstructed.

But there are also important differences in the way in which ethnicity and gender may be mobilized in social organization. Ethnicities or ethnic groups may not always be communities – hence the importance of the distinction between category and group (Jenkins, 1997). But ethnic groups *may* be communities – that is they may become groups by having a real basis of shared life, grounded in region or locale, reproduced through kinship and the social reproduction of cultural forms, and possibly entailing a whole division of labour, shared economy and internal class system, whether or not it is effectively part of a wider system of class and the division of labour. In, for example, much of rural North Eastern Malaysia, Malay ethnicity is socially reproduced under these kinds of conditions. There is no equivalent sense in which a gender forms a community although of course men and women may organize in a more or less systematic way to defend identified gender interests, as in the numerous feminist movements which have historically developed or more recently the 'men's rights' groups which have been formed to defend the interests of men as fathers and as workers against what is seen as a feminist takeover. Gender is also a more general and diffused principle of social organization. With respect to ethnicity it is possible at least to *envisage* an ethnicity-free social order. There are certainly social orders in which ethnicity may be said to play a minor part in comparison to others. Even within social orders in which ethnicity has a general social force, ethnicity may in many circumstances be of minor significance. The situationist theories of ethnicity do not only imply that individuals mobilize different identities in different circumstances but also that in some circumstances ethnic identity is of virtually no account. While gender, too, is not necessarily asserted as an identification in every context or situation, we would argue that gender does inform every aspect of social and cultural life, from school to sport, from classical painting to popular music. In our view Eagleton (1996), is right in suggesting that even after the abolition of social classes there would still be men and women, despite the various feminist Utopian visions of an androgynous future.

THE CONTEXTS OF ETHNICITY: BRINGING GENDER IN

We now turn to the kinds of settings that have formed the context for the analysis of ethnicity. In almost all these circumstances gender too plays an important part, although the literature on ethnicity has not always recognized this. Before discussing some concrete examples, however, we wish to emphasize three points. First, the emphasis on the social construction of both gender and ethnicity should not be taken to be an idealistic emphasis on forms of classification, as if these were primary. Both ethnic and gender definitions *are* socially constructed and to stress this is to correct a prior undue concreteness in the way social thought has discussed 'men and women' and 'ethnic groups'. But it should at the same time be remembered that systems of classification (social constructions of gender and ethnicity) are reproduced within relations of power and social organization. People do not simply invent and re-invent themselves at will, plucking ways of construing their individual and collective identities out of thin air. Second, the concepts of macro-, meso- and micro-levels of social practice should not be regarded as a fixed and final mode of conceptualizing social organization and process, but merely as convenient guides to the different spheres in which both ethnicity and gender move. There is, to give an example, a real and important difference between the social reproduction of ethnicity (or gender) in the household, the schoolroom and factory and in the system of citizenship of a state system. Finally, it should be realized that the concept of ethnicity-in-context (Fenton, forthcoming) involves an intentional weakening of any notion of social determination, especially in terms of class. To say that ethnicity is produced and reproduced within the context of a system of class relations, is clearly a weakening of any argument that ethnicity is in some sense a *product* of class relations or that the analysis of ethnic groups can be simply subsumed under the analysis of class. We say this weakening is intentional because we believe it is evident that theories that attempted to achieve this with respect to both gender and ethnicity failed. At the same time we assert that the class (or political) context of ethnicity and gender remains a critical consideration. Just as we asked the general question – 'who is doing the classifying?' – we may ask this question equally of gender and ethnicity. This serves to remind us that in both instances there are important distinctions to be made between willed, imposed and contested definitions. Within a specific ethnic group individuals may resist the definition of ethnicity urged upon them, for example young adults may challenge their parents' accounts of ethnic belonging. This process of opposition and redefining may be concerned with both ethnicity and gender and indeed may crucially be simultaneously about both – where, for example, specific expectations about what it is to be a woman are at the same time expectations about what it is to be a White, Irish or Sikh person. Also, definitions within communities may be powerfully influenced by changes and pressures outside of them – changes to which *all* women and *all* Whites, Irish or Sikhs are subject. A sensible sociology of ethnicity and gender could not afford to ignore either the internal or the external dynamics. For example, Oonagh O'Brien's analysis of the social reproduction of Catalan ethnicity on the borders of France and Spain (O'Brien, 1993) shows how ethnicity is sustained (within the system of class relations, employment and the household), how gender identities are reproduced, and how women play a critical role as the reproducers of the cultural forms which are seen as conveying Catalan identity and ethnicity.

While studies of migration, colonization and class have formed an important context for understanding ethnicity, they have also frequently understated gender. For example, much of the analysis of migration assumed a model either of family migration led by men, or of men pioneers followed by female and younger dependants. But we know that among Black Caribbean migrants to the UK both men and women frequently migrated independently of each other. Female migration had a quite distinctive trajectory: it was concentrated around the engagement of Caribbean women as nurses in the National Health Service, as discussed by John Carter in Chapter 2. By contrast, among South Asian migrants to Britain early migrants were predominantly men and the arrival of women – as wives, fiancees and other relatives – dramatically altered social practices and identities in the migrant population.

Moreover, some migration has been primarily female-led. This is the case with some North African migrants to Italy and, as discussed in Chapter 1, with respect to females migrating as maids and domestic workers on a world-wide basis, exemplified by the global movement of Sri Lankan, Pakistani and Filipina workers. Sex-worker migration is also highly specific, typically involving women originating from poor countries and regions and working in affluent zones; the influx of East European women working in Germany and other affluent European countries is only the most recent manifestation.

Another set of examples derive from a social process which is global in its impact and intersects vitally with a form of ethnic and national identity. These are the numerous cases where countries have been colonized over the last three hundred years (Canada, New Zealand, Hawaii, the USA and large parts of the Pacific) or where European countries have colonized their hinterland and remote regions (Finland and Norway). In these instances indigenous peoples (commonly termed 'natives') have been decimated, partly decultured, impoverished and pushed to the peripheries of their territories. In the period since World War II particularly, there have been cultural revitalization movements which have, in many instances, been re-stated as nationalisms and sovereignty movements. In such cases, the White European representation of 'native culture' has not only entailed a trivialization and commodified capture of indigenous mentalities and artefacts, but has also done so with special reference to gender identities. This is most commonly perpetrated with reference to touristic promotion, in which not only are 'natives' portrayed as friendly and exotic and as bearers of captivating difference, but women particularly are presented as charming and alluring beauties, with flowers in their hair. Women in these circumstances – and in many instances important leaders of ethno-nationalist movements are women – have to re-present themselves on at least two fronts: to the world at large as, for example, Hawaiians, and to men both from outside and from within their community (Buck, 1993).

A further set of important intersections of gender and ethnicity can be found in the analysis of social mobility and class change among ethnically defined urban minorities: Black Americans in Northern cities, Pakistanis in Bradford, or Black Caribbean women in London and many other contexts. It is clear in the British case that an account of social mobility and of employment and educational success among Black and South Asian-origin populations would have to pay close attention to gender. As the 1970s and 1980s portrayal of class disadvantage and ethnicity gives way to a 1990s recognition of some indications of mobility, there is evidence that some women have been more successful than men. There is need for further study to explain this phenomenon, but contributory factors clearly include: the feminization of the labour force (Bradley, 1997); masculine peer cultures which are antipathetic to success in school (Mac an Ghaill, 1988); African-Caribbean family arrangements which encourage independence in girls (Mirza, 1992); and the greater social control exercised over young women by parents compared to young men. We may also speculate that women have had more success in coping with the double disadvantage of minority status and class position. Certainly, the literature suggests that younger cohorts of minority women have had some success in managing careers in fields untrodden by their parents. By contrast the migrant generation of women often worked in a way which reflected both ethnic cultural expectations and social organization and also limiting gender definitions – working within the household as outworkers or in factories owned and operated by co-ethnic business men.

Again, when we consider the specificities of racism as a doctrine and a practice, we encounter examples importantly compounded by sexual imagery and exploitations. Racial slavery in the USA entailed treatment of Black by White which was frequently gender and sex-specific. Black women were treated as available to White men (with specific consequences for Black men and also White women) and Black men were treated by Whites as sexual threats. At the time of the Black consciousness movements of the 1960s, Eldridge Cleaver captured the nature of this alliance of sexual imagery and racism in his famous essay *Soul on Ice* (Cleaver, 1970). Black/White sexuality has continued to be a major theme of 'racial' imagery and practice. In another instance of interethnic conflict and violence – the civil wars in Yugoslavia – sexual exploitation played a key role. Milosevic in Serbia adorned his assault on Kosovo and its Albanian populations with accusations of rape of Serbian women directed at Albanian men. This was part of a repertoire designed to foster not only Serbian ethnic nationalism but also dreams of a Greater Serbia. While we have no knowledge of the truth or otherwise of his accusations, we do know that subordinated populations are regularly accused of 'raping our women'; this has been a standard item of racisms throughout history. The evidence of rape as a prominent element of the prosecution of ethnic war in Yugoslavia is, by contrast, all too well documented. We should also note, as has Yuval-Davis (1997), that gender themes are frequently an under-recognized dimension of nationalist doctrines and cultures. All these examples are now well enough known to indicate general interest in the interconnectedness of ethnicity and gender.

INTERSECTIONS OF GENDER AND ETHNICITY

As we noted, there are many common aspects of ethnicity and gender (Fenton, forthcoming). Both have in recent years been the basis of political mobilization; both have been the focus of actions within institutional frameworks (employment, education, politics) against discrimination and disadvantage, involving the elaboration of programmes of equal opportunities or of anti-racist or anti-sexist campaigns. But perhaps the crucial sociological point is that both ethnicity and gender, as analytic frameworks, have been central to recent work on the reconceptualization of social divisions (Bradley, 1996), and the displacement of class as the 'master social identity' (Du Gay, 1996). As a result a much more subtle picture of contemporary social structure, involving both material and cultural elements, has emerged.

This theoretical change has promoted the exploration of the way ethnicity and gender mutually interact. Perhaps this tendency is still less developed in the study of ethnicity. Two recent influential introductory texts by David Mason (1995) and Thomas Eriksen (1993) each have only five index items under gender. In contrast, within gender studies there has been an almost obsessive concern with ethnicity as a source of difference among women since the mounting of the critique of early feminist research as ethnocentric by 'Black' feminists in the early 1980s. This concern has been heightened by the theoretical stress within postmodernism and poststructuralism, currently the dominant orthodoxies within feminism, on the need to counter essentialism and to deconstruct the category of 'women'. Indeed, the current preoccupation with the diversity of gendered experience is considered to cast in doubt the whole political project of feminism, based as it has been on some notion of the commonality of the oppression of women.

However, if the stress on diversity is politically problematic it has certainly yielded a rich sociological harvest in terms of an explosion of research into the experience of women of differing ethnicities This has generated a whole new set of research questions. For example: how are ethnic communities gendered and how is the experience of ethnicity different for women? Conversely, how is gender experienced by women of different ethnic origin? How do gender and ethnicity come together to disadvantage women? And what is the effect of class upon both? How do all these factors come together in processes of identification? This book contributes to ongoing debates on these key questions.

1   The Effect of Gender on Ethnicity

Within many ethnic populations, women can be seen as having an important role as carriers of ethnicity, both in terms of ancestry (some communities have strict rules about intermarriage) and culture. Yuval-Davis (1997) stresses that this role of 'symbolic boundary maintenance' is enacted in a very concrete way as women simultaneously 'embody' ethnic culture and gender: 'Women in their "proper" behaviour, in their "proper" clothing embody the line which signifies the collectivity's boundaries' (Yuval-Davis, 1997, p. 46).

Yuval-Davis points to the centrality of the home in this process and thus of women's responsibility as home-makers: it is in the home that cultural rules and practices are transmitted to the next generation, through the switchboard of the home that networks of ancestry and kinship are maintained. Vieda Skultans in Chapter 9 (this book) also stresses the importance of this female task of 'ethnicity maintenance' in extreme situations, such as war and exile. Eriksen quotes a line from the Norwegian national anthem which neatly summarizes the situation described by Skultans: 'The fathers have fought and the mothers have wept,' (Eriksen, 1993, p. 156).

Given the ubiquity of the sexual division of labour, we can be sure that women and men will be ascribed different economic roles within ethnic communities. When ethnic relations are played out in a minority context as a result of migration, women often may contribute to ethnicity maintenance in a more material way, even though initially economic opportunities for men may appear more promising. For example, historical research into Irish migrants in New York shows that while Irish men suffered from negative stereotyping as lazy, irresponsible and drunken, Irish women were sought after as servants and cooks, thus helping to establish the respectability of the Irish community (Walter, 1997). This pattern of differential stereotyping on the basis of gender is not uncommon and may contribute to problems of high male unemployment among some minority ethnic groups (African-Caribbeans in the UK, for example). In Chapter 3 Ineke Van Wetering offers another example of women's crucial role in ethnic maintenance; the saving clubs (ROSCAs) run by Surinamese women in Holland are an important prop to the community's precarious economic situation and help to maintain community ties through positive forms of interaction. Indeed, Van Wetering illustrates admirably the way in which ethnicity and gender come together in processes of both symbolic and material reproduction.

While all this indicates the important position of women within many urban ethnically-defined minorities, the responsibility involved in, for example, maintaining ethnic purity and the status and honour of the community may place a heavier burden on them and constraints upon their actions. Rules about clothing, drinking, eating and so forth are often enforced more vigorously for women, as among some UK South Asian groups (Afshar, 1994). In Chapter 5 Shirley Firth highlights the restraints put upon Hindu widows in the UK by traditional cultural rules and codes of practice and the practical difficulties of survival in following those rules within a different wider culture, although that culture, too, is deficient in its support for older widowed women and in the stigmatization of their social role. This points to a crucial tension and dilemma in the politics and analysis of ethnicity and gender. The trend within 'the new sociology of ethnicities' has been to view ethnicity as something to be celebrated, as opposed to the older 'race relations' framework which was marked by its critique of racial disadvantage and its commitment to a common humanity which would unite across ethnic diversity. This switch to a celebratory concept of ethnicity and the affirmation of difference has been fostered by the fact that many of the new young practitioners are themselves of minority origin and wish to valorize and promote their own cultural distinctiveness. However, there are problems here in terms of gender divisions. The desire to promote a positive view of ethnicity may lead to glossing over of differences of class and gender within ethnically based political movements, in order to present ethnic communities as unified. In turn this may encourage the legitimation of inequalities of gender, especially in the name of community solidarity. Put simply, the desire to preserve the integrity of culture may lead women as well as men to deny the fact that cultural practices may promote gender inequality.

2   The Effect of Ethnicity on Gender

This problem is writ large in gender studies when it comes to the discussion of how ethnicity affects gender. As we noted, feminists from minority ethnicities in the USA and UK have taken the lead in deconstructing the notion of a common experience of oppression among women which was central to 1970s feminist analysis. They argued that initial theorizations of gender relations were ethnocentric and only served further to marginalize the experience of ethnicity and ethnic disadvantage; they called for careful study of the distinctive experience of minority women in relation to social institutions such as the family, employment, the state and the welfare services. Particular objection was raised to the way that some forms of gendering associated with cultural practices in non-Western societies, such as arranged marriages or clothing customs such as wearing the veil, were read by White western feminists as 'backward' and oppressive. It becomes necessary, then, to explore the specific form taken by the dynamic of gender in each ethnic context and to explore the different ways in which gender differences are maintained or resisted in each context.

Here the problem arises. Initial formulations of patriarchy might rightly be read as ethnocentric, even racist, in that they asserted the universality of male dominance and the primacy of gender inequalities over other forms of disadvantage, such as racist exploitation. Newer variants of gender analysis, while recognizing this, still wish to maintain some notion of unequal power between the sexes. However, it becomes quite problematic to explore the nature of male power within cultural contexts where women's and men's lives are more differentiated and indeed segregated than is the case within White western cultures. Do we read this as evidence of male dominance? Or are such gendered arrangements mutually agreed and desirable?

This problem is nicely illustrated by the group of chapters within this book that explore the experiences of young British South Asian women in relation to cultural tradition and religion and interpret them in very different ways. For Kalwant Bhopal (Chapter 6) aspects of South Asian culture are experienced unequivocally as oppressive by at least one group of highly educated young women who refuse to accept the rules of sexual behaviour and marriage and may thus face censure or even rejection from their family. For Bhopal, this is the distinctive form that male domination takes in the South Asian context. Hannah Bradby (Chapter 8) views arranged marriages more ambiguously, suggesting ways in which non-conformist young women are able to work within the rules to juggle different aspects of their lives: in such a view cultural institutions are portrayed as evolving and moderating within a new context, a position which might be supported by recent evidence of the growing proportion of inter-ethnic marriages (Modood *et al.*, 1997). A third aspect is highlighted by Charlotte Butler (Chapter 7), who shows how some young Muslim women positively embrace Islamic religion and some of its rules on gendering, while at the same time rejecting other aspects of Pakistani cultural 'tradition' which seem irrelevant to their lives in Britain. For these young women, ethnic difference of a particular type becomes at once a right, a source of pride and dignity and a basis of positive identity. Taken together these chapters illustrate the complexity of ethnic situations, the wide variety of individual and collective responses to ethnic situations, and the extraordinary adaptability of 'cultural practice' which has often been theorized in too monolithic and deterministic a way. The chapters demonstrate the importance of women's active involvement in challenging gender norms, redefining gendered ethnicity and recreating culture; and, sociologically, they show the need for further sensitive ethnographic and qualitative research to explore these complexities of adaptation and change.

3   Ethnicity, Gender, Class and Disadvantage

Do we view ethnicity and gender, then, in terms of disadvantage and inequality, or in terms of self-determination and celebratory identity? The answer must be both. There is plenty of research showing how gender and ethnicity come together to disadvantage women materially. Discriminatory immigration rules, such as the iniquitous 'primary purpose rule' explored by Werner Menski in Chapter 4, set the context for the position of social disadvantage experienced by many minority women in Britain, as Annie Phizacklea's work has shown. Here Phizacklea extends her study of the way race relations, gender and class combine from the British to the European context. Her previous research explored employment hierarchies in the textile industry and the experience of homeworking, showing how minority women were pushed into the least desirable, lowest-paid jobs (Phizacklea, 1990; Phizacklea and Wolkowitz, 1995). Such forms of labour are often concealed and marginalized because of their link with the sphere of domesticity: family labour within ethnic enterprises, for example, or homework which takes place within, and is surrounded by, the framework of household responsibilities and domestic tasks. Phizacklea is now exploring how this wage labour/domestic labour link is played out within Europe as a result of new patterns of migration: women are typically found in the lowest tiers of the formal economic hierarchy, especially in service work, and in the informal and illegal economy; their roles as domestic workers in hotels and catering and as sex workers exemplify this position of disadvantage. As John Carter's work on the NHS also demonstrates, minority women have in the past typically been confined to such gendered and ethnicized niches – nursing is an example.

But class has a crucial role here too. It has long been possible for women from the upper sections of the class structure to 'buy out' of some of the constraints of gender and ethnicity, for example by employing women of less privileged class origin to perform domestic tasks for them, or by utilizing both material and cultural forms of capital to gain access to elite forms of employment (professional work, entrepreneurial activities). Class privilege allows women of the elite to float above the cultural restrictions imposed by gender ideologies or ethnic cultural rules. More modestly, young women from minority groupings in contemporary Britain (and elsewhere) are making use of the qualifications lever (Crompton and Sanderson, 1990) to achieve upward mobility and escape from ethnic ghettoes; young African-Caribbean women, for example, are distinguishing themselves from their brothers by pursuing opportunities in further and higher education to gain access to jobs in teaching, social work, the media and to other white-collar and professional occupations from which their own mothers were excluded (Mirza, 1992; Modood *et al.*, 1997). This does not free them from the experience of either racism or sexism, but at least elevates them from the bottom tiers of the employment hierarchy and from the threat of finding themselves as part of the excluded 'underclass' which has been the fate of many minority ethnic members in America (Wilson, 1993; Morris, 1994).

4   Ethnicity, Gender and Diasporic Identities

Ethnic disadvantage is a continuing phenomenon, then. But ethnicity also has become increasingly a source of positive as opposed to imposed and stigmatized identification. In this process young women have played a particularly significant part, as reflected in many of the chapters in this book. Refusing to accept views of themselves and their cultures as inferior, alien, the other, the 'second generation' in Britain have been crucially involved in the work of reconceptualizing and deconstructing ethnicity. This has involved disaggregating notions of 'Black' and 'White' to explore the situation of women in particular ethnic categories and also presenting aspects of culture disparaged by White feminists (arranged marriages, wearing the veil) within a framework that treats difference as positive and queries the view of western gender arrangements as more progressive.

Ideas about postcolonialism, diasporas and hybrid or 'hyphenated' identities have been especially influential in this respect. The idea of a hybrid or diasporic identity may be used to challenge essentialist readings of 'race' or ethnic culture and to assert the right to self-definition. This is not necessarily a comfortable process as Jayne Ifekwunigwe's sensitive discussion of the experience of 'métisse' (mixed-ethnic) identities shows (Chapter 11). Individuals may be uneasily placed within differing cultural traditions, vacillating between allegiances and subject to complex processes of multiple stereotypes. It is indeed 'not easy' (Modood, 1992) negotiating the complexities of hybridity, whether in terms of 'British-Pakistani-Muslim' or in terms of a 'Black' father and 'White' mother. However, the analysis of hybridity not only exposes the weakness of essentialist thinking about 'primordial' ethnic ties and the search for one's 'authentic origins'; it also demonstrates that ethnic identities and cultures, both majority and minority, are not static but constantly changing and evolving, in the context of life in postcolonial polyethnic societies.

Moreover, we might posit, the notion of diasporic identities may provide an answer to the problem of how to present ethnic difference positively while also unmasking structures of gendered power. In Bhabha's words (1990) hybridity provides a 'third space', a vantage point from which to regard critically both majority and minority gender relations and to move beyond the constraints of both. Puar describes such identities as 'oppositionally active'; in her words, 'such a form of identity suggests a complete alliance neither with South Asian nor with white society; rather it resists both' (Puar, 1996, p. 131). This is subtly exemplified in Chapter 10 with Helen Kanitkar's account of Meera, the heroine of one of the novels she analyses: Meera moves between England and India, distancing herself from the hierarchies and customs of both while at the same time finding space in which she can place herself and form her own identity – both connected and separate. To do so is to move beyond such either/or categories as Black and White – even beyond ethnicity perhaps – and at the same time to construct new ways of being a woman. As Ang-Lygate (1996, p. 160) suggests:

Unless we insist in moving beyond traditional knowledge production and adopt new forms of understanding that unshackle new meanings, the struggle for the space for self-definition is a fruitless one... Research into women's experiences of diaspora can contribute significantly towards a social dynamics which seeks to ensure that our sons and daughters inherit modern identities and enter into a more egalitarian future.

This understanding has potential to overturn current understandings of both ethnicity and gender and indeed of all other forms of social identification. As Walsh (1997) suggests in relation to the experience of class, gender and ethnicity, hybridity and multiplicity are actually the majority experience of social location in the postcolonial capitalist world. Thus the experience of ethnic and gender disadvantage can be the basis for a transformed critical analysis of society. 'The discomfort of being located "in the margins" is ultimately worthwhile. Experiencing two worlds, but fully belonging in neither, can bring the pain of displacement and alienation. But the exile can become the outlaw: exploding the myths which accumulate around all social and cultural identities, myths which limit and constrain all women, whatever their class' (Clancy, 1997, p. 52). And, of course, their ethnicity.

METHODOLOGICAL IMPLICATIONS

In exploring the questions posed at the beginning of the last section, researchers are able to draw on a rich heritage of techniques of empirical investigation. The study of both ethnic and 'race' relations has encompassed the use of national and local social surveys, so typically associated with mainstream empirical sociology, alongside case-study research and the full-blown ethnographical work central to social anthropology. In this way the study of ethnicity has straddled the uncomfortable qualitative/quantitative divide which has sometimes disrupted the unity of the discipline of sociology. Feminist researchers too, while notably defending the validity of 'softer' qualitative methods, have embraced the whole repertoire of investigatory techniques: a special interest has been in deploying personal or autobiographical material as a way of overcoming the conventional binary oppositions between 'subject' and 'object', 'researcher' and 'researched' and thus more sensitively and effectively tapping into the experience of gender in women's lives.

Such methodological tolerance is reflected in the wide range of tools and strategies employed by the researchers in this book. While survey research and case study investigation in the past have tended to be pitched at the level of the locality, if not the nation, the trend now is to explore how ethnic relations are played out in more specific loci or sites.

Examples here are Carter's investigation of the micropolitics of equal opportunity in one NHS hospital trust, or Van Wetering's careful unpicking of the economic and symbolic significance of Roscas among Surinamese communities in Holland. Another trend is to focus on the differentiated experience of particular sub-groups, as, for example, Firth's exploration of the dilemmas facing Hindu widows in Britain.

This emphasis both on the local context and the diversity of ethnic experience is in line with the epistemological prescriptions of postmodern sociology, with its distrust of foundational theory and rejection of the predominant forms of structural sociological explanation, such as Marxism or feminist theories of patriarchy. Postmodernism has something to offer here especially in its reaffirmation of the challenge to the imperialism of positivist 'scientific' sociology. But we would also stress that a concern with the local and the diverse is hardly new. Good sociology has always appreciated that social relationships manifest themselves in specific concrete forms. Thus the old and the new can both contribute to the best research practice.

A further recent methodological trend has been the attention given to the role of narrative within the practice of social science. This arises from the challenge offered both by postmodernism and feminism to the claims of natural science and its associated methodologies to hold privileged access to truth. There are two ways in particular in which such a challenge encourages close attention to narrative, in the sense of the telling of stories and the ways in which they are told. First it is suggested that 'non-scientific' forms of knowledge such as fiction may offer just as much insight and understanding into social relations as do conventional scientific methods. Second, it is argued that the practice and writing of science (and similarly of sociology) is itself inevitably impregnated by narrative structures and rhetorical devices which serve to impress forms of 'truth' on the reader.

This concern is reflected in three of the chapters in this book which deal with the issue of narrative in rather different ways. In her analysis of novels written by women, Kanitkar uses them to unlock the experience of hyphenated identity in contemporary Britain; the heroines, as they move between cultural and spatial locations, embody the dilemmas of ethnicity, gender and class. She argues that novels can be used to supplement conventional sociological analysis, illuminating the nature of individual subjectivity. In contrast Skultans explores the devices of narrative, demonstrating how the life stories of her Latvian respondents were shaped by their use of religious, mythic and folklore elements to give structure and meaning to their accounts of loss and exile. While

Ifekwunigwe also uses life stories, in her case the interest is to show how the métisse women she interviewed juggle the various elements of their hybrid identities and come to terms with their 'difference' within a diasporic culture.

The methodological diversity displayed in the research reported on in this book bears testimony to the vitality and richness of the study of ethnicity in the 1990s but also highlights the positive contribution made to sociology by postmodern and feminist extensions to what counts as 'normal science'. This is not to say that more tried and tested methodological tools are outmoded. More conventional approaches are represented here by Phizacklea's overview of gendered and ethnicized hierarchies in the European economy and Menski's careful dissection of the primary purpose rule. Older and newer strategies co-exist here in the search to unravel the complexities of changing ethnic relations. As we have argued elsewhere (Bradley and Fenton, 1999), mainstream sociology could profit from adopting the methodological tolerance displayed in the sub-disciplines of gender and ethnicity, to bring an end to the often acrimonious and arid disputes between proponents of quantitative and qualitative work which, for example, have bedeviled British class analysis.

ETHNICITY, GENDER AND SOCIAL CHANGE

At the 1995 conference contributors were invited to consider processes of social change. We close by considering the importance of comprehending change at a time when relations of ethnicity and gender are especially volatile and dynamic. Colonial and postcolonial transformations have played a decisive part in the emergence of ethnicity as an issue on a global scale. The authors in this book take up and extend this theme further in their own researches. A common concern is the relationship between metropolitan centres and the ex-colonial society with respect to migration, settlement and social change. Carter's contribution on nurses shows that colonial racist ideologies had a lasting influence on the career prospects of nurses from ethnic minority backgrounds and that the emergent rhetoric of egalitarianism failed to mask this. Wetering's contribution also illustrates the significance of the colonial connection and the way in which the Surinamese women organize rotational credit systems to meet their particular social needs in terms of their own cosmological ideas. But both colonial legacies and cultural practices associated with membership of ethnic populations may shift in the postcolonial context. Shirley Firth's erudite contribution on Hindu widows highlights the adaptive responses of widows and their families to their new habitat in Britain – processes of change that allow for modification of tradition in a new milieu. Bhopal, Butler and Bradby focus on the different situation facing young South Asian women when they confront the choice of marriage partners. Having been socialized into the normative patterns of their own caste-like communities, as well as being exposed to the ideology of individual choice, for some South Asian women the question of establishing relationships with young people of their own or other communities is particularly difficult. It may involve either temporary or long-term alienation between family members which in itself is a significant change. However, this change has a more universal resonance. As women become more self-confident and self-reliant, they are likely to demand greater degrees of participation in family decision-making that affects their lives. While Bhopal's material demonstrates a greater degree of autonomy for women, Bradby deals with respondents whose affiliation to their 'community of honour' is a matter of concern for them. Breaking away from the community of honour can bring shame and dishonour, and sometimes unbearable isolation, that can affect the immediate and extended family in its transnational relationships, especially in towns and villages in South Asia where the families are anxious to maintain their social standing. The wider context of opportunity, especially in higher education and the labour market, can engender social change that alters the future prospects of women. They may enjoy the choice and freedom that can also cause anxiety and insecurity.

These examples clearly show the changing relationship between ethnicity and gender and some weakening of patriarchal family relationships as women rise to influence the course of their own lives. Kanitkar's analysis of two novels depicting the lives of a Black British and a South Asian woman emphasizes the search for meaning and identity in a metropolitan world which creates conditions for new relationships and new dilemmas and suffering for both Indian and Caribbean women living in Britain. The question of being is something that one can not take for granted as in a traditional community. What one is has to be a self-conscious process of discovery that is influenced by social and material conditions as well as by self-expression.

Ifekwunigwe deals with some of the most subtle effects of racism with respect to shades of whiteness and blackness which influence the relationships and self-conceptions of the women she interviewed. In an example such as this, the dynamics of racism combine with a reassessment and even reinvention of identities, which empower the respondents to sustain their own self-respect and honour without the stigma and traumatization that can undermine confidence.

The contemporary world is a dynamic one, in which a complex range of forces combine to shape the particular identities and fates of individuals and groups. The contributors to this book emphasize that ethnicity may act as a creative and positive force, in a world that is rapidly shrinking through globalization and revolutionary changes in systems of communication. The old unilinear arguments about the disappearance of ethnicity in the face of modernization and democratization are certainly problematized, as the resurgence of ethnic identifications in the post-communist world has demonstrated. But all too often membership of minority ethnic groups involves exposure to racism, material disadvantage and social exclusion. As John Rex (1993) has observed, it is vital that modern European and other states pursue social policies which respect diversity and difference, enabling citizens to perceive equality of opportunity for themselves in societies where ethnicity and gender cease to be markers of inequality, oppression and exploitation.

Section 1
Ethnicity, Gender and
Economic Disadvantage

1 Gender and Transnational Labour Migration
Annie Phizacklea

Over the last thirty years the theorization of transnational population movements has taken, I will argue, four main forms; 'push-pull' theories which emphasize agency; structural accounts; household strategy theories and the role of social networks in supporting transnational movements. Much of this theorization has taken a very ungendered form and has been largely disconnected from developing debates within feminist theory, particularly those relating to a recognition of difference and diversity within the category of 'women', and more generally from social theory. This chapter works through in a gendered way, each of these different models and their relationship (or lack of it) to each other. It begins by considering the context within which these debates are situated.

HAS GLOBAL LABOUR MIGRATION BECOME INCREASINGLY FEMINIZED?

In the early 1980s a number of researchers were keen to correct what they considered to be a misplaced emphasis on migration as a largely male phenomenon with women getting a rare look-in as wives or daughters of male migrants. Even in situations where emigration data indicated quite clearly that during the 1950s and 1960s women were independent labour migrants, (for instance from the Caribbean to the UK and France) their presence was ignored (see Phizacklea, 1982 for an analysis of labour migration from Jamaica). Thus when Castles and Miller (1993) claim that the 'feminization of migration' has become and will continue to be, an important tendency of transnational migratory movements, one response is that it always has been an important tendency. Nevertheless the quantification of transnational movements in a gendered way has become increasingly imprecise since the introduction of strict immigration controls in the affluent countries of the world since the early 1970s.

Some migration specialists challenge what they refer to as the 'conventional wisdom' that female labour migration has outnumbered male since 1974. The argument is that 'the fact remains that the majority of women who migrate internationally do not do so for work purposes. That is especially the case of women migrating legally from developing to developed countries' (Zlotnik, 1995, p. 230). On the basis of official entry data Zlotnik is correct. Apart from professionals with scarce skills, it has been very difficult for anyone to migrate legally for employment purposes from the developing to the developed world since 1974. But if we examine the gender composition of regularization programmes over the last ten years then we can conclude that indeed women do constitute a significant proportion of labour migrants in transnational movements.

Even though the criteria for regularization of immigration status were tough under the 1986 Immigration Reform and Control Act in the US, of the 1.2 million Mexicans who fulfilled the criteria, half were women (Hondagneu-Sotelo, 1994). In Italy there have been numerous regularization programmes since 1986. Even though the criteria for regularization have become increasingly tougher in Italy and involve the cooperation of employers, in the twelve months up to November 1996, 220,000 foreigners were regularized under what was called the 'Dini decree'. The results of the programme indicated that around 25 per cent of Italy's foreign worker population was undocumented. The single largest nationality group to benefit from the regularization programme were from the Philippines, virtually all of whom were women (*Migration News Sheet*, June 1996 and January 1997).

These kinds of calculations provide us with very rough-and-ready estimates of the gender and ethnic composition of contemporary transnational movements, but it is important that we make that effort. It is with this general picture in mind that we can begin to consider some of the more common conceptualizations of transnational population movements in a gendered way.

WHY DID YOU PACK YOUR BAGS?

The answers to that question are many and varied, not least from a gendered perspective; women may have very different reasons for migrating from those of men. The model of migration which has been most strongly criticized is the 'push-pull' thesis. While it is now generally regarded as an inadequate tool for the analysis of what are highly complex and diverse processes of migration, (see critiques in Castles and Miller, 1993; Phizacklea, 1997) it is a model which has had a significant influence over official attitudes to migration in many developing countries.

'Push-pull' and Rational Decision-making

Neo-classical economic analyses of migration can be considered at both a macro level, in terms of global differences in wage rates and employment opportunities, and a micro level, in terms of individuals as rational decision makers. While they appear to provide very 'obvious' explanations for transnational population movements, they have been heavily criticized.

The work of Todaro is representative of the neo-classical economic approach (Todaro, 1969) and can be summed up as a prediction that the volume of transnational migration is significantly related to the real or expected international earnings gap (Massey *et al.*, 1993, p. 455). Thus at a macro level we are analysing a situation where the 'push' factors determining outward migration are low wages and living standards, and in many cases high levels of structural unemployment, while the 'pull' factors are migration destinations that offer employment and higher wages. At a micro level the model assumes that individuals make rational choices about migration, that they weigh up the costs and benefits and will move to the destination which maximizes the net return on migration. Part of this equation will be individual human capital characteristics, such as education and training, that will increase the individuals likelihood of gaining employment or higher wages in the migration setting (Borjas, 1990).

While such assumptions have been criticized for their tendency towards ahistoricism and an over-emphasis on agency, they may well have influenced the policies on migration adopted by a number of developing countries, the Philippines being a prime example. In the latter case, migration has long been positively encouraged to relieve internal poverty and to service foreign debt. By law migrant workers must remit between 30 and 70 per cent of their earnings and in 1992 the Government collected $9.6 million in passport fees alone (Chant and McIlwaine, 1995, p. 33).

Remittances do constitute an important economic contribution to governments and families alike, but increasingly migrants themselves are saddled with debts to intermediaries (such as employment agencies, traffickers, etc.) which mean prolonged absence and vulnerability in the migration setting. As the human capital part of the equation might predict, it is not the least educated and trained that migrate, but rather those with qualifications and skills to offer. But if individuals believe this will improve the probability of their gaining employment commensurate with their qualifications then they are likely to be disappointed.

There is in fact considerable evidence to show underemployment of migrants from poor countries and few opportunities to acquire new skills or further education in the migration setting. For instance a study of Filipina domestic workers carried out in Rome and Milan in 1991 indicated that half of the 101 women interviewed had college education and complained bitterly about the obstacles to their gaining better employment or qualifications in the migration setting (LIFE, 1991). Research carried out in Spain in 1996 indicated that Filipina women were the preferred nationality group as maids in families with children precisely because they could teach the children English. Their bilingual skills were taken for granted and there was no additional financial reward for the provision of this specialized skill (Anderson and Phizacklea, 1997).

Thus whether the account is pitched at the macro or micro level, neo-classical economic accounts provide a limited understanding of transnational population movements. Individual, 'rational' choices must be analysed within the context of external constraint such as immigration policies which are in the main not difficult for individuals to manipulate. For instance, immigration laws and rules determine the 'legal' or 'illegal' status of the migrant in the migration setting, which in turn will have a significant bearing on the employment options of the individual. Nevertheless these accounts are important in stressing the role of agency, for while individuals may act on very imperfect information as regards the migratory decision, the decisions they make clearly are not wholly shaped by external constraint.

While these early accounts are ungendered it is possible to indicate how the argument would run if one adopted this model in relation to women's migration. Basically the argument would run that, faced with poverty and unemployment, women in poor countries would view access to low paid work through migration 'as better than nothing'. Not only would migration offer the possibility of providing access to a wage and therefore to remittances but this would have an 'emancipatory' potential for women strengthening their position and power within households. As we shall see later this argument has been used more generally in analysing women's employment in world market factories in developing countries and is usually referred to as the 'integration' thesis.

An alternative perspective to these neo-classical economic accounts are the household strategy models. These models are often regarded as providing a more adequate account of migration and in so far as households are an important unit of analysis mediating between individuals and the larger structural context then I would agree. Nevertheless from

a gendered perspective there are aspects of extant theorizing in this area which are open to criticism.

HOUSEHOLDS AND MIGRATION

It is often assumed that, because women are members of households, accounts of migration that start with household decision-making must provide more adequate accounts. In the early 1980s certain economists moved beyond models of migration predicated on individual rational choice to one where the 'family' was recognized as the effective decision-making unit (Stark's work is an example of this, 1984). Some see these 'new economics of migration' accounts as overcoming the shortcomings of neo-classical models based on individual rational decision-making, (see Cohen's introduction, 1996, p. xv).

Unless this move is accompanied by an analytical shift which recognizes that households are deeply implicated in gendered ideologies and practices then we have advanced very little. In fact, one might argue that we have simply introduced another set of problematic assumptions. For instance, it is quite common to find the following assumptions in accounts of migration that utilize the household strategy model: that households represent shared income, resources and goals; that migration is a reactive strategy to a lack of fit between household consumption and locally available resources and that household-wide decisions are made about migration (see for instance Wood, 1982; Selby and Murphy, 1982).

Some of the more recent accounts have overcome these weaknesses by acknowledging, for instance, that 'the household, as we conceive it, has its own political economy, in which access to power and other valued resources is distributed along gender and generational lines' (Grasmuck and Pessar, 1991, p. 202). They also recognize that the household cannot be analysed in isolation from extra-household relations in particular the social networks and other migrant institutions which support transnational migration (Hondagneu-Sotelo, 1994; Boyd, 1989).

Empirical work which has explored decision-making within households regarding migration point to the hollowness of the assumption that households make collective decisions. In her research on Mexican migration, Hondagneu-Sotelo shows that men who migrated ahead of wives and children did so quite autonomously with little regard for the rest of the family's views on this decision. Rather than the women who were left behind viewing this decision as based on a recognition of family need, they were in fact fearful that they might be abandoned altogether. As male remittances rarely met household consumption expenditure in Mexico, many women effectively became sole heads of households. The result was an increased desire by women to move North in order that husbands resume at least partial social and economic responsibility for family welfare. Hondagneu-Sotelo (1994, p. 95) concludes:

> Opening the household 'black box' exposes a highly charged political arena where husbands and wives and parents and children may simultaneously express and pursue divergent interests and competing agendas. How these agendas become enacted draws attention to the place of patriarchal authority in shaping migration... a household cannot think, decide or plan, but certain people in households do engage in these activities.

Radcliffe's research in the Calca area of the Peruvian Andes indicates that in peasant households unmarried daughters' labour is of minimal value because the sexual division of labour dictates that they cannot participate in extra-household exchanges of labour. They are 'surplus' to the agricultural base and packed off to work as maids in urban areas. Radcliffe (1993, p. 283) sums up the process as follows:

> As female offsprings' labour does not contribute to the household economy, its expulsion becomes an option for poorer households. This is not necessarily for reasons of high returns on labour as posited in the neo-classical models. When female members enter external labour markets, the return on their labour power is not significant, and in comparison to that predicted in neo-classical models... it is not the potentially higher wage-earning labour which leaves the peasant unit, but the members whose labour is of minimal value, owing to its gender and peasant origins.

To reiterate, households do constitute an important unit of analysis in accounts of migration but there are a number of qualifications to their use. First, there is the problem of definition, what is a household and who is a member? Given the very different cultural meanings attached to the concept 'household' and the heterogeneity of family forms there are real problems of boundary marking on a transnational basis. Second, households as a unit of analysis cannot be examined in isolation from the broader structural and ideological context within which they are situated. Finally and this follows from the last point, they can only be viewed at an intermediary level of analysis. Thus it is to macro-structural accounts that we now move.

STRUCTURAL ACCOUNTS AND MIGRATION SYSTEMS

A very different macro account of migration rooted in Marxist political economy became favoured in the early 1970s. Drawing heavily on dependency theory and world systems theory the work of Castles and Kosack (1973), of Manuel Castells (1975) and Marios Nikolinakos (1975) stressed not only the political economy of migratory processes but the common class position shared by migrant workers in the host countries. With hindsight we now identify these accounts as overly economically determined, analyses which employ a functionalist notion of the needs of capitalism as the prime determinant and which consequently leave little space for the role of human agency. As Boyd (1989, p. 641) puts it; 'A real danger also was the replacement of an undersocialised view of migration in which all action reflected individual wishes and preferences with an oversocialised view in which people were passive agents in the migratory process, projected through time and space by social forces'.

At the end of the 1970s I began to explore how a gendered analysis of migration within this political economy based model could be developed. These early attempts now seem to me to display the failures of a systems theory which explains all phenomena in terms of the logic of capitalism, with migrant women cast as a racialized and gendered class fraction whose migration was largely determined by the uneven economic development of capitalism on a global level (Phizacklea and Miles, 1980; Phizacklea, 1983). Thus capitalist relations and ideologies maintained primacy even though it was acknowledged that gender and racism could constitute significant structural features of societies

Nevertheless this theorization did emphasize that women as well as men migrate in search of work. It raised questions about the relationship between female labour and transnational capital and whether women's labour migration could be regarded as a positive, emancipatory development. Finally, it endeavoured to produce an account that recognized migrant women as agents, individual and collective, while at the same time being subject to external constraint. In the latter case it was argued that colonialism and the trade and investment practices of post-colonialism have produced vast regional inequalities on a global scale. In the short to medium term economic development does not reduce the pressure on individuals to migrate in search of a livelihood. On the contrary it actually increases that pressure because of the economic and social dislocation that accompanies the development process. But the penetration of the cash economy, the mechanization of agriculture and the industrialization process itself are not gender neutral in their impact. For instance, it is often women, deprived of traditional subsistence and cash-generating activities on and around the land, who become a relative surplus population in the poorer developing countries of the world. Even though from the late 1960s these same countries became the favoured sites for low wage manufacturing production in world market factories set up by transnational companies, the supply of women workers outstrips available employment. Migration provides an economic escape route (Phizacklea, 1983).

Sassen-Koob's work went one step further in linking the industrialization process in developing countries (particularly through the investment practices of transnational companies in Free Trade Zones) with emigration to the USA and other 'core' economies. Her argument is that the integration of women into employment in world-market factories affects migratory processes. She argues; 'Incipient westernization among zone workers and the disruption of traditional work structures combine to minimise the possibilities of returning to communities of origin. In sum these developments can be seen as having induced the formation of a pool of migrant workers' (Sassen-Koob, 1984, p. 1151). Unfortunately subsequent research on these issues has been patchy, either concentrating on the conditions and consequences of employment in world-market factories or concluding that the 'stepping-stones' to transnational migration are more likely to be tourism and entertainment work, areas which bring women into contact with foreigners (Chant and McIlwaine, 1995, p. 37). Much subsequent research on women's employment in world-market factories has in fact reflected the concerns of the early attempts to analyse women's labour migration and to evaluate its meaning within the debate between agency and structure paradigms. It is useful to illustrate the main arguments with reference to Tiano's research on the Mexican Maquila industry. Tiano argues that there are two alternative paradigms for looking at the predominance of women as employees in world market factories: the first, is the *exploitation thesis* which asserts that transnational companies invest in poor countries such as Mexico because they can exploit cheap female labour and take advantage of women's vulnerability in the labour market and in the household. According to this view women do not participate in employment as independent agents but as members of patriarchal families dependent upon women's wages (Tiano, 1994, p. 45). The alternative paradigm she argues is the *integration thesis*, which regards employment in world-market factories as a significant improvement over other employment options available to women whose earning power provides essential financial contributions to household income as well as the self-respect needed to negotiate with male household members (Tiano, 1994, p. 46). Tiano concludes from her research that there is a good deal of evidence to support both the exploitation and the integration theses; wages in the world-market factories that she studied were indubitably low and the work monotonous. As a result, women who could find alternative work, for instance in the service sector, did so. But these tended to be younger women with fewer domestic responsibilities and better education.

Thus the feminist political economy accounts of migration in the early-to mid-1980s focused on the role of female migrant labour and its linkages with transnational capital. At the same time an alternative focus began to dominate accounts of transnational migration, that of social networks, though it was some time before theorizing took a gendered form in these accounts (see Boyd, 1989).

SOCIAL NETWORKS AND MIGRANT INSTITUTIONS

Portes and Bach (1985) describe migration as a process of network building which depends on and in turn reinforces social relations across space, linking migrants and non-migrants. By the late 1980s Boyd (1989, p. 639) argues that a growing body of research existed; 'regarding the role of social networks in the etiology, composition, direction and persistence of migration flows, and in the settlement and integration of migrant populations in receiving societies'. Boyd goes on to argue (1989, p. 645) that: 'A starting point for research on social networks is that structural factors provide the context within which migration decisions are made by individuals or groups. However, at this microlevel analysis, the decision to migrate is influenced by the existence of and particpation in social networks, which connect people across space.' The main arguments are that social networks comprising personal networks (household, friends and community ties) and intermediary networks (employment agencies, traffickers, etc.) are crucial for an understanding of settlement patterns, employment and links with the homeland. Once migration begins these networks come to function as causes of migration themselves because they lower the costs and risks and increase the expected returns (Massey *et al.*, 1993). Networks constitute an important resource for migrants who use them to gain employment, housing and other assets in the migration setting. Without the existence of these social networks migration involves high costs and risks.

Massey *et al.* also argue that because affluent countries have introduced stringent immigration controls this creates a lucrative economic niche for entrepreneurs and organizations who will facilitate clandestine transnational population movements. Their activities include smuggling across borders, fake papers, arranged marriages and other illegal ploys. In turn because these practices create a highly vulnerable underclass of migrants, humanitarian organizations are set up to provide a range of services such as legal advice, shelter and help with obtaining papers.

Massey *et al.* conclude that these processes lead to a number of results that are completely different from those projected from micro-level decision-making models. They argue (1993, p. 451) that:

> As organizations develop to support, sustain, and promote international movement, the international flow of migrants becomes more and more institutionalized and independent of the factors that originally caused it...Governments have difficulty controlling migration flows once they have begun because the process of institutionalization is difficult to regulate.

The ensemble of social networks and intermediaries is referred to by Goss and Lindquist (1995, p. 319) as 'migrant institutions': 'a complex articulation of individuals, associations and organizations which extends the social action of and interaction between these agents and agencies across time and space'; they use Giddens's structuration thesis as a conceptual device to frame their discussion. The latter does not view structure as necessarily external and constraining to individual and collective agency. Rather, Giddens views structures as both constraining and enabling; as individuals, he argues, we make, remake and transform structures in the course of our daily lives (Giddens, 1984, p. 25). He also suggests that while both knowledge and power are unequally distributed, even the seemingly powerless have the capacity to mobilize resources and secure 'spaces' of control. Accordingly, Goss and Lindquist (1995, p. 345) argue that: 'Individuals act strategically within the institution to further their interests, but the capacity for such action is differentially distributed according to knowledge or rules and access to resources, which in turn may be partially determined by their position within other social institutions.'

While the Goss and Lindquist use of structuration theory is innovative and constitutes a long overdue attempt to resolve the agency/structure impasse of migration theory, Giddens's claim to have resolved the 'phoney war' between structure and agency through his thesis of structuration, is not without its critics (see for instance, Archer, 1995; Mouzelis, 1995). Layder (1997, p. 22) argues that Giddens's proposed solution gives analytical primacy to agency and that external constraints; 'do not operate independently of people, but...have properties that are not reducible to people or the reasons and motives that they give for their behaviour'. Rather he argues that we need to recognize the distinctive characteristics of different social domains however heavily they are intermeshed and mutually dependent. As we shall see in the final section I am sympathetic to the argument that; 'human activity is the outcome of the dual influence of external [macro] and situational [micro] factors' (Layder, 1997, p. 21). Moreover, while the notion of migrant institution works well in the case of Filipino migration which has been formally encouraged by successive governments and where the process of migration to a large extent has been 'institutionalized', we would want to look carefully at other situations where migration is far less institutionalized as a process. We must also look critically at how a gendered view of social networks complicates the picture, since much of the literature assumes that these networks are male dominated and that women follow men. But in the case study of migrant domestic workers I use to illustrate a gendered model of migration, we see the importance of migrant women's social networks both in learning of employment opportunities and in providing the basis for transformatory politics.

Hondagneu-Sotelo's analysis (1994, p. 96) of Mexican migration concludes that:

> Traditionally, gender relations in the networks have facilitated men's and constrained women's migration, but this is changing. While patriarchal practices and rules in families and social networks have persisted, through migration women and men reinterpret normative standards and creatively manipulate the rules of gender.

GENDERING MIGRATION THEORY

At this point, I wish to draw out of the foregoing sections what is useful in a gendered theory of migration. To reiterate, my view is that to explain an individual's decision to migrate we need to combine analysis of structural and external factors with situational, micro-level under-standings in a gendered way. Gender roles, ideologies and practices are an integral part of all social structures and as we have seen affect all aspects of transnational population movements.

Accounts that emphasize agency are useful in focusing attention on the rational calculations made by individuals about migration. This is important for a gendered account of migration because it is so often assumed that women simply 'follow' men, that their role in migration is reactive rather than proactive. As we have seen this is not necessarily the case. Nevertheless we must analyse these migratory decisions within the context of gendered social, economic and legal structures. For instance, analyses of Irish and Yugoslav migration indicate that this did not sim-ply represent an enforced response to economic hardship by women but also a deliberate, calculated move on the part of individual gendered actors that migration could provide an escape route from a society where patriarchy was an institutionalized and repressive force (see for example Gray, 1996 and Morokvasic, 1983). Given the very low social esteem and worth accorded to girls in many societies, we should be paying much closer attention to this as a motivating factor in women's migration. As the media, particularly through satellite television, has become a major feature of globalization processes then more attention might be given to what are regarded as the predominant images of women in affluent societies.

Thus agency-driven accounts are far less likely to cast migrant women as victims, as passive bodies tossed around in the turbulent seas of trans-national capital. Rather they will focus on women's economic contri-bution and their efforts to improve their own and in some cases their families' standard of living. They also provide space for the role of col-lective agency in instigating political change through alliance and coali-tion building.

A focus on household strategies can also be useful in a gendered model of migration in enabling us to unpack the gendered distribution of power within households and examine how economic transformations affect households in a gendered way. It allows us to explore the costs and benefits of migration at the micro level, particularly how 'rational' from a gendered perspective those decisions are. In addition it allows us to interrogate not just the economic contribution of labour migration for women to households at home and in migration setting but also how this effects power relations in the home.

Past structural accounts may have erred in the direction of over-emphasizing the logic of capital but this is not to say that the notion of external constraint *has* to be analysed in this way. Immigration legislation and rules are a useful way of examining the question of external constraint in migration in a gendered way. Since 1974 it has been difficult for anyone, other than professionals with scarce skills, to enter affluent societies except for reasons of family reunion. The vast majority of migrants entering in this way are women. In cases where women do enter as a spouse they are bound, usually for at least a year, to a marriage that may be unhappy even violent, because immigration laws stipulate that the woman's right of residence is dependent upon her husband (Potts, 1990).

Women's experience of migration is mediated by immigration policies and rules which in very subtle ways continue to treat women as confined to a male-regulated private sphere. Women's groups in the Netherlands have drawn attention to the fact that for the many undocumented migrant women working in the sex trade in the Netherlands, it is the women who pay through deportation if they leave the 'protection' of their procurer in the migration setting. Rather than the trafficking laws being used to punish the procurer, the worker is punished as an 'undesirable alien' (Truong and del Rosario, 1994). In addition the fact that globally women are crowded into a much narrower band of 'feminized' occupations than men, often lower paid, presents very real external constraints on the opportunities that labour migration can offer women, particularly in a situation where work permits may be difficult to obtain.

The role of social networks and intermediaries (such as agencies) is important in a gendered conceptualization of migration and I will argue in the next section that their role goes well beyond that of facilitators of migration. Finally, the theorization of migration has become increasingly divorced from the theorization of ethnic relations and this is problematic. The problem partly springs from the fact that the study of ethnic relations is pre-occupied with exploring the meanings of multiculturalism in settled communities, while the study of migration increasingly reflects issues around undocumented migration, refugee flows and asylum seeking. While this chapter cannot begin to redress this problem, the case study which follows raises many issues for the study of ethnic and gender relations, as well as for the study of migration, issues which are currently ignored in all of these literatures.

THE MAIDS INDUSTRY

The demand for domestic services world-wide has increased dramatically over the last ten years (Gregson and Lowe, 1994). As the number of dual-earner couples has increased in the affluent countries so too has the demand for maids, very often a demand which requires the domestic to live with the family. Rather than couples questioning patriarchal household and work structures (such as the 'man-made' day) and reorganising domestic labour and child-care on a shared basis, the preferred option has increasingly become one of buying in replacement labour for these chores. Women from poor countries throughout the world are now allowing couples in affluent countries to pursue well-paid careers without sacrificing children and all the comforts that the 'housewife' would have provided.

The classic illustration of this development was in 1993 when President Clinton in his zeal to find women to fill top jobs in his administration nominated Zoe Baird for Attorney General. It transpired that the Bairds employed an undocumented migrant woman as a live-in domestic worker and her husband, also undocumented, as a chauffeur. Not only were the Bairds breaking the law in employing undocumented workers, they also admitted non-payment of social security and others taxes in respect of the couple, (Macklin, 1994, p. 14).

The Baird case is not exceptional and research in the USA suggests that while in theory it is illegal for employers to hire undocumented workers, in practice the Immigration and Naturalization Service refrains from investigating such employers. This situation may be attractive for undocumented workers because they are less likely to come to the notice of the authorities if they are hidden in the privacy of the home, but it increases their exploitability as workers if the threat of deportation hangs over their head (Macklin, 1994, p. 30).

Research carried out by Anderson in five European countries in 1996 indicates that the practice of employing undocumented migrant women to carry out a wide range of domestic tasks is also widespread in Europe, (Anderson and Phizacklea, 1997). Not only are we looking at a situation in Europe of improving educational and employment opportunities for female European Union citizens, we are also looking at a situation of an increasingly ageing population. In Southern Europe, welfare services are poorly developed and whereas in the past women in extended families would have been obliged to care for the elderly, the breakdown of the extended family and the obligations that went with it are leaving a very large gap. Countries such as Italy and Spain recognize the demand for domestic services by either regularizing large numbers of undocumented domestic workers at frequent intervals or actually setting aside a certain quota of work permits every year for this occupation. This is also the case in Spain, though the quota is usually used to regularize domestics already working there. There is widespread admission that migrant workers are carrying out work that EU nationals are no longer prepared to do (such as live-in domestic work). For instance the OECD migration country report (OECD, 1995, p. 93) for Greece in 1994 argues that 1 in 12 employed persons in Greece is a foreigner:

> Most foreigners who work in Greece do so illegally... Immigrants without work permits can find jobs despite high unemployment. Their wages, perhaps three to six times more than they can earn at home, are half the market rate in Greece... foreign labour is used by many households for the care of small children and older people... the large size of the informal economy and established networks that assist newcomers with information and accommodation contribute to the continuing flows.

This is a state of affairs which recognizes that there is a two-tier labour market, one for EU nationals, and one for nationals of 'third' countries who provide cheap and flexible labour power. But examining the social relations that characterize the employment of migrant domestic workers suggests reasons other than purely financial considerations. Domestic service represents the commodification of highly personalized and emotional relationships, yet the employment of a third-country national seems to mean for many employers the opportunity to treat the worker with less respect (see Anderson and Phizacklea, 1997, p. 45). Any guilt is assuaged by the assertion that 'this is the Greek way to help foreigners' (employer interview, ibid., p. 48).

The vast majority of migrant domestics interviewed in Greece and elsewhere in Europe implied that they had no choice but to migrate in search of work. Some suggested that this compulsion was more than economic, so that the lines between economic migrant and refugee can be very blurred. But for the majority, migration was the only way in which money could be sent back to an extended family at home, a family which in some cases was caring for the migrant's children. Women from all nationalities had found work through agencies who 'loan' the women the airfare and the fee and who keep their passport in the migration setting until the 'loan' is paid off. Others had used kin networks to find work, usually a sister finding employment for another female relative.

Many of the accounts of domestic work are very grim from both a physical and emotional viewpoint, long hours of arduous work often involving emotionally demanding work with children and the elderly. But it would be wrong to paint a picture of the migrant domestic victim.

Most women are able to send home remittances and most will work towards improving their situation, particularly to regularize their legal status. In this respect the social networks of migrant workers can be more than simply a social support system in the migration setting. For instance, in 1979 in the UK the Commission for Filipino Migrant workers was set up to support Filipino migrants in the UK many of whom were maids (Anderson, 1993, p. 59). The Commission increasingly gave support to maids of many different nationalities who had left or wanted to leave abusive employers. While the Commission could provide support it became increasingly clear that immigration law as it applies to maids who enter the country with foreign employers had to be changed. Maids entering in this way have no immigration status in their own right, but are treated as 'chattels' of their employer. Alliances were forged with many other diverse groups, including trade unions, lawyers and other immigrant groups, to form KALAYAAN. The latter has campaigned vigorously for the law to be reformed and the present Labour government in the UK has pledged to change the law, in order to give domestics entering the country in this way an immigration status in their own right. A similar successful campaign waged through alliance and coalition building is reported by Macklin in Canada (Macklin, 1994).

CONCLUSION

The agency versus structure debate has preoccupied the conceptualization of migration for over 30 years. As a way of resolving this, many switched attention to an intermediate level of analysis, particularly social networks and their role in facilitating, even institutionalizing transnational migration. While many of these accounts failed to make conceptual progress, more recently there has been a recognition of the conceptual impasse and the extent to which gender sensitivity in that conceptualization is still weak. Some attempt has been made here to indicate where the main weaknesses lie in extant theorizing from a gendered perspective; and the case study of the maids industry has indicated the importance of drawing on each model if a more adequate account of the factors stimulating and facilitating migration is to be given.

2 Ethnicity, Gender and Equality in the NHS
John Carter

This chapter examines the position of minority ethnic workers in the National Health Service (NHS). It investigates the processes that lead to the concentration of workers of different ethnic origins in different types of work. Nursing is a highly gendered profession. In the two hospitals where my research took place, which I have called the Royal Bridgetown Infirmary and Lime Grove Psychiatric Hospital, the nursing workforces were 91 per cent and 74 per cent female respectively. This reflects the fact that, traditionally, there have been more male nurses in psychiatric hospitals partly because of the occasionally violent nature of the patients.

Until recently there has been relatively little empirical research into 'racial' discrimination in nursing. My research shows the way in which gender and ethnicity relate to and overlap one another. Much of the research relating to gender, ethnicity, and equality of opportunity has paid close attention to the way in which formal equal opportunities policies are frequently circumvented by line managers (Jenkins, 1986). Gender segregation within the NHS is well-documented with nursing being an almost exclusively female occupational area while administration and management have tended to be dominated by males. However, few studies of the NHS have taken account of the way in which social divisions on the basis of ethnicity also profoundly affect the sorts of segregation which exist within the nursing profession. Moreover, evidence from my research suggests that there are patterns of social change within the nursing profession which are beginning to emerge. The most significant of these is tentative evidence which suggests that few young people of minority ethnic origin are entering the nursing profession. The obvious corollary of this is that, once those women who migrated to the UK in the 1950s and 1960s to enter the nursing profession have retired, the nursing profession is likely to become increasingly an ethnically homogenous and white occupational area.

During the two detailed case studies of hospitals run by South West Health Trust I interviewed approximately sixty staff including nurses, ancillary workers and managers at the Trust. The interviews covered a

range of different workers, both male and female and from different
ethnic groups. To complement the qualitative material, questionnaires
were distributed to all the workers in the two divisions concerned,
namely Medicine at the RBI and Psychiatry at Lime Grove Hospital.
The purpose was to examine the relative positions of different ethnic
groups within the occupational structure and to attempt to gain some
quantitative information about the promotion process.

The RBI is close to Bridgetown city centre and is regarded as the
Trust's flagship hospital. It employs around two thousand staff. The
hospital deals with all major specialities and is considered to be one of
the leading hospitals in the country for organ transplants. Lime Grove
Hospital is roughly five miles outside the city and, owing to the policy of
care in the community, is the last of the city's long stay mental hospitals.
Bridgetown has a diverse ethnic population which is similar to the proportion of ethnic minorities in the population of the UK as a whole. My
research shows that nursing was one of the key occupations into which
women, particularly from the Caribbean, were recruited during the
1950s. During the course of my research I interviewed a large number of
retired nurses from the Caribbean and those nurses of Caribbean origin
who were still working were approaching retirement. Most of the minority ethnic nurses in my research worked in Lime Grove Psychiatric Hospital. The concentration of minority ethnic nurses in psychiatry reflects
the patterns of recruitment that prevailed during the 1950s when the
acute shortage of nursing staff was felt most keenly in psychiatry and
geriatrics, and it was to these two areas that most minority ethnic nurses
were recruited. However, at the RBI there were very few nurses of
minority origin. The National Health Service union, UNISON, estimates
that approximately eight per cent of the NHS work force is comprised of
minority ethnic workers. However, in the two Bridgetown hospitals in

Table 2.1   Ethnic origin of work force at RBI and Lime Grove

Ethnic origin	RBI (%)	Lime Grove (%)
White	97.86	93.62
Black Caribbean	0.80	2.13
Black African	0.27	0.30
Black Other	0.27	
Indian		0.61
Pakistani		0.61
Chinese		0.61
Other	0.80	2.13

which my research is based, the figures are particularly low for the RBI at around 2 per cent and about 6 per cent at Lime Grove Psychiatric Hospital.

The respective numbers of minority ethnic workers in each of the hospitals in my research bears some comparison with the national figures in Table 2.2:

Table 2.2   Ethnic origin of health service workers

	White (%)	*Black (%)*	*Asian (%)*	*Other (%)*	*Not stated (%)*
All nursing and midwifery staff	88.9	3.3	1.0	3.7	3.2

Source: Department of Health Statistical Bulletin 11.10.94

Nationally the figure of minority ethnic nurses is approximately 11 per cent. The figures from my own research show that the RBI has a figure well below that, while at Lime Grove the figure is closer with nearly 7 per cent of staff of minority ethnic origin. The concentration of non-white workers in the two least desirable specialities of geriatrics and psychiatry within the NHS is already well documented. Indeed the Equal Opportunities Commission (1991) noted that:

> A survey undertaken in 1986 found that black nurses were repeatedly passed over for promotion. 96 per cent of white nurses were promoted to sister or charge nurse within 18 months of qualifying, compared with only 45 per cent of black nurses. The survey confirmed black nurses' concentration on night shifts and in the less prestigious medical specialities, such as geriatric care and mental health. *Black nurses were encouraged to apply for departments and specialities where considerable numbers of black people were already employed* (p. 5 my emphasis).

Both quantitative and qualitative data from my research within the Trust suggests that there is a noticeable division of labour based on ethnic lines. One of the most striking examples of this is the proportion of minority ethnic staff who work on the night shift at Lime Grove Hospital with 73 per cent of the non-white staff working the night shift compared to 36 per cent of the white staff. This pattern is structured partly by the process of recruitment in the 1950s but also by the choices made by staff. That is, there is a process of self-selection in that minority ethnic staff tend to move to areas where they believe they have the best possible chance of promotion.

During interviews with minority ethnic staff who worked nights, the reasons that were cited for preferring nights were that it was easier for child care arrangements, there were considerable numbers of other minority ethnic staff also on nights and that this was therefore likely to create less tension between white staff and minority ethnic staff. The other dominant factor which helps to explain the concentration of minority ethnic staff in the least desirable nursing areas is the success of white nurses in socially closing the other, more desirable areas to minority ethnic staff. This has been achieved through the use of informal networks which allows discriminatory practices to flourish, but also through the use of qualifications. Many minority ethnic nurses are (State Enrolled Nurse) SEN qualified, a qualification which has now been abolished and is considered a 'poor relation' to the (State Registered Nurse) SRN qualification. There remains the very real possibility that minority ethnic nurses may be relegated to the lowest echelons of nursing precisely because they are unable to convert their SEN into qualifications which allow for upward mobility.

Fewer training opportunities were available to Black nurses. A high proportion of Black nurses are SENs. This grade is now being phased-out so that the availability of conversion courses for registered practioner grade is crucial if Black nurses are not to be downgraded to the role of nursing auxiliaries. However, many Black SENs are mature women with children, who may not be able to move to where courses are available. Virtually no conversion courses from SEN to SRN are available on a part time basis (EOC, 1991)

ASPECTS OF ACCEPTABILITY IN THE RECRUITMENT PROCESS

A useful sociological distinction is drawn by Jenkins (1986) between suitability criteria and acceptability criteria. Suitability criteria refer to the skills, qualifications and experience a candidate has and that are relevant to a particular post. Acceptability criteria refer to more subjective opinions about whether or not a candidate will fit-in with the existing workforce, factors such as appearance, manner and attitude, maturity, gut feeling, labour market history, personality and ability to 'fit in', and English language competence. In my research there were several aspects of acceptability which proved to be highly significant in determining the outcome of the selection process. It should be remembered that in situations where there are a number of candidates with similar qualifications and experience a decision about who should get a job can *only* be based on how acceptable that candidate is to the interview panel.

All the ward managers who were interviewed stressed the importance of 'fitting-in' with the team. Clearly in a working environment where a large proportion of the workforce are white it is possible that one of the key criteria for 'fitting-in' will be that a person should be white. There is also a considerable emphasis on the importance of 'steady' and 'reliable' workers, as Richard Jenkins (1986, p. 49) notes:

> Although the specific content of notions of acceptability will obviously alter with the nature of the job, its position within the class hierarchy of organizations and occupations and the nature of the organization concerned, the principle of a threshold of suitability beyond which criteria of acceptability come into play, is common to all job recruitment. The emphasis throughout, in all notions of acceptability, is upon the predictable and reliable person who will not cause management any problems.

During interviews with ward managers at the RBI and Lime Grove Hospital it was emphasized that fitting-in was decisive for successful applicants. One ward manager noted that: 'I look for the person who is going to fit-in with the team best, someone who won't rock the boat. My senior staff nurse and I usually know who to appoint'.

Within the Trust there seemed to be many common sense assumptions about what sort of candidate would or would not fit-in with existing workers, many of them highly ethnocentric and stereotypical. The issue of English language competence for example, was regarded by minority ethnic staff as *crucial* to success in the job seeking process. One Asian nurse I interviewed explained the importance of English language competence:

> Most of the Black and Asian workers in the Trust tend to be at the bottom of the hierarchy. It is partly to do with interviews. There is a big cultural gap between the panel and the Black and Asian applicants. Black and Asian people may apply but they do not get shortlisted. It all comes down to a way of articulating their opinion...it is an issue of language. I could know all the right words, but I do not know some of the nuances of grammar, or the right way of synthesizing sentences, because I come from a different culture. Whereas, with two

white people all that is unspoken. They have grown together culturally. They are in-tune if you like.

Sometimes it comes down to understanding the question. For
example, compare the way the Americans speak English to the way
the English speak English. Americans will tell you straight what they
think. Britain is somewhat different. There is a roundabout way of
saying things so that you do not offend someone and there is a lot of
non-verbal communication which is taken for granted and is tied up
with the culture. This country is very Americanized, through the
media and so on, and with all the influence of America there are still
fundamental misunderstandings between the British and Americans. So
imagine a situation where you come from a culture that has had no
impact on Britain. It is a hundred time harder to communicate. For
example, Asian people, well, at least those born in say India or Pakistan, will tell you their history before they actually answer your question. If you ask them how do you like living in Bridgetown? They will
say oh well we don't have relations here so we are not very happy, or
we have lived in Cardiff and Cardiff was better because so and so.
They just won't say that they don't like it here, they have to give you
some history. It is just a particular way of speaking and explaining
things that is different, and that sometimes lets them down when it
comes to the interview panel. The panel think, 'I don't need all this,
all I want to know is can they give an injection?' So there needs to be a
way of coping with that.

The issue of language competence was frequently mentioned by staff at
both hospitals. Ward managers referred to the importance of speaking,
'The Queen's English'. Reasons for the stress on language competence
include being able to understand instructions and communicating with
other workers, patients and the public. All of these are closely tied-up
with managerial control. Thus, speaking 'The Queen's English' could be
seen as another aspect of 'fitting-in', that is, of being an ideal worker who
does what they are told. Few ward managers were actually able to give
any objective indication of how they measured a candidate's ability to
speak English. Indeed, what is good English seems a highly problematic
concept. What a particular ward manager defines as good English seems
likely to be bound up with their own cultural expectations which may or
may not be ethnocentric. English language competence could indeed be
regarded as a central aspect of acceptability. However in interviews with
ward managers and minority ethnic staff another issue proved to be
even more significant, that of the number of minority ethnic staff who

had been formally disciplined. Responses from my questionnaire show that approximately 2 per cent of white staff at Lime Grove Hospital had been formally disciplined compared to approximately 20 per cent of minority ethnic staff. A Black African charge nurse described what he saw as an inequitable application of the rules:

> About 98 per cent of all disciplinary cases here involve black staff. Managers are just not flexible. They could deal with problems very differently, you know informally, but they always go through the disciplinary machinery. If you have a Black nurse and a white nurse and there is a problem, then it will always go to disciplinary procedure for the Black nurse but rarely for the white nurse.

Similarly, an African-Caribbean manager at Lime Grove Hospital suggested that:

> The disciplinary policy is used in a very heavy-handed fashion. The basic problem is that most of the white staff here are not used to working with Black people and the inexperience shows. Problems arise because of cultural differences. White staff don't know how to deal with it and it blows up into a conflict.

There *is* a tendency among key figures in management to view minority ethnic workers within the Trust as potential 'trouble-makers'. In situations where there are a number of candidates for promotion with similar qualifications and experience the label of 'trouble-maker' which has frequently been attached to minority ethnic candidates seems likely to influence often mainly white selection panels in a negative way. During my research many white staff seemed indiscriminately to attach the label of trouble-maker to *all* minority ethnic staff. It is not possible to accurately gauge how widespread such views were. None the less, it is clear from informal conversations in canteens, waiting-rooms and corridors with a range of staff that such views are not unusual among white staff. In a hospital like Lime Grove which is effectively a small village, the informal networks which exist between ward managers may have a profound influence over the promotion prospects of minority ethnic staff who have been disciplined. Once someone has acquired a label as a 'trouble-maker', regardless of the actual outcome of a disciplinary hearing, it is very difficult for that person to shake off that label. Given the preference of ward managers to choose candidates for promotion who 'fit-in' and who are not likely to 'rock the boat' it seems probable that since minority ethnic workers are more frequently disciplined than their white peers, they face a considerable obstacle in the promotion process.

There seems to be an underlying assumption about the employment of a candidate who is not personally known to a ward manager. That is, that it constitutes a risk. The risk in appointing a candidate is increased when that candidate is from a minority ethnic group because of the belief prevalent within the Trust that minority ethnic workers are trouble-makers. Similarly, when the candidate is female the risk is again increased because it is considered that she may leave to have a family. There is a sense in which 'whiteness' is one of the most significant criteria for recruitment and promotion.

The distinction between suitability and acceptability criteria is not a rigid one and there are occasions when the two sets of criteria converge. That is, there are certain jobs that are socially constructed as female jobs rather than male jobs. Thus, one of the principal elements of both suitability and acceptability is that the candidate is female rather than male. Mainwaring (1984) refers to the concept of tacit skills that are involved in certain jobs. Nursing is a good example of a job in which both suitability and acceptability criteria converge to make nursing a predominantly female profession precisely because the skills that are required in nurses are believed to be present 'naturally' in women.

BAD FAITH

There is undoubtedly an antagonistic relationship between some of the minority ethnic workers in the Trust and senior managers. This stems in part from a lack of minority ethnic managers at the highest level. Several minority ethnic workers have been promoted to an intermediate level within the Trust but only one has reached the highest level.

Table 2.3   Current job grade and ethnicity

	higher (%)	intermediate (%)	lower (%)
White group	20.57	34.49	44.94
Black group	18.18	63.64	18.18

The absence of minority ethnic staff at higher levels is taken by some minority ethnic workers within the Trust to be *ipso facto* evidence of discrimination. There is a widespread feeling of disenchantment among different groups of minority ethnic workers. Accusations of 'racist' discrimination have been frequent. This has led to considerable friction between some minority ethnic groups and senior managers at the Trust. During interviews with minority ethnic nurses the feelings of disenchantment were apparent. For example, responses to questions about the Trust's equal opportunities policy included:

> If you ask managers about it [the equal opportunities policy] they always say that they have something in progress. Of course you never see the end result. If you ask about the equal opportunities policy they show you some glossy brochure but *nothing* ever gets done. (Chinese nurse)

> The Trust is just like everywhere else, the equal opportunities policy is just a piece of paper but it does not mean very much. (African-Caribbean psychiatric nurse)

> The policy does not mean anything because it does not change people's attitudes. (Asian psychiatric nurse)

One particular group of minority ethnic workers have formed The Black Workers' Forum. This is a vocal and highly politicized group of minority ethnic workers who work mainly at the Trust's mental health team. The Forum has been openly critical of the Trust's attempts to implement equal opportunities. The Black Workers' Forum articulates an aggressive, anti-racist stance and has proved unpopular with some senior managers. It regards the absence of minority ethnic workers from positions of power as *de facto* evidence of the failure of the equal opportunities policy. Their political stance in relation to equal opportunities is one in which: 'Equality of opportunity is not seen as something to be granted by white society. Rather it is a right which must be wrested from a racist society' (Jenkins, 1986).

There may exist a conflict between the political objectives of those workers involved in the Black Workers' Forum and their professional objectives. It is clear that some of the members of the Black Workers' Forum have become preoccupied with advancing the cause of minority ethnic workers leading to allegations that their work has suffered as well as to accusations of unprofessional conduct.

FORMAL POLICIES AND INFORMAL NETWORKS: EQUAL OPPORTUNITIES AT SOUTH WEST HEALTH TRUSTS

South West Health Trust has had a formal equal opportunities policy in operation for some ten years. All ward managers are obliged to attend a two day training course run by the Trust's personnel department on equal opportunities in the selection process. The selection process was described by one of the personnel managers thus:

> Ward managers draw up the job specification and are sometimes helped by personnel, often so that there is some element of self-selection in terms of experience and qualifications... but in the end it is the ward manager who draws up the criteria using the Trust-wide stated criteria and *any others they feel are relevant.*

The absence of minority ethnic managers is partly a result of the Trust's own policy of internal recruitment. Their current policy is to recruit managers from within the organization and to give them in-house management training. There is extensive internal recruitment within the Trust at all levels. The use of an internal labour market is clearly one of the factors that militates against the recruitment of minority ethnic nurses and managers, as Jenkins (1986, p. 121) notes:

> In those organizations with a small number of black workers, or with the majority of black workers in low status jobs, an organizational preference for internal search may have detrimental consequences for black job seekers. In the case of organizations with small numbers of black workers such a policy is likely to ensure that the situation does not change. Given that the majority of the workforce is white, it is white job seekers who will be more likely to receive information about vacancies prior to their appearing on the 'open' market.

The use of an extended internal labour market combined with the sorts of informal networks which clearly exist at the two hospitals works to undermine formal recruitment processes and the Trust's equal opportunities policy. The most significant informal network is the one between ward managers who meet on a weekly basis to discuss clinical issues. It is at these meetings that details of possible candidates for internal vacancies are passed on either formally or informally. Ward managers are in a powerful position *vis-à-vis* the recruitment process. Much of the work of the personnel function has been devolved to ward managers. It is official Trust policy that in the final analysis the ward manager should have the most influence over decisions regarding appointments. In interviews with ward managers at both the RBI and Lime Grove it was clear that they believed themselves to be the best judges of who would or would not fit with their team. Some were openly hostile to the influence of personnel and regarded their presence on interview panels as an unwelcome intrusion. The issue of the autonomy of line managers is crucial to the understanding of how formal policies are circumvented. As Collinson *et al.* (1990) state:

> Line managers attach a particular importance to their functional autonomy. When refusing to accept the incursions of professional personnel managers, line managers often articulate a bread-winner ideology through which they justify claims to exclusive power over recruitment by emphasizing their significant contribution to the success of the organization as the producers of profit and wealth. (p. 86)

As a line manager interviewed stated:

> Of course people know how to get round it [the equal opportunities policy] ... what usually happens is that if there is a vacancy they often have someone in mind for that post, they know people who would be good in that particular job, it makes the recruiting process more difficult because you have to go through the process formally, to show that you have been fair. But you end up taking on the person who you thought would be good in the first place, *but you have to be seen to be doing it correctly*.

Compare this to the views of nurses at Lime Grove hospital:

> Sometimes if they know somebody before they advertise the job they have got a better chance than a candidate from outside. I know of a couple of occasions when they advertised a post but they already decided who was going to get the job before it was advertised. Everybody knew that Mr A was going to get the job and sure enough he got it. (Mauritian health care assistant)

> There are occasions when a job is advertised and the interview is a bit of a farce. You know the job has to be advertised but they are just going through the motions because they have already got someone in mind for the post. (African-Caribbean staff nurse)

> Fixing jobs? Is that what you mean? Yes it happens here, but it goes on everywhere not just in nursing. To a certain extent you can understand it because on a ward like this you need someone who knows the patients and who knows what they are doing, so if you know that someone can do the job then it makes sense to appoint them. (White health care assistant)

Much has been written about the formalization of the recruitment process. The formalization of recruitment practices is generally regarded as more, rather than less, desirable. One of the central conclusions of Jewson and Mason's 1986 research is that formalization of the recruitment process does not necessarily result in more equitable outcomes. Formality is, however, more desirable than informality. On the basis of the research carried out at these two hospitals there is little to suggest that formality has any effect on the recruitment and promotion process at all. The difference of emphasis on process and outcome is the source of considerable tension within the Trust. There are a range of reasons for the lack of senior minority ethnic managers including the persistent failure of minority ethnic applicants to break through the barrier between intermediate management posts and senior management posts. One of the few female African Caribbean managers at the Trust expressed considerable disillusion with the way the Trust operated its recruitment and promotion policy:

> They just don't want Black and Asian managers. The whole management set-up here is totally closed. They use the cadre system to redeploy managers internally because the Trust has a policy of no compulsory redundancy. The cadre is a pool of managers within the Trust and they have weekly meetings to discuss overall management strategy. When I got my job here as a manager I was not in the cadre. When I asked the director of personnel why I was not in the cadre he said he would sort it out, but if it had been anyone else they would have been in the cadre from the beginning.

PATTERNS OF PROMOTION

A comparison of different rates of promotion for men and women and white and minority ethnic groups shows that there are very different

Table 2.4 Ethnicity and education

	White group (%)	Black group (%)
No formal qualifications	15.94	13.64
Apprenticeship	1.56	
'O' Levels	38.76	40.9
'A' Levels	15.31	13.64
Diploma	15.62	18.18
Degree	12.81	13.64

career paths for the different groups. There are a number of factors that might explain the different rates of promotion for white and Black staff. Foremost of these is the educational background of the different groups. Table 2.4 shows that, if anything, the Black sample is slightly better qualified than the white sample. It would therefore be difficult to attribute differences in promotion to educational background.

Despite a similar educational background the Black and white groups within the directorate of psychiatry had diametrically opposed rates of promotion as shown in Table 2.5 below:

Table 2.5 Ethnicity and number of promotions

	0 promotions (%)	1 to 4 promotions (%)
White group	23.58	76.42
Black group	75.00	25.00

There are similar (although slightly less pronounced) differences in rates of promotion for men and women as shown in Table 2.6:

Table 2.6 Gender and number of promotions

	0 promotions (%)	1 to 4 promotions (%)
Males	19.15	80.85
Females	30.95	69.05

One of the most obvious consequences of the lack of minority ethnic staff is that there are very few minority ethnic members of staff who can sit on an interview panel. One of the Asian workers who had experience of sitting on an interview panel stated that more minority ethnic group workers on interview panels would help:

It will help but it won't sort the problem and doing that imposes pressure on those staff who are Asian, you know we still have a job to do, and it is very time consuming to get involved with interviews. Of course not all Black and Asian people share the same dialect or meanings in their speech, people have a very different understanding. There is also the problem that some African and African Caribbean and Asian people are very racist themselves, they have internalized white values and have rejected their own culture because they see it as the culture of failure. But it is still a good check on the interview process. The panels I have been involved in have been pretty good, but then I react if someone says something and I don't mince words. The interviews I have been involved with have all followed the process very well and I have seen some successes for Black people. But you have to remember that white people will always tone down what they think, but then later after work, down at the pub you can hear them talk about Pakis and niggers. They just don't say it at work.

The simple numerical under representation of minority ethnic staff makes it difficult for interview panels at the two hospitals to be ethnically diverse. When combined with the preference of ward managers to appoint internal candidates, often those known to the ward manager, there is an increased possibility of discrimination on the grounds of ethnicity.

CONCLUSIONS

My research shows elements of continuity and change for minority ethnic workers in the National Health Service. Continuity in that the patterns of segregation that predominated in the 1950s and 1960s have persisted to the present day. There is evidence that minority ethnic nurses are located in the least desirable types of nursing (psychiatry and geriatrics) and on the least desirable shift (the night shift). Minority ethnic nurses also seem to be located at the bottom of the nursing hierarchy often as heath care assistants with few reaching management positions. The key aspect of social change is that there is some evidence to suggest that the numbers of minority ethnic nurses in the Health Service are beginning to decline. Also of considerable significance is the introduction of equal opportunities policies which represents an acknowledgement of the existence of segregation and discrimination even if only at a symbolic level. While the efficacy of such policies has been extensively debated they are a sign that overt discrimination is rarely tolerated. Of course critics of such polices quite correctly point out that this has made discrimination covert rather than overt. Those non-white nurses that remain in the NHS tend to be first generation migrants who were recruited in the 1950s and 1960s. There is also little evidence to suggest that young people of minority ethnic origin regard nursing as fulfilling career.

My research also supports the findings of others such as Jenkins who argue that informal networks often determine selection outcomes. Given the disproportionate number of Black workers who go through the discipline process it seems highly likely that they are at a real disadvantage in the recruitment and promotion processes. One ward manager acknowledged the significance of the disciplinary process in the promotion and recruitment process: 'Whether I like it or not there *is* a problem with Black workers and absenteeism in this Trust. There have also been a lot of disciplinary cases involving Black workers and I have to say that it is always at the back of my mind when I am interviewing Black and Asian candidates.'

The introduction of a formal equal opportunities policy at the Trust has helped to eradicate the most overt forms of discrimination. However the ability of ward managers to manipulate selection outcomes is evidence that informal networks remain highly significant in the recruitment and promotion process. Thus a vicious circle exists with Black workers effectively excluded from the informal networks which determine selection outcomes as few are in positions of power. The consequence of this is that those Black workers who remain in the health service are likely to stay stuck on the lowest rungs of the nursing hierarchy. There is, therefore, little evidence to suggest that equal opportunity policies have had a marked impact on breaking the cycle of discrimination and disadvantage experienced by non-white workers in the Health Service.

3 Roscas, Ethnicity and Strategy: Suriname Creole Women's Saving Clubs in Amsterdam
Ineke Van Wetering

Roscas are associations by means of which people save funds collectively and are able to 'draw out' in such a way as to enable them to afford things which would otherwise be beyond their financial reach. One typical setting within which these forms of collaboration are found is among migrant communities in urban centres. In the present case study the migrants are Surinamese settled in Amsterdam after the independence of Surinam from the Netherlands. The savings and credit associations not only provide an excellent site for the observation of ethnicity 'in action' but also raise the question of whether they are to be primarily understood in economic (economistic) terms or with a primary emphasis on the cultural and symbolic. It is clear too that women have a leading role in the organization of the Rosca in this case study and present a close-up view of the intersection of gender and ethnicity.

The materials on which this chapter is based were gathered in the 1980s in Amsterdam. Roscas, or Rotating Savings and Credit Associations, that is: associations formed upon a core of participants who make regular contributions to a fund which is given, in whole or in part, to each contributor in rotation (Ardener and Burman 1995, p. vii), were not part of the research design. My main interest was the reproduction of an African American worldview in the diaspora. As lower-class women have been singled out as the guardians of Creole popular religious culture, I focused on the ritual life of elderly female migrants. Gradually, I found that religion and finance are closely interrelated, that all women involved in the religious subculture also participated in Roscas or *kasmoni*, as they are referred to in *Sranan Tongo* or Suriname Creole language. Although I noted the significance of this way of managing financial affairs for women, research on this matter has been mainly exploratory.[1] My data refer to women's strategies only, and conclusions about this system should await the results of further inquiries (Bijnaar,

1996). Yet, it is possible at this stage to redefine research questions, to go into the issues of gender and class differences, and discuss some of our basic assumptions about migrants' financial strategies.

In a recent publication, Ardener and Burman (1995) have raised a number of important questions concerning Roscas. They have noted (1995, pp. 16–17) a lingering controversy between those who favour an economistic approach – based on allegedly 'hard facts' – and anthropologists who stress the embeddedness of economics in culture. Also, significant lacunae in our knowledge about the functioning of 'money-go-rounds' are found: the participation of women (Ardener 1995, p. 11) for instance, has been a neglected issue. In the same volume, Besson (1995, p. 269) signals this lack of data on women's use of Roscas for a specific region, the Caribbean, and suggests the topic as a field for future research. The former Scandinavian and Dutch territories are singled out specifically (1995, p. 278) as areas where information on this system of handling money matters is wanting. The same holds, Besson maintains (1995, p. 281) for the financial strategies of Caribbean migrants, a subject on which data are contradictory.

Since Roscas have been placed on the research agenda, the main perspective has been an assessment of their potential for economic development. Based on assumptions about 'modernization', the evaluation of indigenous associations – the measuring rod being the incentives given to business enterprise and so-called 'rationality' of individualist accumulation – has often been ethnocentric.[2] These concerns have not vanished, although research questions have been reformulated and specified. Rowlands (1995, pp. 120, 123) has suggested that Roscas follow a different logic and are part of an active appropriation of capital for socially desirable purposes. This approach seems to hold great promise. The argument presented here is that Roscas are embedded in a subculture that protects a vulnerable sector of the population from the onslaught and vicissitudes of world capitalism and sustains a counter-offensive.

ELDERLY CREOLE MIGRANT WOMEN IN AMSTERDAM

In 1975 Suriname, a former Dutch colony, gained political independence. A large number of its citizens, however, feared for their country's future, opted for Dutch citizenship and settled in the Netherlands. In Amsterdam's Bijlmermeer, a newly built city quarter, facilities for housing the new wave of immigrants quickly made a cluster of highrise apartment buildings into a 'little Paramaribo'. About 25 per cent of

Bijlmermeer's inhabitants are Surinamese, predominantly Creole, and in some flats the percentage is higher. The high ethnic population density of the quarter has enabled the residents to maintain a community life that is in many ways reminiscent of that in their home town. Gradually, middle-class Creole residents moved out of what they feared was like a ghetto, and by the mid-1980s most inhabitants were unemployed and depended on social security. Many households are female-headed; a pattern familiar from the Caribbean has re-established itself across the Atlantic (Buschkens, 1974; Hoolt, 1988). The newcomers show allegiance to various 'traditional' institutions related to kinship and religiosity, both in its orthodox-Christian and popular varieties. One of the 'traditional' practices is participation in *kasmoni*.

KASMONI

The definition of Roscas as given by Ardener and Burman fully applies to Creole *kasmoni*. The participants contribute a sum each month to a fund, which is immediately handed over to one of them. In principle this is continued until all have had their turn. As a reason to take part the women mention a wish to have access to a lump sum which would be difficult to gather by other saving methods. In a survey of Creole single mothers' life situation in Amsterdam, Lenders and Van de Rhoer (1984, pp. 52–4) found that women whose incomes are low but – thanks to welfare payments – regular, use the *kasmoni* system for requirements not met by formal Dutch institutions. Partly, these are expenditures which are problematic for all women in this income bracket: the purchase or replacement of durable consumer goods. Partly costs are involved that are specific for Suriname Creoles. A birthday celebration, and particularly a jubilee year or *bigi jari* is an occasion that is cherished as a key point in ethnic group life, is an oft-mentioned aim to save up for. Travel to the home country, for burials and other rituals, is also financed in this manner. Savings are also earmarked for the long-term project of buying a compound in Paramaribo, and to return there is the great ideal. Often, day-to-day expenses hamper carrying this out, but still, many succeed in realizing this project. The present exchange rate of Dutch and Surinamese money favours the attempts.[3]

Although the economic situation of the women participating in the Roscas discussed here would define them as a residual category at the lowest rungs of the social ladder, this characterization would create a lopsided impression. It is hard to clearly delineate the class position of the women whose strategies are my concern, and to link the type of *kasmoni* they favour with class interests. Their position on the labour market would make them into proletarians, but, as Wolf (1982, p. 360) has it: 'Working classes are not made in their place of work alone . . .' This is certainly true of these women, as we will note. Their aspirations are not only to survive, but to reach a status of proprietorship and respectability.

RISKS AND SANCTIONS

Lenders and Van de Rhoer (1984, pp. 52–4) noted that women are aware of the risks of misappropriation in the prevalent system; the respondents mentioned the dangers of default and mismanagement. They replied they hoped to obviate these drawbacks by a careful selection of participants. Most women accept only those participants they know well, kinswomen for instance, and rely on the effects of social control and sanctions: exclusion from further participation in case of non-payment. Ardener and Burman (1995, pp. 4–5) discuss a number of cases where such sanctions and other measures seem to be reasonably successful. Besson (1995, p. 272) and Bijnaar (1996) stress the social importance of reputation and personal worth in the Caribbean. The role of a *kasmoni* organizer confers prestige, and fear of loss of social status is a powerful incentive to meet expectations. This is certainly true of Creole *kasmoni*. Nevertheless, complaints are voiced about commercialization and a hardening of the system. Organizers no longer are content with a modest compensation, settled by mutual arrangement, but sometimes charge a considerable sum, occasionally amounting to a month's contribution. The sanctions have sharper edges now and then: the two researchers report one interviewee's remark, that her *kasmoni*'s organizer would not hesitate to set her gun-armed son upon defaulters.

Lenders and Van de Rhoer (1984, pp. 52–4) found that 90 per cent of the women they interviewed had run up debts. They regard this as a consciously planned strategy. The impression is created, that most Creole women have a different view of financial management than is thought of as desirable in western-oriented middle classes.

Quite striking is the continuity in the system, which begs the question of the 'why', and the failure of change to materialize. To some extent the financial position of women has greatly improved after migration to the Netherlands. The plain fact that there is a financial basis that was lacking in the home country could – as might be argued – affect the way people deal with money matters. Welfare agencies for migrants have taken initiatives – courses in budgeting have been started, for instance – which did not lead to tangible results. This will not imply that no changes have occurred at all, or that Creole women have shied away from the modern world. The contrary is true. Also, great differences are to be expected between *kasmoni* groups, in style of management and social control as well as in financial strategies of individual participants.

A mentality favouring entrepreneurship is manifestly present among Creole women; they are busily engaged in hustling. However, due to a slender starting position, as a rule these initiatives remain modest. I have not come across even one case of a lower-class female entrepreneur who had switched to a larger-scale type of business, or who had achieved some independence or autonomy from the mutual aid system and the supportive networks to which the *kasmoni* known to me belong. There is a lot of speculation about great economic successes, daydreaming about them, but the ideals are rarely realized (cf. Sansone, 1992). It is striking, that any gains won are reinvested in the same cooperative networks.

THEORY AND METHOD

In migrant studies, theorizing has remained stuck with the notion of 'survival strategies'. Invariably, the attempts are characterized as stopgap solutions, failing to take off in a more promising direction due to restricted opportunities or opposition from a discouraging environment.[4] The image of pitiable victims lacking business sense is reinforced unintentionally. Lenders and Van de Rhoer (1984, p. 53), for instance, stress the importance of the investments in feasts as an underpinning of emotional ties so badly needed in the diaspora. It is doubtful whether we do well in reinforcing the oft-cited opposition between emotion and interest. A conclusion on a single item, too quickly drawn, can lead to a wrong evaluation of the whole situation.

Apart from the prevailing theoretical approaches, the research methods used contribute to the difficulty. Social research into 'minority' issues mostly is a short-range affair, which implies that the only feasible technique is the interview. Though indispensable in some matters, as a sole source of information this almost inevitably leads to misinterpretations.

Rash conclusions, drawn from data based on interview material, abound. The questions put to interviewees concern for example the expectations as to help from relatives. The answers uniformly showed low hopes: in these verbal assessments, kinship no longer was what it used to be. Ratings as 'high' or 'low' are notoriously relative and subjective, as is well-known. The way an interviewer classifies such answers may contribute to distortion. The interviewer often has a middle-class background and kinship has different connotations in this sector than among lower-class Creoles. Students are inclined to infer, that social ties are weakening. Respondents will voice such statements with great eloquence; it is part of social rhetorics, and of the strategies to keep these ties intact. Complaints are a powerful weapon in a social struggle, certainly within the bosom of this subgroup. So the question arises whether the inference is correct, and to which social sector it applies. The conclusion has been drawn prematurely, the reactions read in an ethnocentric way. Several data suggest the opposite. The amounts of money involved in the mailing of parcels to the folks back home are in themselves an indication of an impressive solidarity. But it is conceivable that differences between social sectors are large. The inhabitants of Bijlmermeer, at any rate, the female heads of households who participate in *kasmoni*, are actively involved. The question has been presented, whether participation in *kasmoni* serves as a protective device against claims from relatives or other levelling forces. This is, to some extent, true. In day-to-day life so many requests for support turn up, that it would be impossible to gratify all, which would prevent one from laying aside anything. But on the other hand, this is obviously not true. The striking fact is, that all savings are channelled back into current circuits. The birthday celebrations referred to above, for instance, provide a free meal to a great number of persons, and create employment for young musicians. As a first impression, and a preliminary hypothesis, all economic dealings of this social sector could be taken as attempts to keep the collectivity afloat in a sea of insecurities. The extent to which people are willing to shoulder such responsibilities is simply amazing. An observer unfamiliar with anthropological approaches and the tendency to look for a rationale behind behaviour that is apparently inexplicable, could be seduced into speaking of irrationality.

RESEARCH ON MONEY AND CULTURE

When financial matters and other sensitive issues are involved, insight into alternative courses of action people select cannot be gleaned from interviews, which yield a harvest of socially desirable answers. If this is true of the European 'natives', it applies even more to migrants. With a professionalization in social sciences, a pretence has arisen that we have gained a grip on reality by our theories and methods. But, in fact, what we often do is to create an appearance of true knowledge and advance allaying formulas. A topic like Roscas among people in uncertain situations is an awkward subject, and hard to tackle.

Bijlmermeer's inhabitants are averse to all interviews, even about matters that are seemingly innocent and hardly problematic. Direct questioning on any subject is generally looked upon by Creoles as impolite.[5] Inquisitivess or openness are not regarded as virtues but as stupid, and a token of a lack of social sophistication. The pursuit of valid information, so highly valued in modern middle classes, is distrusted. Even when allegedly used to take away prejudice and correct misunderstandings, the quest for information is interpreted as idle curiosity and a violation of a social code. Self-respecting women display disinterest in other people's doings. 'I am in no way involved' and 'I mind my own business' are standard expressions used on all occasions. In fact, the preoccupation with peers is great and there is little that remains hidden in a gregarious community, but the front stage presented to others does belie this.

I have lived in Bijlmermeer for five years and joined a women's club that has the preservation of Creole culture as its main aim. *Kasmoni* are looked upon as part of that culture. Money and 'traditional' or popular religion are both matters people hang a shroud of mystery around, even when, in the eyes of the outsider, there is little cause to do so. At the meetings of the women's club, the members call each other apart to discuss some monetary transaction, trivial though it may be. People keen to investigate 'real life' in financial matters are thrown back upon shreds and snippets of information, derived from everyday interactions. Some examples about dealing with money:

- One of the club's members proudly shows a note of fl 25 – that she received the day before. She had gone to a party, where she had helped the hostess to model a starched kerchief into an appropriate Creole-style headdress. Such services are usually rewarded with a simple gift of a few guilders. However, the woman had been so pleased with the result that she spontaneously had offered the tenfold and had added: 'Lady, I appreciate you for the accomplished way you have done this.'
- In front of the baker's shop I meet a woman, who, as I know, is constantly short of money. She has a grown-up son who is a drug addict and steals everything he can lay his hands on. I am quite

surprised when she presses a note of fl 5 – into my hand, adding that she celebrates her birthday next Thursday and hopes I will attend. A possible explanation for the unexpected gift is that there are so many such occasions. It is hard, at times, to get a company together, and all are keen to have an all-out occasion. Besides, this woman has a reputation of being a prostitute which makes her unpopular. It is clear that every person must be very active in organizing her own enterprise, although this will only have levelling effects. It creates a basis for a social reputation, though.

- I go shopping with a friend who hasn't got a penny in her purse. What will we have for dinner ? Dutch vegetables that cost a guilder a kilo, or imported cow-peas at 5 guilders a half kilo? There is not a moment of doubt; our ethnic duties are clear. We support Suriname's vegetable cultivation.
- A group of women is ready to leave for the community centre, half a mile away. We are in broad daylight and the weather is fine, so I suggest that we walk there. But this meets with strong objections. All ladies are worn-out, and there is a whole night of dances ahead of us. So we watch out for a cruising taxi, a driver of Creole ethnic background who can make fl 5 – out of us.

SOLIDARITY AND ETHNIC ENTREPRENEURSHIP

Kasmoni are to be classified as 'tontines de solidarité' (Rowlands, 1995, p. 122), and their meetings symbolize the theme of mutual aid as a totalizing, unifying event. As Rowlands (1995, p. 111) so aptly phrased it, rotating credit associations show that people strive to conserve scarce cash within social domains that define morally suitable goals and objectives. Creole moral economy is a special type of moral economy, though, one that is not based on an assumption of basic scarcity. Not only a striving towards conservation prompts Creole women; they are also keen to enhance the common fund available. They are fully aware that lots of money is afloat in the world around them, and they try to get a bigger share of the pie. Moreover, they are convinced that all should share in the affluence.

These economic attitudes have not been recognized for what they are, and are mostly discussed in a standard way. According to a generalized and gradually popularized view, thrift is not a Creole quality. Stereotypes being what they are, they should not lead us to infer that social and economic foresight or planning is absent. Among the lower classes as well as in other sectors, there is a guideline that group members should not be left out of financial circuits. An unspoken assumption is that money should flow, and the rate of circulation is certainly enhanced by Creole strategies.

The rationality behind the system is an ethnic one, and class-linked to some extent. As Ardener and Burman (1995, pp. 15–16) noted, economic attitudes among Caribbean migrants are variegated. West-Indian born members of Queen Elizabeth's kitchen staff were found disdainful of Roscas – a fact which should hardly cause surprise. It can be assumed that their material life base was rather sound, so for what would they need supportive networks? Persons with political aspirations might think differently, and closeness or looseness of family ties should also be taken into account as factors determining attitudes towards Roscas and economic behaviour in general. As Besson (1995, pp. 272–3) rightly stresses, participation in such organizations and networks is a way to build a reputation, and this holds for lower-class women as well as for others. Some apparently enigmatic attitudes and actions can be meaningfully interpreted when looked at as ways of group mobilization and promotion of interests. For those whose position is basically insecure, investments in supportive ethnic networks can be counted on to bring rewards when the worst comes to the worst. The way to participate in *kasmoni* and to run these organizations is geared to an overall lifestyle.

The embeddedness of Roscas in a way of life can be illustrated by some examples. These will bring out the informality of some of these organizations, and their versatility in adjusting to the personal needs of participants. Ardener and Burman (1995, p. 3) have mentioned these as qualities which can not be matched by distant, impersonal banking systems. Rules can be adapted to the exigencies of the moment and the situation.

OLD LOVE WON'T RUST

Eva is, socially speaking, a 'loser' She is a mother of ten, foundered in the home country, and arrived too late in the Netherlands to obtain a residence permit. She earned some money with a cleaning job, and contracted a marriage of convenience to get a Dutch passport. However, she was saddled with her ex-partner's rent arrears when he left. But, Bijlmermeer is full of piety and God exists, Eva is sure of that. And lo and behold: suddenly she finds herself the recipient of the jack-pot of a *kasmoni*, although she, as far as I know, had never contributed. But I am not sure of that, for I have no access to her financial bookkeeping. The only thing I am aware of, is that the organizer of the *kasmoni* is her former *mati*,[6] a friend who is willing to help her out. Whether this has been discussed with the other participants or not, or whether Eva has payed her dues later, I do not know.

THREE SISTERS

The eldest of three sisters, Gisela, has embezzled the fund of fl 8000. Her two younger sisters have contributed and fear that disbursement will fail. Gisela is known as one who is quick to anger. Sometimes she will use abusive language at the slightest provocation, and become violent. So it is not easy to call her to account. Cynthia, the second sister, does not feel up to that. She 'does not conduct her life well', which means she lives like a Dutch woman, a *bakra*, which implies that she neglects her ritual duties to protective spirits. She does not want to have anything to do with *Winti*. She is hard-working, has two jobs, does all she can for her children and partner, but her *yeye*, her soul or vital force, is diminishing. This, at least, is the definition of the situation given by the youngest sister, Wonnie, who has embarked on a career as ritual specialist. She convenes the sisters and organizes a ritual for Cynthia, an occasion to make up old quarrels, and for Gisela, to deliver contributions. Wonnie has the means now to make the trip to Suriname she had planned. The sanctions for infringement of rules were backed up by religious arguments; the organizer was touched in her weak spot – 'culture'.

SANCTIONS FOR ABUSE?

Florrie has become entangled in her own strategies. She had been caught for fare-dodging in the subway and had thrown a tantrum on the spot. Two ticket inspectors had held her to the floor. Then, 'they' had started to investigate, and it was found that she owed rent in arrears and was a moonlighter. She had got a summary dismissal and had lost both apartment and furniture. She was evicted from her home, a bailiff called and Florrie went into hiding. Although there was no lack of support, public opinion turned against her. 'She has got only herself to blame' was the most frequently heard comment. The suspension of ethnic loyalty had its background in the fact that she had used an association's *kasmoni* she was entrusted with for personal ends. She had gone through other women's money fast to finance her private *Winti* rituals. Such rituals, it was felt, would never do her any good.

What consequences this will have is hard to say, though. Will it mean that she will never be admitted to any other *kasmoni*? This is improbable. Loss of reputation is a powerful sanction, as Ardener and Burman (1995, pp. 4–5) have stressed, but its effectiveness depends on the subgroup, its norms and coherence. Also, Creole women's organizations are hierarchically ordered, and many respectable Creole women would never associate with a type like Florrie anyway. But this does not apply to her peers. In the Bijlmermeer subculture discussed here, gossip is so pervasive, and so frequently changes its topics and objects, that the effect is uncertain. Moreover, a victim often has recourse to a tried and tested method of reprisal, and will launch a counter-attack, which often is no less successful. Whoever feels that something is wrong, immediately opens an offensive to hit back. And then, it is hard to say who lends credibility to what rumour, and will take steps accordingly. Proverbs and songs are very clear about this: 'Scandal is not for me alone, but overtakes us all'.

DOUBLE STRATEGIES

Ethnic loyalty is extensive, and moral indignation about financial misconduct may become heated, but is also a relative matter. Although this is never stated in so many words: identification with the heroine/victim also plays a part. Today's righteous can be tomorrow's transgressors, as is fully realized. One senses that anyone, oneself included, might fall to censured practices, and hopes for the clemency that often is so abundantly forwarded. This outlook is shared by sexes and generations. The trickster figure, *Ba Anansi*, lives on in fantasy. As indicated above, all dream of big financial successes and matching lifestyles. Solidarity implies that one incurs losses occasionally, but that there are opportunities of gain as well.

There is a material base for this kind of speculation in the Netherlands now. The opportunities for gainful employment in the formal sector may be slight for the unskilled, but in the informal sector, its white, grey and black circuits, chances are greater. Creoles gained a foothold in the catering industry; the many Creole-run coffeeshops that mushroomed attest to that. In coffeeshops not only 'white', but also 'black' money is circulating. As Buiks (1983, p. 208) found, successful dealers, the *wakaman*, spend their money on sweethearts for instance. Sansone (1992, p. 126) also noted that black money siphons back into the ethnic subculture by channels of kinship and other networks, though he shows little optimism about the lasting effects of these forms of entrepreneurship. In Bijlmermeer, it can be observed at first glance that not all inhabitants belong to the poorest-of-the poor. The standard of living and consumption pattern – the showy cars and golden jewellery – suggest that, for many, the young in particular, welfare cheques are not the only source of income. In view of the close relations between kin, it is natural to assume that the elder generation, particularly the mothers, cashes in indirectly. Black money is also laundered by the sponsoring of rituals (Van Wetering, 1988). To some extent, some ambivalence about norms is within the range of expectations (cf. Scott, 1985, 1990), and the outgrowths of the *kasmoni* system should also be looked at from this angle.

AN INTERPRETATION OF *KASMONI*

The strategies of lower-class women suggest that the advantages of a welfare state are built into their overall policies. The women I know mentioned that they had been under pressure in Suriname to migrate. As the old age pensions in the Netherlands are considerably larger than those in Suriname, kinsmen felt that the elderly should lighten the group's burden and get support overseas. Similarly, men back out of their obligations to support their families in the Netherlands, arguing that welfare cheques are available now (Lenders and Van de Rhoer, 1984, p. 90; Ferrier, 1985, p. 124). This reinforces the pattern of matrifocality, familiar from Suriname. The policies of making investments in subcultural supportive networks similarly underpin the reproduction of a culture formed in the slavery past. The attitudes are based in a colonial practice, that arose when the plantations had given out and the state had to make good deficits: *Winti wai, lanti pai* (the wind blows and the administration pays), so the proverb runs (cf. Kruyer, 1973, p. 176; Kagie, 1980, pp. 169–70). New opportunities are taken up into familiar practices. Countercultural attitudes formed during slavery, reinforced in an economically stagnant colony, are reproduced after migration.

Creoles from Suriname are acutely aware of exploitation in the past, and of present risks of similar experiences. Legitimations in modern terms for attitudes and practices of long standing are supplied by well-trained spokesmen from Creole ranks: 'We are here because you were there'. Sansone (1992, pp. 138–9) for instance, found that young

Creoles openly state they blame colonialism and discrimination for their hustling practices. The elder generation would not spell this out in so many words. But the generations share the conviction that they are entitled to a greater share of prosperity than they have enjoyed so far. As a rule, this 'hidden script' (Thoden van Velzen and Van Wetering, 1988) or 'hidden transcript' (Scott, 1990a) is not expressed verbally, but in rituals. More is involved than resistance against repression or domination. The sociability and shared consumption, so pronounced in many types of Roscas (Ardener, 1995, pp. 7–8), and also quite marked in the Creole ethnic subculture, has more than Durkheimian connotations of enhancing solidarity, but serves an ethos that hopes to neutralize the effects of western penetration. These preoccupations crop up in magico–religious discourse: a fear of pollution and loss of vital force. These dangers are created by the contradictions in social relations, and are experienced in daily life (Van Wetering, 1995).

Empirically, there is ground to assume that Roscas among lower-class Creole women are part of an anti-colonial counter-offensive. All along, women have been active in creating cultural policies, in which financial matters are embedded. Besson's (1995, p. 273) observations about women's involvement in the Caribbean counter-culture of reputation as well as in the creation of Creole institutions most certainly hold good for Suriname as well, and apply also to its migrants abroad. From the 1920s onward, when Herskovits and Herskovits ([1936] 1969, p. 9) noted this, Creole women have been the guardians of culture. Culture – for the Herskovits primarily an African heritage – has all connotations of a counter-culture. Nevertheless, it would be wrong to stress the aspect of resistance to the neglect of accommodation. Women acted as the prime intermediaries with the dominant sector, as Mintz (1971, pp. 28, 39) has argued, and they have not given up that role in postcolonial times. Accommodation did and does yield its profits, which are legitimized by the fact that they are shared with peers. Rosemary Brana-Shute (1976) highlighted the activities of women in political mobilization at the grass-roots level of Paramaribo's neighbourhoods, and their abilities to gain part of the spoils in the arena of national politics. Women's objectives are two-faced: to maintain soldarity within kin group, neighbourhood and class, and to 'sell' this backing to those in power and gain from other windfalls. These forms of entrepreneurship, and the quest for reputation, are looked upon as subservient to the aim of respectability. Reputation and respectability, introduced by Wilson (1973) as key concepts in Caribbean studies, should certainly not be applied only to characterize opposed orientations of classes and genders; reputation as a male and lower-class domain, and respectability as a cultural orientation for women and the middle class. Nor will it be enough to argue (Besson 1993, 1995), that women have had a full share in cultural resistance. They had, but they do more. This pair of concepts expresses a contradiction in society which women try to overcome. Recently, Ortner (1995, pp. 180–2) has critized resistance studies, so influential in anthropology, for 'cultural thinning'. Responses to domination are simply represented as opposition, and no justice is done to the full range of reactions, to ambivalences and, we might add, an awareness of contradictions.

The link between private and public policies in a colonial context has been neglected. Kruyer (1973, p. 53) noted that the incurring of debts was 'normal' practice in Suriname among people of middle-class background as well as among the lower classes, but is content to attribute this to mere consumerism. He also found that the liberal granting of loans which were never repaid, was a part of political machinery. The funds for development projects, to the extent that these were not recycled back to foreign experts and organizations, was dissipated through a politically controlled civil service (Kagie, 1980, pp. 166 ff.; Gowricharn, 1983, p. 208). Lagerberg (1974, p. 96) speaks of a 'hand-out economy', in which income was redistribued along family lines.

Creole women's strategies to maximize debts seems to be in line with the policies of men, and anchored in ethnic and nationalist interests. Rosca systems, which have the spreading of risk as an aim, do not lose their significance when more money becomes available. As Rowlands (1995, p. 123), discussing Roscas in Cameroon, observes, Roscas are part of an active appropriation of economic capital. There is no assumption, for most Cameroonians, that money borrowed should be repaid. He refers to state-controlled funding agencies that supply easy loans, and he adds: 'People look immediately to the possibilities of rescheduling debts through collective bargaining with creditors and converting debt into a social resource', and 'Credit typically implies a means of obtaining resources which are likely to be used for many other purposes than the enterprise for which the loan was ostensibly intended'. In his view, Roscas develop and expand at the interface of two logics, representing different, incompatible priorities. One is the rationality of well-known western, individualist accumulation, the other that of siphoning off circulating cheap money into channels controlled within a socialized context. 'To settle a debt...would be unthinkable, since it destroys a social network on which it is founded' (p. 115). This seems to have an exact parallel in what has happened in Suriname, except for one aspect: women's active participation.

This raises the question whether the difference between male and female strategies is as great as Rowlands suggests. Although it seems quite plausible that women control far smaller amounts of money than men do, the guidelines for economic transactions seem strikingly similar for both sexes. It appears, that both men and women use their economic resources in the same way, within the range of their networks and the scope of opportunities open to them. In the above-cited passages, that author stresses that men, just like women, have the maintenance of networks as a prime goal. Were that correct, we might infer that women's policies are an extension, on a modest scale, of those of males, and obey the same economic logic. Rowlands seems to have been taken in by Cameroonian male grumblings about female and household spending, but such squabbles will occur almost everywhere in variegated forms. In Suriname and among its migrants abroad, disputes about the allocation of funds within households, families, and networks are as heated as anywhere else, but it would be wrong to let these detract us from the main issues.

WORLDVIEW AND BODY SYMBOLISM

Rowlands's main hypothesis – Roscas thriving at the interface of two logics – is striking and persuasive. To substantiate this view, he (1995, p. 122) refers to body symbolism, an original move, particularly in its relation to economics. Money, he argues, is seen as a vital force, on a par with bodily substances that have to be transmitted in order to make a continuation of life possible. Thus, money and all globalized opportunities are taken up and reinterpreted in a culturally based vernacular. To money (Rowlands, 1995, p. 118) procreative qualities are attributed; money is 'magic'.

This attitude, based on a similar ontology, is shared by Suriname Creoles. In *Winti* philosophy, no opposition between material and spiritual forces is acknowledged. If there is a bias, it tends towards the earthly powers in the pantheon (Van Wetering, 1995). The concrete – in the form of food, money, services – is valued above the abstract or words, which may prove deceitful. If real, the spiritual will manifest itself in material form. All traffic with divine powers is mediated by material offerings, and the deities are expected to grant prosperity. Indeed, as in Cameroon (Rowlands, 1995, p. 118): 'Money is blessed.'

Rowlands (1995, pp. 122–3) implicitly assumes that the notions of male supremacy current in Cameroon Grassfield societies are basic to the ontology. In that part of West Africa, he notes, ancestrally derived life essences are passed on in the paternal line, and he infers: 'The idea that men are containers of transmissable vital substances provides an idiom and an ethos for contemporary and past accumulation.' Women's body fluids, on the other hand, particularly of women of reproductive age, are regarded as dangerous, as are those of all affinal kin. This suggests, the author argues, that symbolism may be a powerful influence in determining women's relative access to capital.

Body symbolism can be worked out in different ways, however, depending on the nature of kinship and power relations. The idea that men would be able to monopolize the transference of vital substance is foreign to Creole thinking. As pervasive in African-American Suriname as it is in Cameroon, these representations have received an imprint of the fact that women are the main force behind the reproduction of *Winti* culture. This form of agency, and men's relative indifference and absence from partners' households, enabled women to put a stamp on their worldview. *Winti* allows the prime role to women and female vital force in the procreation of life (cf. Wooding, 1981, p. 68). As in some other cosmologies in West Africa, of the Ashanti (Rattray, [1929] 1979, p. 318) for instance, transmission of vital essence in the form of the 'blood soul' is predicated upon the maternal line of descent. Although the Creole kinship system is bilateral and not matrilineal, there is a consensus that ties through female kin are stronger than patrilateral relations. In *Winti* rituals, the congregation is recruited primarily through matrilateral kinship, and relations connected through other ties are regarded as outsiders. The African heritage in Suriname has drawn on different traditions; there are aspects of culture that point to connections with places as far apart as Ghana and Cameroon or Angola. This is not the place to go deeply into this matter. It is sufficient to note that symbolism is not only an independent factor, reinforcing power relations, but also is a dependent variable, moulded, preserved and manipulated in accordance with the interests of the main reproducers.

Wealth in Creole thinking is, moreover, explicitly associated with a female power, Mother Earth or *Aisa*, regarded as the first among her peers, the other spirits. Mother Earth is, in Geertz's (1973, p. 93) well-known terms, both a model *of* and a model *for* reality. Her image is cast in that of a traditional Creole mother or grandmother wearing a *koto misi* costume; the honest, common woman to whom all can apply for support. Mediumship of an *Aisa* spirit gives authority in family groups, is much-desired and hotly contested. The deity is looked upon as the main unifying force who can bring people together whose fortunes have varied. This is highly important for the Creole group that has gone through far-reaching processes of social differentiation. She is credited with the power to grant riches through sharing; through rituals devoted to the *Aisa winti* of one's kin group, the sponsor as well as the other participants will fare well. Rituals in her honour are expected to bridge the opposition between private accumulation and collective well-being.

So, in the eyes of Creoles, there is nothing in money that makes it inherently evil. This does not imply that the handling of money is regarded as without danger under all circumstances. The cultural repertoire is very rich in notions stipulating conditions which make money into a threat to communal well-being: beliefs in witchcraft, demoniac possession and devil's pacts spell this out, and have marked the negotiation of money's meanings throughout the group's history. On the whole, though, accumulation is not condemned, provided a flow of gains is not disrupted.

The Creole case could be cited as one of those mentioned by Parry and Bloch (1989, pp. 20 ff.), where short-term exchanges associated with individual appropriation are morally acceptable, as long as they remain subordinated to the long-term restorative cycles which focus on a collectivity. As they have stressed, the articulation between these two spheres is far from unproblematic. In order to sustain the long-term cycle, and not to reduce it to the transient world of the individual, they must be kept separate, but also be related. Hence the transformative processes, of which Creole women's rituals provide such a clear instance.

NOTES

1. The focus of the research programme on which this paper is based was on women's ritual lives. In the media in the early 1980s, attention had been drawn to a lingering or even revitalized popular culture, mostly referred to as *Winti*. This literally means 'winds', denoting the possession-causing spirits that play a large part in it. This religion was said to flourish in one of Amsterdam's new suburbs, Bijlmermeer, where many migrants from Suriname had settled in the mid-1970s. The project has been sponsored between 1984 and 1987 by ZWO, now NWO, the Foundation for Scientific Research in The Hague.
2. In Suriname studies, evaluations of *kasmoni* and lower-class women's financial strategies have been part of what Patterson (quoted in Hannerz, 1975, p. 15) labelled as 'catastrophism'. No special study has been made of the way this saving system functioned in Suriname. As a rule, it is

mentioned only in passing, and in a disparaging way. Helman (1978, p. 86), Buschkens (1974, p. 162) and Kruyer (1973, p. 53) file it among the 'social problems'.

3. The gigantic rate of inflation of the Surinamese guilder – in the early 1960s worth N.fl 2.50, now less than one cent – placed migrants, even those depending on social security, in a financially advantageous position on a holiday or upon return in the home country.

4. In mainstream sociology and in migrant studies, an assumption of marginalization (Buiks, 1983, Cross and Entzinger, 1988) has precluded an interest in the interrelation of financial strategies and a, mostly reified, cultural system.

5. My interest in rituals was more or less accepted, gradually. Whenever I showed a tendency to probe into other matters, though, this immediately evoked a response: 'What are you after?' Only patience and participant observation gave me some insight into the practical, day-to-day dealings with money.

6. A *mati* relation among women has been important for lower-class Creole women since the turn of the century (Van Lier, 1986; Wekker, 1994). In the Netherlands, these relations also matter. Such friendships cannot be properly characterized as 'lesbian', although sexual and emotional connotations are undeniably there.

Section 2
Institutions and Culture:
Continuities and Change

4 South Asian Women in Britain, Family Integrity and the Primary Purpose Rule
Werner Menski

Modern state masculinism in Britain takes many forms. With particular reference to immigration law, it is not difficult at all to point not only to the racist but also the gender-biased nature of the British entry control system which has been put into place gradually, since the Aliens Act of 1905, the Commonwealth Immigrants Acts of 1962 and 1968, and especially under the Immigration Act of 1971, with its complex web of constantly changing Immigration Rules and secret instructions to immigration officials.[1]

One of the most disagreeable effects of state masculinism manifested in British immigration controls, especially as far as Asian ethnic minorities are concerned, constitutes an outright violation of the basic human rights of British Asian women, about which far too little is known in the general public and even among academics. In essence, the male-dominated, xenophobic immigration regime of the UK has, during the past two decades, systematically singled out certain non-white, ethnic minority groups by treating perfectly genuine marriages in such communities virtually as marriages of convenience, alleging that the primary purpose of such marriages has been to facilitate entry to Britain for the foreign spouse.

It is in this context that Asian women have been particularly victimized by the law. They have become a prominent target group for the primary purpose rule (ppr) because through the continued immigration of male South Asian spouses, apart from asylum seekers and business people, the leaking tap of British immigration controls has continued to drip. While this raises the important question whether any immigration control system actually can and should switch off family migration altogether, we shall focus here on the predicaments for Asian women, caused by the state's policy of refusing entry clearance to their lawful spouses.[2]

Ethnic minorities in Britain often perpetuate their manifold links with the countries of origin and/or other centres of diaspora settlement through marriages (Pearl, 1986; Mole, 1987; Evans, 1988). A major reason appears to be the scarcity of eligible spouses of the same group in Britain. Apart from that, the continuation of marital alliances across continents confirms that Britain's ethnic minorities today are part of global social structures that depend, to some extent, on the freedom for individuals to move between countries. Such a scenario presents, therefore, a powerful and ultimately insuperable challenge to an immigration control system which seeks to implement watertight entry controls.

This chapter argues that tailor-made exclusionary immigration rules aimed at certain groups not only marginalize the structure of all ethnic minorities in Britain, they also wilfully disregard the legitimate expectations and socio-psychological needs of Asian and other ethnic minority women in Britain. Exploring the consequences of such systematic disempowerment for Asian women, it is argued here that, while Asian women as a class or social group, as well as individually, are being victimized and disadvantaged by the effects of British immigration laws, there is growing evidence that inequalities between Asian women are being exploited. In particular, less prosperous Asian women in Britain are being marginalized still further by multiple strategies of exclusion that focus on financial aspects.

At the Bristol Conference in December 1993 several researchers reported on their work with Asian women, whose symptoms of discomfort and illness were often clearly related to immigration trouble, in particular the notorious ppr (Bradby, 1993; Mumford, 1993). Building on my own paper on the development and effects of the ppr (Menski, 1993), this chapter focuses more specifically on the legal evidence of consistent disregard for the needs and wishes of Asian women through the application of this rule at the appeal stage. In particular, I present an analysis of the limited options available to Asian women whose spouses are prevented from joining them in Britain by the ppr. Judicial perceptions of the predicaments of Asian women entangled in this rule reflect and illustrate the power that the law exercises over ethnic minority women's private lives. They show, in particular, that the purported division of the private and public spheres does not exist in the day-to-day experience that Asian women and their families have of the law. The English legal system, built on axioms of equality and assimilationist assumptions, purports to offer a contract to the effect that the state will respect the private sphere of individuals, while citizens/residents should accept that the state dominates the public sphere. However, the arbitrary nature of control of the public sphere demonstrates to ethnic minority women, and certainly not only to them, that this contractual arrangement is constantly violated by the state because the dividing line between 'private' and 'public' is not, and cannot, be neatly drawn. In our context, an Asian woman, having made her choice of spouse, may have scrupulously followed the law on marriage. Yet, despite the existence of her legally valid marriage with a man from overseas, the law will not honour that validity by letting the spouse enter Britain. Historically, it has been easier in Britain to apply such discriminatory exclusion strategies to non-white women (Bhabha and Shutter, 1994). We need not be surprised, therefore, about the massive evidence of anger, insecurity and anguish, resulting in various forms of illness among Asian women which some researchers have now begun to uncover. Such evidence reflects a wider pattern of state-induced disadvantaging of many South Asian women in Britain today who, as part of ethnic minority communities, know only too well that the axiom of legal equality is merely a convenient fiction.

THE PRIMARY PURPOSE RULE AND ITS EFFECTS

As Sachdeva (1993) has shown in detail, the ppr was gradually fine-tuned during the late 1970s and early 1980s, especially after 1983, as an effective key element of British immigration controls regarding the entry of foreign spouses. It was designed to target Asian family formation in Britain, seeking to slow down, if not totally prevent, the addition of new family members from overseas through marriage.[3] Apart from asylum, family formation is now a major source of immigration in most European countries (Menski, 1994). Immigration controls have therefore focused on the exclusion of spouses. Inspired by a desperate sense of urgency to control the numbers of non-white new entrants, Britain's uniquely cruel ppr, a 'rule without a purpose' (Justice, 1993), serves, in fact, the obvious purpose of keeping as many non-white spouses out of Britain as possible. The brief history of this control mechanism shows that as long as the UK-based spouse is also non-white, there is little public reaction to the exclusionary policies. Ethnic minority spouses, men and women, are expected to suffer in silence and will not have the benefit of public support for their rights. The leading British handbook on immigration law correctly emphasized that there are indeed no known primary purpose cases involving two white spouses (Macdonald and

Blake, 1991, p. 260). Poignantly, it is treated as a different matter if white British men now face greater obstacles in being united with their overseas spouses, especially if such women happen to come from the Philippines or Thailand.[4]

The primary purpose rule was so cleverly devised that for the past fifteen years, whatever was said by applicants to support their claim for entry clearance, the immigration authorities could (and still can now) claim that entry to the UK was the primary purpose of the marriage and therefore, the claim should be refused. The law has – intentionally – not developed clear, unambiguous rules but has left ample scope for discretion by officials who decide such applications. This, together with an onerous burden of proof, requiring applicants to show that achieving settlement in the UK was not their primary purpose for marrying the sponsor, has created virtually insurmountable hurdles for applicants. How does one prove that one did *not* have certain intentions at some point in the past?

Let us take the case of a UK-based Asian woman who travels to India, Pakistan or Bangladesh with a view to arranging a suitable marriage. It is not relevant here whether the arrangements are a matter for the families involved rather than the individuals. But if such a woman expects her prospective husband to settle with her in Britain, any suitable partners must, in the first place, be willing to join her in Britain. Strong anecdotal evidence shows consistently (and to an increasing extent) that not all eligible young men in South Asia want to move to Europe. Thus, British-based Asian women actually find their choice of partner restricted to those men who are willing to contemplate a move overseas – which is one of the precise reasons why the ppr has been so effective. For, following an application for entry clearance, the Entry Clearance Officer (ECO) may simply ask a number of innocent questions about the motives of the man: Is he a good Muslim/Sikh/Hindu? Does he believe in tradition? Then why does he agree to move to his wife's place of residence? It must be his primary purpose to come to Britain!

Legal analysis tells us much, at this point, about changing patterns of customary practices. No doubt, apart from the patrilocal norm, matrilocal and – more so – neo-local residence patterns after marriage have always been known to South Asians. During the process of applying for entry clearance, however, if there are any indications that the applicant actually wanted to live in Britain, the subjective test of primary purpose allows the ECO to form an opinion in his/her mind that it was the main aim of the applicant to move to Britain. This opinion is formed regardless of the fact that he married the sponsor some time ago, they may have children already, the marriage clearly subsists, and there is every indication that this is a perfectly genuine marriage.

The case of Sumeina Masood ([1992] ImmAR 69) illustrates this scenario very well.[5] The wife, born in Halifax in Yorkshire, was well-settled and even owned her own house. She expected her husband to join her. She went to Pakistan and married a cousin there on 15 January 1987. Clearly, here was a British Muslim family making sensible family arrangements. They had provided a house for their daughter, had helped her find a suitable husband, and there was no question of becoming a burden on public funds, because a job in a bakery in Bradford had already been arranged for the man, too.

In July 1988, the husband's application for entry clearance was refused. The couple kept in touch and the wife spent whatever time she could in Pakistan, but the immigration authorities continued to view the marriage as a 'conditional marriage', since the sponsor had made it clear that she would not live with her husband in Pakistan. Based on a number of statements in the husband's interview, including the fact that a job had been arranged for him in Britain, his spouse application continued to be viewed as a hidden application to enter Britain as a worker. When, three years later, Mr Justice Glidewell in the Court of Appeal sat in final judgement over this case, the uncaring approach of the state's immigration control system was fully revealed. While the case report does not explicitly verbalize this, the young man's decision (or that of his family) to marry a girl from the UK was found to infringe the immigration control system, which bans the entry of workers unless they are key personnel or possess special skills. In the present case, Mr. Masood was just a labourer, clearly not entitled to challenge that control system. Lord Justice Glidewell held, at p. 78:

> I know that it puts some intending immigrants in a very real difficulty, but it is not enough for somebody like Mr. Khalid Masood to convince the entry clearance officer that he likes his wife. It may be he even loves her though that question did not arise in this case and, that if given the chance he intends to make a permanence of this marriage. This could be a perfect genuine long-lasting marriage. But that is not enough. If those considerations were secondary, the primary consideration was that he should first come to the United Kingdom. That was the primary purpose of the marriage and, if the entry clearance officer was not persuaded to the contrary, then he was entitled to refuse consent.

This last sentence should alert us: here is a couple who have been lawfully married for years. Why is someone else brought in much later to grant or withhold consent? This illustrates the inflated claims of the law and its personnel, controlling people's most private actions by simply declaring that some matter of public concern overrides their private decisions. Of course, the word 'consent' in the case report is supposed to refer, *prima facie*, to the entry clearance application, but it appears purposely ambiguous. Significantly, nothing is found in this case report regarding the anguish caused to the young woman and the infringements of her legitimate expectations as a British citizen. Still, the dilemma of South Asian women in Britain who are determined to remain settled here, married to a husband from overseas, is clearly demonstrated in this case. The judge (Sachdeva, 1993, pp. 155–7) focused on the technical question of intention to live together permanently and challenged the assertion that there was such an intention, because the couple's joint future depended not on their wish, but on the discretion of British immigration officials or, as it turned out, the higher judiciary. Thus, before the Court of Appeal, the case turned on the question of intention to remain together. Since the wife had made it clear that she was unwilling to live in Pakistan and expected her husband to join her in the UK, the court came to the conclusion that there was no real intention to live together, because the marriage would be broken if the husband was not allowed to come to the UK. The key passage is found on p. 78 of the report:

> In this case, not to put too fine a point on it, the wife had the whip hand. She was the person who was saying quite firmly, 'I am established in the United Kingdom, I am a British citizen, I have a job, and I have a home. I very much hope that you can come and join me, but I am not going to live with you permanently unless you can'.

From this perspective, it was a simple step for the judge to conclude that this particular marriage was entered into primarily to obtain admission to the UK. Although this approach is in fact contrary to one of the guiding principles in primary purpose cases laid down in an earlier case,[6] this is typical of ppr cases as, 'the extensive case law has swung backwards and forwards between a liberal and a stricter approach' (Macdonald and Blake, 1995, p. 343). The signals given to Asian spouses are obvious: Marry among yourselves in Britain if you want to be safe from primary purpose trouble. Do not expect the state law to underwrite and uphold your private decisions about marrying someone from overseas. In other words, the case powerfully re-asserts the state's prerogative to govern the lives of citizens, a classic scenario of male-dominated legal centralism.

The dismay expressed by several commentators about this approach concentrates on the fact that the male spokespersons of the law appeared here to disapprove of the fact that a woman, notably an Asian woman, should be able to make private decisions which should then bind the English public law. A good legal analysis of this case was produced by Rick Scannell (1991 and 1992). After Sumeina Masood, it appeared for a while that henceforth any British Asian woman who made it clear that she was unwilling to settle outside the UK delivered her partner into the jaws of the ppr arguments advanced in that case.

Slightly earlier, however, in the Court of Session in Scotland, a similar case had been decided in favour of the applicant.[7] Here, Lord Prosser took a more broad-minded view of 'primary purpose' (Scannell, 1991, p. 2):

> It would be silly as well as cynical to believe that where a marriage brings advantages, the acquisition (or conferring) of those advantages must be seriously regarded as the primary purpose of the marriage, justifying not only the marriage itself but lifelong union.

Developments after 1992 in this field show that the ppr has lost none of its venom and that perfectly good cases still result in refusal. Despite some more positive decisions, Sumeina Masood remains technically authoritative. Meanwhile, the debate among women activists, spearheaded by Southall Black Sisters, has concentrated on the abolition of the one-year rule, the probationary leave to remain in Britain for a year after entry clearance as a spouse has been granted. Problems for Asian women arise in that context if the husband (or other family members) use violence against the woman and she cannot leave him or the family because that would lead to deportation from Britain. While some attention is currently, and rightly so, focused on this issue, such public debates continue to portray South Asian marriages as the problem, rather than the immigration law. In other words, elitist perceptions of South Asian women and their legal position in Britain can easily be misused by the male-dominated state system to justify further repression mechanisms which target Asians and other ethnic minorities, and often victimize women. The result is that the state can continue to play havoc with the lives of Asian women in Britain, denying them, in essence, any space for the private sphere.

THE CURRENT LAW

UK immigration law keeps changing all the time, partly to plug perceived 'loopholes', partly to keep immigration on the public agenda. At
present, attention has shifted from the ppr and family migration to asylum law and internal immigration controls. Since the legal framework of
the ppr was already perfected in the 1980s (Sachdeva, 1993, pp. 43–105),
the most recent modifications to British immigration law have not
affected the ppr. The exclusionary system is now entrenched to the satisfaction of the Home Office; calls for its abolition have been ignored.

The latest set of Immigration Rules (HC 395 of October 1994) explicitly purported to abandon gender discrimination but introduced some
new restrictions with negative effects for women, hitting unmarried
daughters between 18 to 21 and widowed mothers especially hard. There
is, in addition, increasing evidence that more female spouses from the
subcontinent are being refused entry clearance now, which raises new
problems of adjustment to an already complex situation for South Asian
women who married a man based in Britain. Some existing literature
(see Barton, 1987) as well as ongoing research indicates that such women
are severely disadvantaged and further marginalized by the law.

The ppr is now found in paragraph 281 of HC 395, the current set of
revised Immigration Rules, which came into force on 1 October 1994.
This provides as follows:

> 281. The requirements to be met by a person seeking leave to enter
> the United Kingdom with a view to settlement as the spouse of a per-
> son present and settled in the United Kingdom or who is on the same
> occasion being admitted for settlement are that:
> (i)   the applicant is married to a person present and settled in the
> United Kingdom or who is on the same occasion being admitted for
> settlement; and
> (ii) the marriage was not entered into primarily to obtain admission
> to the United Kingdom; and
> (iii) the parties to the marriage have met; and
> (iv) each of the parties intends to live permanently with the other as
> his or her spouse and the marriage is subsisting; and
> (v)   there will be adequate accommodation for the parties and any
> dependants without recourse to public funds in accommodation
> which they own or occupy exclusively; and
> (vi) the parties will be able to maintain themselves and any depend-
> ants adequately without recourse to public funds; and

(vii)   the applicant holds a valid United Kingdom entry clearance for entry in this capacity.

Such well-chosen, innocuous wording does not disclose the burden of proof which lies with the applicant, and illustrates the power of the law by leaving sufficient discretion for the persons deciding upon the application to declare themselves 'not satisfied' that this burden was discharged. It thus allows for as many refusals as are deemed necessary. It is known that the Home Office periodically issues secret instructions to its staff, providing guidance, for example, on how strictly the burden of proof is to be handled (for an early example see Sachdeva, 1993, p. 47). It appears that Britain actually operates hidden quotas for certain categories of immigrants, although this continues to be vigorously denied. It is well known that refusal rates are extremely high in some overseas missions, and that the Home Office is hiding the real figures by 'massaging' statistics, as publications from the Joint Council for the Welfare of Immigrants have been pointing out for years. The ppr and its application is undoubtedly designed to protect the UK from further South Asian immigration. In view of human rights obligations, such family migration cannot be switched off altogether, but the immigration control system seeks to slow it down to a trickle.

Focused on immigration agenda and constrained to fulfill predetermined targets, the law therefore purposely disregards the wishes and aspirations of South Asian women who live in Britain and want to remain here after marriage. Clearly, the law also ignores the fact that such spouses are actually legally married. While others have researched the mental effects of such predicaments on Asian women and the resulting social complications, I shall focus below on the legal scenario, showing how badly many Asian women are treated by a legal system which purports to stand for equality, dignity and human rights.

Looking at the conditions which the law itself has set, we must note first of all that even if conditions (i), (iii) and (iv) in para 281 of HC 395 are shown to be satisfied, the application can still be rejected simply on the primary purpose ground under (ii). ECOs now have to provide some reasons for their decisions and can no longer simply assert that they are not satisfied that it was not the primary purpose of the applicant to come to the UK. This remains very easy to do as the law has purposely left this matter to subjective assessment. Reported and unreported cases alike show that evidence collected in formal interviews is routinely held against the applicant, even though quite different interpretations of such facts are possible. Thus, an earlier application for a passport or for entry to another country than Britain is routinely treated as evidence that the applicant was desperate to leave India, Pakistan or Bangladesh. Evidence of income is turned into arguments that the applicant must be desperately poor, when in fact he is often comfortably off by South Asian standards. This technique remains very simple because even substantial rupee sums, when converted into pounds, look comparatively meagre. The exclusionary rationale ruthlessly exploits such arguments. Any perceived discrepancies are held against the applicant and ECOs regularly use entrapment techniques to achieve a finding that the applicant is not credible (see Lal and Wilson, 1986). Given the scope for such subjective interferences, even the most genuine couple may fall foul of the ppr and have to face the full consequence of the rule, with instant refusal, long delays over appeals, and repeated rejections of the case. Recent unpublished research shows that even a well-sounding Home Office concession, made in June 1992, for spouses whose marriage had lasted for more than five years and for applicants with British-born children, is not in fact implemented in practice. The Home Office virtually expects applicants and their advisers to remind officials of this concession (Sachdeva, 1993, p. 168; Macdonald and Blake, 1995, pp. 343–4).

THE SOCIAL IMPLICATIONS OF THE PPR

As the above cases show, the ppr is not really focused on detecting bogus marriages. Rather, it is a device to wean South Asians in Britain, both men and women, away from the system of intercontinental marriages. The official approach seems to be, that the continued occurrence of such marriage arrangements increases the ethnic minority population of Britain directly and, through later births, indirectly. While, from a white majority perspective, this appears to make sense, the almost obsessive focus on immigration, backed up by selective statistical information, overlooks the parallel phenomenon of emigration. A significant number of young South Asians marrying spouses from abroad actually leave Britain and it speaks for itself that this fact is not made known in the public debates.

While the ppr has now been discredited as thoroughly immoral and openly discriminatory, many spouse applications continue to be refused. Because of vocal protests about the ppr, refusals are now given on a variety of grounds, which increasingly include financial and 'public funds' arguments (Gillespie, 1992; McKee, 1995), and which are in-tune with recent British debates about public funds generally. This in turn further disadvantages certain groups of South Asian women. Applicants and their sponsors face the key issue of resources. One experienced adviser (Mole, 1987, p. 37) put it as follows:

> Those couples who are determined that no number of obstacles laid in their way will in the end prevent them from living together in the country of their choice may eventually be allowed to make their matrimonial home in the UK. The faint-hearted and the ill-advised will, unfortunately, often forfeit their rights along the way. Few will find the journey easy.

While one could say a lot about how this reflects state masculinism and adds to a general image of governmental lack of openness, we need to focus here on the effects of such policies and actions on the lives of Asian women. First, it has been a consistent pattern that the refusal rates for fiancé(e)s are much higher than for spouses (Mole, 1987, pp. 26–7; Menski, 1994, p. 118). If the couple are actually married, but not allowed to live together in Britain, the alternatives facing Asian women in Britain are difficult, even stark. I briefly discussed the options facing British Asian women, regarding decisions relating to getting married in the first place, in an earlier paper (Menski, 1993). Here, I focus on the predicaments for women whose spouses have actually been refused entry to Britain by an ECO or any of the appellate authorities. Their options could be summarized as follows:

(a)   give up and move to the subcontinent to resume marital life;
(b)   go back and forth between Britain and the subcontinent;
(c)   live as an 'immigration widow', apparently an increasing phenomenon;
(d)   at least have a child, so that something of the marriage is salvaged;
(e)   do nothing, let others decide, perhaps similar to (c);
(f)   give up on the marriage and seek its dissolution;
(g)   fight on through legal and other channels to achieve entry of the husband.

As indicated, it remains a task of future research to address the impact of the exclusionary mechanisms on South Asian women who have been told that they cannot come to Britain to join their husband or fiancé. If such women are subsequently successful through the appeal structures or other interventions, there will be all kinds of fallouts on the interpersonal relationship as well as the frame of mind of such women. How are they expected to settle into a country that appears to reject them through institutional forms of differential treatment from the very start? A further complication has arisen because campaigners against arranged marriages have actually offered an attractive new argument to the Home Office. The phenomenon of the 'reluctant bride' has been exploited so that female applicants for entry clearance are asked pointed questions about whether they actually wanted to get married to this particular man. If a female interviewee in such a situation shows signs of reluctance to answer, or is merely too hesitant to talk about her emotions, this may quickly be interpreted as evidence of some kind of 'forced marriage'. In the next few years we will probably see a number of appeal cases in which this issue will surface. Clearly, just as male applicants have been unsure whether life in Britain would be a positive and satisfying experience, so are female applicants apprehensive about life abroad with a partner who is still more or less a stranger.

Either way, whether the female partner is in Britain or in the subcontinent, the procedurally oriented, establishment-focused and male-dominated immigration appeals system offers only a semblance of legal recourse. In the practical experience of such women, justice remains at best an unfulfilled promise. British Asian women are led to believe that through the appropriate legal channels they can ultimately claim their rights as citizens of this country. Few realize that the purposely discretionary set-up of the law is deliberately set against their frame of mind and expectations and is, in fact, designed to defeat those expectations rather than to help the individual. The result can be various pathological symptoms presented to medical practitioners and social workers. These may remain unexplained if one is not aware of the complex negative impact which the ppr has had for many Asian women in this country.

THE OPTIONS FOR ASIAN WOMEN

A closer look at the options for women, as listed above, shows that (a) to (f) represent a victory of some sort for the UK immigration control system. Option (a), joining the spouse overseas, is exercised much more often than we realize. Yet, because the UK migration statistics and the media focus on immigration, not emigration, we are not told about re-migration to South Asia or places such as the Caribbean.[8] The reverse has recently been shown for Hong Kong, demonstrating how selectively we are informed by the press and governments.[9]

While option (a) is clearly an absolute victory for the immigration control agencies, so is option (f), a decision to terminate the marriage, which then raises the question what such women will do next. The Home Office would obviously hope that, having learnt the intended lesson, such women would marry a man from Britain or remain unmarried. Somehow, this is now a private matter. Such women are left to cope by themselves with the problems created for their private lives by the public law.

Options (b) to (d) also appear to occur much more frequently than we realize. The problem of 'immigration widows' has been raised in various studies (most recently Bhabha and Shutter, 1994). It seems that medical practitioners, other health care professionals and social workers would come to know much more about the negative fall-out from those options than lawyers. Thus, one should not expect legal researchers to make a significant contribution to this field.

Some legal attention has been focused on option (d), the decision to have a child or children of the marriage, despite the fact that the parents are not allowed to live together in Britain. From a technical legal angle, this represents evidence of 'intervening devotion', a sign that the marriage is intact despite immigration barriers and that the spouses are cohabiting, if only from time to time, and want the marriage to continue, come what may. Whether, in many such cases, pregnancies 'happen' as a result of overseas visits by the British-based woman, or because of pressure from the man and/or his family, or as a deliberate strategy to fall under the June 1992 Home Office concession for well-established marriages, would need to be further researched. The implication for Britain has been a not insignificant growth in the number of 'single' Asian mothers, no doubt with some negative repercussions on the use of public funds. In the prevailing climate of concern over public expenditure, this has sparked off some thinking about the undesirable economic impact of separating families. Surely, in many cases, to allow the husband to join his family in Britain offers a greater chance of economic self-sufficiency. It is possible that for this reason, rather than compassion, the Home Office made the important concession of June 1992 for spouses in marriages where there is a British-born child of the parties. Since this scenario has not been researched by anyone in detail, we do not know how many Asian women are found in this particular predicament, nor how they cope with it.

Several participants in the previous Bristol Conference confirmed that Asian women with refused husbands were advised to get pregnant and to rely on the Home Office concession. Once the child had been born, perhaps even during the pregnancy, one could then hope for family reunion. In a reported 1994 case,[10] it was held that the concession should not operate before the child is born, illustrating the mean approach of the immigration control system to something like 'primary purpose pregnancies'. While there is limited evidence that some spouses benefited from the concession in 1992/93 (Sachdeva, 1993, p. 168), many practitioners are concerned that the concession is applied with such reluctance.

Option (f) would require the termination of an existing and legally valid marriage in the respective South Asian jurisdiction rather than in Britain. So far, I have not come across any such case in the official law reports of South Asia. One reason for this is certainly that any termination of a marriage which became an immigration casualty will probably be settled amicably, and without court involvement. Since this is normal practice in South Asian laws, and the familiar elements of shame and loss of status are also involved in terminating such marriage arrangements, nobody in South Asia would have any real interest in publicizing such cases. Thus the pernicious effects of British immigration control on many South Asian families are not in fact made public. Any fieldwork on this topic would need to be done in the subcontinent rather than in Britain. One can anticipate – given the dismissive approach to legal documents from South Asia – that the findings of such studies would merely be treated as 'anecdotal', which is an additional powerful disincentive for a researcher in the first place.

What we can study already, because it is happening in front of our eyes in Britain, concerns the implications of option (g), a decision to battle on through the appeals structure of the English legal system. The question would then be how successful British Asian women have been in the last few years if they decided to fight for their marriage and their right to family life in Britain.

While there are a large number of cases, the reported evidence is meagre and has also remained largely unresearched. It is apparent that recourse to European law still looks like the best strategy and that the simplest option – if one can afford it – is to rely on the free movement rights for European citizens under EU law. This involves a temporary move for the British citizen woman to any country in the EU, where she would have to settle for a limited period, certainly not more than six months. In accordance with the law of that country, she would then call her spouse to Europe, which is often quite simple, because no other country in the European Union has an equivalent to the British ppr. After six months or so, the couple would then be able to rely on the important test case of Surinder Singh (reported at [1992] All ER 798) and claim entry to the UK on the basis of free movement rights within the

European Union. The new specialist legal term created as a result of this technique, 'to surinder singh oneself', obviously also involves climbing all kinds of traditional hurdles against Asian women moving alone to strange places. Still, my advice would be that it is cheaper (and probably better for the relationship between the spouses) to take an extended holiday in Portugal, for example, than to fight against the ppr through the UK court system, which seems still little more than a lottery draw in this regard because of the large scope for discretion.

Again, we urgently need research into how the European route works in practice and what problems can and do occur. Technically and legally, the above bypass through Europe seems to be the most viable alternative, but most women with ppr trouble are probably never told about the Surinder Singh strategy. One suspects that this has as much to do with ignorance in the legal profession about the now highly specialized area of immigration law as with legal self-interest. For, if all British spouses whose overseas partners have been rejected on primary purpose grounds actually chose to 'surinder singh' themselves to Europe, the ppr problem would be solved rather swiftly (Menski, 1994, p. 113). The indications are not only that lawyers would lose business but also that quite a few couples (several cases have been reported) would find greener pastures in Europe and might never actually settle in the UK. It remains a fact, though, that cultural reservations about the mobility of Asian women prevent many couples from choosing this route.[11]

The other form of recourse to European law, working through the court system, is tedious, more expensive, and only for the most hardy souls, since the Home Office is a formidable, resourceful opponent. However, threatening the British court system with recourse to European law does not work effectively if the case languishes in the lower immigration appeals system. Before an appeal can reach Europe, one has to exhaust the domestic remedies. For Asian women, the journey to the peak of this mountain of legal hierarchies bears all the characteristics of a difficult obstacle race. After all, we are not dealing here with some accidental maldevelopment which could be remedied by legal reforms. Asian women are faced with the planned effects of a purportedly colour-blind law and deliberate refusals to consider reforms which would assist ethnic minority individuals. Obviously, taking away the hurdles of the ppr would open what some perceive as floodgates for non-white migration to Britain. In addition, a close look at the case-law shows that European law offers no magic legal remedy about the right to family life. It has been held that there is a right to family life, but this does not imply a right to enjoy family life in a particular country![12]

Few studies, so far, have researched the ppr and its implications from a victim perspective. The important WING study of 1985 (Bhabha *et al.*, 1985), its revised edition (Bhabha and Shutter, 1994), the only detailed British study of the ppr (Sachdeva, 1993) and the recent work of South-all Black Sisters on the abolition of the one-year rule, have laid important foundations for more detailed research. Much of this will have to be done through fieldwork and case studies. Such work may bring to light the suffering of many Asian women (and their families) in Britain as a result of the systematic operation of the ppr and its deliberately inhuman implications.

OPTIONS FOR THE FUTURE

As Sachdeva (1993, pp. 107–69) shows in detail, the case-law on the ppr has vacillated between concern for the right to family life and worry about the immigration implications of a liberal approach to family formation. A set of early cases in 1984 showed, with extreme clarity, that the recognition of South Asian arranged marriages as genuine marital unions would deny legitimacy to the ppr (Sachdeva, 1993, pp. 119–22). Consequently, if a marriage was treated as genuine, the applicant should be allowed to join the UK-based spouse. The only way forward to achieve exclusion was to insinuate that these were somehow not genuine marriages.

The same predicament continues to exist today. Despite several legal challenges to the ppr, ECOs still exercise discretion, so that genuine marriages are being destroyed by the ppr in the same way as ten years ago. It appears that immigration phobia has blocked all thinking about rationally and morally justifiable solutions to this conundrum.

An analysis of cases in the past few years shows little evidence of progress. Lawyers have been arguing about niceties of phrases and shades of interpretation, but see no light at the end of the tunnel unless the ppr is abolished. More judges are becoming impatient, while some resent such kinds of cases. While some judges appeared to feel earlier that the ppr is indeed inhuman (Scannell, 1992, p. 3), others have come to view themselves as protectors of the immigration control system. The politics of law reporting affect the present context, as the official Immigration Appeals Reports contain decisions mainly in favour of the Home Office, and one must search closely for the more positive cases in collections produced by the Immigration Law Practitioners' Association, the JCWI and others.

At the same time, the aspirations, not to speak of legitimate expections, of applicants and their British sponsors appear to count very little. As the *Sumeina Masood* case confirms, this is one of the clearest messages: You are just a little person, a woman at that, and you are not entitled to claim rights from the state on the basis of your own private actions. If you marry a man from abroad, this is your problem, the state has no obligation to support your case for his entry and may simply withhold consent! The masculinist message is that the state determines the law, not individual citizens, and certainly not Asian women and their spouses! What better illustration could one find to show the hollowness of modern democracy in which commoners (and more so, women and ethnic minorities) still live so obviously subject to the discretion of those who are 'more equal' than others.

Such negative conclusions appear inevitable if one views the ppr problem from the victim perspective. The perpetuation of this kind of structural disadvantaging through our modern legal system is neither good for 'race relations' nor, in fact, an effective remedy against the leaking tap of family formation. While this chapter should not be read as an appeal for open borders, there is certainly a need to work towards a more humane implementation of the ppr for Asian and other ethnic minority women.

I hope to have shown, in addition, that the current climate of concern about public funds further disadvantages many Asian women because of persistent assumptions about immigrant deprivation and the resulting costs of immigration for the country. It seems that Britain is confused about the relationship between race relations and immigration, and between immigration and economics (Spencer, 1994a, b). At the same time, more privileged Asian women may not suffer the direct consequences of the ppr but, as Asian women, they are still perceived to be in the same social category and the discriminatory structures of state masculinism remain directed against them, too. The xenophobic attitudes underlying the day-to-day application of the law continue to treat and target all Asian women as inferiors, somehow less entitled to the protection of the law than one should expect.

NOTES

1. The standard handbook on British immigration law is Macdonald and Blake (1995). There is now a large specialist literature on the subject. A useful, accessible bibliography is found in Sachdeva (1993, pp. 179–83).

2. Since this article was originally written, the ppr has been abolished under the new government, through the introduction of HC 26 of 5 June 1997, which has deleted the explicit reference to 'primary purpose' in paras 281(ii), 284(iii) and 290(ii) of HC 395 of 23rd May 1994, as amended. However, there are many signs that this amendment is merely of a formal nature and that the restrictive approach to South Asian spouse applications, and the consequent disregard for the legitimate concerns of South Asian women in Britain, will continue virtually unabated.

3. The migration literature now distinguishes family formation, when an overseas spouse joins a British-based spouse in a neo-local arrangement, and family (re-)unification when family members move to Britain from overseas to join other members of their family or household.

4. In the first reported case of that kind, *R. v. IAT ex parte Victoria Ofiana Hansford* [1992] ImmAR 407, the judge was obviously concerned about the welfare of the English husband. For details see also Sachdeva (1993, pp. 162–4) and Macdonald and Blake (1995, pp. 341–2).

5. For details see Scannell (1992) and Macdonald and Blake (1995, pp. 340–1).

6. See *R. v. IAT, ex parte Hoque and Singh* [1988] ImmAR 216 and Macdonald and Blake (1995, pp. 338–41).

7. On the case of *Safter (Mohammed)* v. *Secretary of State for the Home Department* ([1992] ImmAR 1) see in detail Scannell (1991 and 1992); Macdonald and Blake (1995, pp. 341–2).

8. Several recent reports in national newspapers indicated that there is a constant stream of non-white emigrants from Britain to Jamaica, South Asia and North America. I myself have met many returnees and their families in Pakistan and India.

9. Thus, we hear of emigration from Hong Kong, but there is actually more immigration than emigration (see in detail Menski, 1995).

10. See *R. v. Secretary of State for the Home Department, ex p Shahed* [1994] ImmAR 200 QBD.

11. I am grateful to Ms. Nuala Mole, Director of the AIRE Centre in London, for emphasising this particular point.

12. Sachdeva (1993, pp. 80–4, 165–9). The latest position is authoritatively reflected in Macdonald and Blake (1995, pp. 198–202).

5 Hindu Widows in Britain: Continuity and Change
Shirley Firth

Widowhood marks a most important change in gender relations in all human societies. The aim of this chapter is to examine how becoming a widow affects lives of Hindu women in the UK. This is based on anthropological fieldwork that I carried out in Westmouth (a pseudonym), over a period of many years in the late 1980s and early 1990s.[1] During this time I developed a close contact with the local Hindu community and eventually interviewed 12 widows in depth in their own homes. The lives of these widows show that traditional Hindu values continue to influence their self-consciousness as well as communal attitudes to them. The effects of change on widows as a result of Western influences and migration to Britain can best be understood against the background of the traditional Hindu views of marriage and widowhood, which is explored briefly. The experiences of individual women are then discussed, and the changes are analysed in the final section of this chapter. This analysis shows that traditional norms of widowhood among the Hindus are inextricably bound together with processes of social change.

It is probably safe to surmise that most of the Hindu widows in Britain are of a generation which grew up in India or East Africa, where the ideal of womanhood is based on the concept of *sati-stri*, the good woman or the perfect wife, who dedicated herself (*vrata, vow*) to the well-being and long life of her husband (*pati*). She is thus a *pativrata*, committed to the *dharma*, or moral obligation of ensuring her husband's health and welfare. Her own *dharma* was thus inextricably linked to both his and her own fate in the next life. In earlier times it was such a woman who followed him on to the pyre if he died first, hence the anglicized term, 'suttee' for the act of widow burning.[2] The true widow was a woman who had failed to live up to this model because she had not managed to keep him alive, and failed to go along with her husband on the pyre, whether from choice or coercion. While the emphasis on the act of suttee has been blown up out of all proportion to its actual numbers,[3] the ideology associated with it seems of continuing significance. Even in a rapidly changing society, with more women being educated than ever before, the continued emphasis on arranged marriages indicates the importance of traditional religious, social and – as bride-burning shows – economic values.

In Britain Hindus are living in a society with different concepts of women's rights, sexuality, marriage and divorce, which bombard them through television, work contacts, the influence of education and the general social milieu. Thus, while the older widows and those of the same generation forming their social network may retain traditional attitudes, the younger generation's attitudes are changing, which influences, among other things, the social and economic position of the widow and the kind of care she receives. The willingness of the state to assist with benefits and housing is also a factor in her situation.

HISTORICAL PERSPECTIVES

The *sati-stri* viewed her husband as a god, embodying, 'the ideals of utter unselfishness and complete self-sacrifice' (Ross, 1961, p. 158; cf *Garuda Purana* II.4.91–92; cf Evison, 1989, p. 301). Married before or at puberty, her life had meaning only in relation to her husband and sons. Sons were essential not only for the economic survival of the family, but also for its spiritual and religious continuity by performing the death and ancestral rituals (*Brhadaranyaka Upanisad* 1.5.17; Kakar, 1981, pp. 73–9, 88). She would have internalized the view that a virtuous and auspicious wife died before her husband, and that his premature death indicated both her own bad karma and failure to fulfil her vow of ensuring his well-being. If she died on the pyre with her husband she never became a widow as that title was reserved for the one who survived the cremation pyre. The real widow was the woman who had not immolated herself. Her most honourable (and usual) alternative was the life of the widow-ascetic, expurgating both her own sin and that of her husband in a life of devotion both to him and on his behalf in the hope of reunion with him in their next lives (Dubois, 1906, p. 361; Kane, 1973, p. 604).[4]

Such a rigorous life of asceticism may not have been practical for the young widow who was living in her husband's extended family household. A young woman was in a vulnerable position where other men were concerned, especially if there was property and if she was young and childless. In a common form of levirate liaison, *niyoga*, a childless widow bore a child by a brother-in-law or male relative of her husband's, to whom she was not married, and with whom she did not otherwise live as a wife, to ensure sons who would inherit the deceased man's property and perform the essential ancestral sacrifices.[5] Remarriage, often to a younger brother-in-law, was permitted to lower castes, and the practice was sometimes abandoned when they attempted to improve their status through Sanskritization.

WIDOWS IN CONTEMPORARY INDIA

The position of the widow in more recent times has depended on her age, whether or not she has children, the relationship she has forged in her husband's family, and whether or not she stands to inherit property from her husband or father. Support from her father and brothers is crucial if she is turned out of her marital home or treated badly. Adult sons also give her status and protection. If she is young and without sons, she is often blamed for her husband's death and held in great scorn, bringing ill-luck to those who meet her, and forbidden to participate in auspicious rituals. According to Bayly (1981, p. 175) she is, 'perceived almost literally to be part of her husband's body [so that] her presence in a household raised questions of pollution; she was in effect, in a "liminal" and dangerous state'. Because of this, she would be regarded as 'another man's physical leavings,' and thus unsuitable for remarriage.

Early ethnography describes rituals reversing the marriage ceremony, which still occur today. The new widow was dressed in her marriage finery. Her *mangala-sutra*, the marriage necklace, was cut off, and other jewels removed. Her bangles were broken on her husband's Giev and placed on it, or at the river and then thrown into the water. A Brahmin widow had to wear a single coarse garment. Her head was shaved, which Stevenson describes as, 'the widow's scarlet letter, which, together with her terrible name, Randiranda (one who has been a prostitute), testifies that she is now penalised for the sins of a previous life.'[6]

The practice of dressing the widow in her bridal finery, breaking her bangles and stripping off her jewellery still continues in parts of India. Tonsuring is now rare, but older women may choose it, partly because of fear of offending public opinion. Ideally, a widow should lead a simple ascetic life of devotion to God. But this ideal is very difficult to achieve in the face of the struggles she may face to feed, educate and marry her children. Thus, many widows gravitate to pilgrimage centres such as Hardwar and Varanasi where they can, 'expiate the bad karma to which the prior death of their husband testifies,' (Parry, 1994, p. 51; cf Eck, 1983, p. 329), often driven away by in-laws (Menon, 1984, pp. 80–6). Some widows deliberately choose religious asceticism which enables them to recover their lost honour and feel they are playing a part in society (Ojha, 1981, p. 278), a view shared by Gandhi, who advocated remarriage for child widows but thought that adult widows should adopt 'satihood'. For him, the Hindu widow is a treasure who should cling to her suffering:[7]

> She would prove her *sati*, not by mounting the funeral pyre at her husband's death, she would prove it with every breath that she breathes... She would shun creature comforts and delights of the sense... Knowing that the soul of him who she married is not dead but still lives, she will never think of remarrying.[8]

Given both the religious legitimation of suttee and the dismal alternatives facing many widows, it was not surprising that many women, historically, chose this route voluntarily; others were forced into it particularly in Rajasthan and Bengal (Altekar, 1956, p. 137). Although officially outlawed in 1829, thanks to the efforts of Ram Mohan Roy and Lord Bentinck, the 1987 case of Roop Kanwar in Rajasthan indicates that it is still a contemporary issue in India, reflecting both a resurgence of the popular ideology of the *sati* as a good woman who becomes deified on her husband's pyre, and a feminist reaction to what is perceived as a patriarchal system which connives at murder. Leslie observes that, 'Even today, while this powerful ideology is rejected vehemently by many Indian women, it is accepted without hesitation by others.[9] Roop Kanwar, an eighteen year old girl, died on her husband's pyre, apparently willingly, and according to Leslie, sat 'showering blessings and benedictions on the crowds while chanting the Gayatri mantra' even when 'the fire consumed her torso and flames enveloped her neck'.[10] While the thousands who still flock to her shrine regard this as a religious phenomenon of the indwelling of the goddess Sati, many Indian writers have seen her death as a revival of a traditional view of womanhood and marriage (Shekhewat, 1989, p. 47), and as a move to restore the concept of the *pati-bhakta*, the woman who worships her husband as God (Mishra, 1989, pp. 50–1). Mishra views the suttee, 'as the outcome of a systematic ideology working hand-in-hand with criminal design suitably garnished with religious obscurantism... patriarchy triumphant, unmoved by the buffeting winds of modernization' (Dandavate and Verguese, 1989, p. x).

REMARRIAGE

Reformers encouraged the remarriage of 'virgin widows', often against much opposition, since many upper castes forbade the remarriage of any widows on the grounds that once a chaste daughter was given in marriage (*kanya dana*), she could never be given to any one else.[11] Many Brahmins still hold this view. Castes which permit remarriage sometimes adopt this stricter stance to improve their status (Stevenson, 1920, p. 206). Marriage to a younger brother is common in a number of castes, 'to keep the same blood' or honour in the family. There may also be material considerations as well if there is a dowry or the woman and/or her children stand to inherit a share of the husband's property.

Among educated families remarriage is taking place more frequently, even among Brahmins, as registered civil marriages become more acceptable. The economic prospects of educated women have made a difference to the position of widows, giving working widows the possibility of independence and making them more desirable as an economic asset both to their present in-laws and as a marriage partner.

The second marriage is not a formal marriage but based on caste traditions, often reinforced by a civil ceremony. In law it has to be a publicly recognized ritual according to, 'the customary rites and ceremonies of either party', (Menski, 1995a, p. 15) in which the widow is recognised as the wife of the new husband, and their children are recognised as legitimate.[12]

While women's *dharma* is inextricably linked to their husbands', the reverse is not true. Widowed men are not regarded as permanently inauspicious and wounded, less than whole; indeed, they are fortunate if their wives die before them. Men from all castes have always been able to remarry, and if they have young children, are often encouraged to do so. A man who intends to remarry, or whose family insists that he do so, might not even attend his wife's cremation, but tears a piece of cloth off her red garment and hangs it over the door when the corpse departs, to signal his intention (cf Madan, 1987, pp. 129 ff.).

HINDU WIDOWS IN BRITAIN

In Westmouth the Hindu community is a small one of about 2000 Hindus, of whom about 60 per cent are Gujarati and about 40 per cent Panjabi, with a few from UP and other regions. Most of the Gujaratis and some of the Panjabis migrated from East Africa in the late 1960s and early 1970s. There were five Panjabi and seven Gujarati widows in my sample. All the Gujarati widows and two of the Panjabis were 'twice migrants', having grown up in India and gone to East Africa on their marriages – a factor influencing their adjustment both to life in Britain and to the loss of their husbands, since many women who had grown up in extended family situations, and possibly lived in one in East Africa, found themselves living in nuclear households in Britain. They were all middle class in the sense that their husbands had been involved in business, but there was considerable variation in their own educational backgrounds, command of English, and employment experience or potential. The Panjabi women were from Brahmin, Soni and Khattri castes. The latter women were Arya Samaji; the others from Sanatan Dharmi families. The Gujaratis were Brahmin, Lohana, Patel, and Kumhar, and included followers of Sanatan Dharm, Pushtimarg and Swaminarayan.[13] Other variables were size and the extent of their local caste groups and extended families, especially the absence or presence of their natal kin in Britain. The older informants had married at around fifteen or sixteen. Finally, they all had children; which in India is one of the crucial elements influencing the status of widows.

Obtaining detailed information from widows in my study was not easy, particularly from younger ones who were anxious lest the information they gave me about their difficulties would be published and prejudice their relationship with their husband's family. Others were reluctant to make comments which might upset the son or daughter-in-law who might be present. It was even more difficult to find out much about widow remarriage, because of the stigma attached to it, although clearly there are a number of cases in Britain. I did not meet any remarried widows, some of whom are apparently second wives, nor did I meet any childless widows.[14]

The factors which affect the situation of a widow in Britain include her social position and the expectations of those around her, economic status and whether or not she has her own resources or supportive natal kin and/or sons who can play an active role in ensuring her welfare, and her own and other people's attitudes to widowhood. Older women, especially those without employment or an established religious or social position, are more likely to keep to a longer period of mourning and to internalize beliefs about the inauspiciousness of the widow. Gujaratis from East Africa, in particular, who in my sample belonged to strong caste groups, were apt to be more conservative in retaining old traditions and attitudes, often reinforced by the widows themselves. An exception was a leading Brahmin woman who already had an important role in the life of the mandir and in the community, conducting various rituals both in the home and temple, and was a surrogate recipient of gifts for the departed. Her public role continued after her husband died, altered only by the coming of a resident pandit.

At the other end of the spectrum, an elderly Kumhari woman internalized this sense of being impure and inauspicious to such an extent that she did not go out for ten years. She had loved bright colours and she had worn 'the biggest *bindi* in town'. After her husband died and her *bindi* (the red dot on the forehead denoting marriage) was removed she felt 'that this was it'. Now she would be a bad omen and people would look at her and avoid her. She adopted an ascetic lifestyle, wearing white and spending much of her time in prayer, and honouring her husband daily with offerings. She followed a strict, simple diet, taking an unobtrusive position at any auspicious functions. Another, Lohana, widow commented, 'You have to cover your face at festivities in case you are thought of as bad luck. You can't be there when the bride and groom come or do *arti* (prayer before the gods with a lamp) for the new couple.'

Widows are not supposed to perform any auspicious rituals, such as the *havan*, the Vedic fire ritual, although in practice many of Panjabi women who participate in the weekly *havan* in the local temple are widows. Many of these are of Arya Samaj backgrounds, which places less stress on death impurity and inauspiciousness than those following Sanatan Dharm. This can cause tension between the groups. A Sanatani Panjabi Brahmin man reflected a common view when he commented that the participation of widows in these rituals was 'not religiously right because while they are not impure, they are not complete, not part of a unit'.

A more ascetic, devotional lifestyle may be adopted, not because of external pressure, but from a continued sense of dedication to the husband and a desire to find meaning in the bereavement. However, for the Gujarati woman, above, who did not go out for ten years because she felt so inauspicious and unlucky there seemed to be no other option than to concentrate on her religious life. Even when she resumed a limited social life she remained on the periphery and left early.

A Punjabi Arya Samaji widow had already adopted a religious life style before her husband died, participating in the weekly *havans*, and regularly discussing religious issues with her friends. This deepened as she tried to understand her loss:

Sometimes when I am alone I think, 'Oh, what is life now, the children were here, now I am alone, what about me?' Then I think, the *atman* (soul) is eternal, he has gone and my turn is coming...Nobody is dead if you believe the *atman* is eternal...When my turn comes my children will miss me, as we miss our parents, but in *samsar* (the cycle of birth and death) it is like this. When you read the *Bhagavad Gita* this reminds you that we change our bodies, like clothes, and we have a new birth. People come and go, come and go, and you think, 'My parents have died, others have died'. Then your visitors say, 'My son has died, my daughter has died', and share with you. In every house death has come. When you realize it you have *santi* (peace).

Even when the marriage is less than satisfactory and her husband's death releases her from an unwelcome bond, the widow has to cope with a dramatic change in her position in the family and her social status on top of any economic problems that may arise. The ritual of stripping her of her wedding finery and marks of marriage as occurs in some Gujarati communities reinforces this in no uncertain terms, encompassing loss of the marriage, of role, position and worth, and reinforcing her new role as one of the unlucky marginalized widows. When the body is brought in, her glass or plastic bangles are removed, often by older widows, or smashed on the coffin. A Gujarati pandit finds this is so painful that he will not watch it and tells the widow to take them off herself and place them in the coffin. She may be asked to take a coconut around the coffin since, 'she entered marriage with the coconut in her hand, so this is the moment when it should be returned'. Her *bindi* is removed. If she does not normally wear one it is put on and then rubbed out by the older widows. Her *mangala-sutra* (marriage necklace) may be broken, with a piece of the gold used for the mouth of the deceased. She is not supposed to go to the cremation.[15] This was said by a pandit to be out of respect and emotion and because of her bondage to the deceased: 'If she went she would sacrifice herself.'

One young Gujarati Brahmin had her bangles forced off by a senior widow and was made to put them in the coffin. She was also made to remove her nose ring. After the body left the widows took her into the bathroom, sat her in the bath and poured water over her. She then had to put on a white sari and carry a *diva* into the living room to place before her husband's photo. All the married women turned their backs on her so they did not have to see her face, since that would be bad luck. She was hurt and shocked because it had never occurred to her that this might happen to her. She was told she could never wear make up or a *bindi* again. Because she was young her widowed mother-in-law told her she could wear beige or blue but never red, green or yellow. She could wear gold bangles, but her *mangala-sutra*, which was not broken, was being kept for her daughter. She knew that the lot of widows was better than it used to be, but she was lonely, despite a sister living nearby. Her widowed mother-in-law ended the mourning period after three months, instead of the traditional year, so that the family could arrange auspicious events such as marriages and the tonsure of children; this is common practice in Britain.[16] According to a recently widowed Lohana woman, such rituals only takes place if the mother-in-law is still alive, which seems to suggest a punitive element legitimized by custom. Knott (1996, p. 23) comments that, 'it is the senior women who police the home and the *dharma* of its women members, ensuring the principles and laws are passed on to and upheld by the junior women.' The practice of married women turning their backs on the new widow when she first appears in her widow's clothes reflects the traditional view of the inauspiciousness of the woman whose husband predeceases her, and indicates the pressure placed on the widow at her most vulnerable to conform to such views.

There are also expectations as to how much grief the widow expresses. If she does not show enough sorrow she may be criticized. I was sitting with one recently bereaved woman when she was ordered to cry by some of her visitors, who also wept as they remembered their own bereavements. While this can be therapeutic, it may also seem artificial, as a young Gujarati woman found when her Panjabi friend's father died:

> She had all these people coming, and her mother just had to be in that room with them, all that time, and if they cried, her mother had to cry, because if her mother didn't cry they would get the wrong idea. They were upsetting her mother more by mourning than if they had just kept quiet. What can you say? 'I'm awfully sorry?' Because sorry doesn't bring a dead man alive again, does it? A lot of Indian women, when they grieve, they sort of beat their chests, and that's how they demonstrate their grieving and if you don't do that they say that you don't care.

Several of the Panjabi widows felt less constrained by public opinion than the Gujaratis, partly because of a more liberal Arya Samaj tradition, and partly because they were not members of such large, closely knit caste groups. One widow (aged 60) chose to remain at home for the first month because she did not want to be judged to be lacking in the proper feeling for her husband, but was not concerned about 'proper behaviour' as such. Another refused to wear white or pale colours as she felt it was hypocritical, and continued to wear the same clothes as before, although she always chose dark or muted colours. A graduate, she secluded herself because she was so devastated by her husband's unexpected death and lost all interest in social and religious activities. She had had an arranged marriage in India, seeing her husband for the first time at the wedding. He brought her to England to set up a nuclear household, and she became completely devoted to and very dependent on him. She had no family in Britain apart from her children. This widow was one of the only informants in my study who questioned God for taking such a good man, and struggled for some time to find an explanation for his unexpected death in terms of karma or God's will. For several years she fasted and spent more and more time reading the scriptures as she came to terms with the loss. She felt she had no role in Westmouth, and eventually emigrated with her family.

While there is no longer an insistence that widows wear white or the colour of mourning acceptable in their caste, many older women wear white or pale colours because, as an elderly Gujarati Brahmin woman said, 'In our hearts we don't want to wear bright colours. I have lost a husband and a son'. Conformity is expected, and a young woman who tries to carry on as before can encounter severe criticism, even from her own family. The Gujarati woman, whose Panjabi friend's father died, described the widow's behaviour and her mother's reaction to it:

> She wears bright colours. A widow is supposed to wear white, but she doesn't believe in that; she wears lipstick and make up and colours. Her mother really tells her off, she goes, 'You didn't care for him,' that's coming from her own mother. She says, 'Look, grieving isn't just what you see physically, it's what you feel inside that matters'. I suppose because her mother is old she is finding it hard to believe that anyone could grieve inside when they look so colourful outside.

This young widow at least had her mother with her in Britain, but those without relatives in Britain may feel particularly isolated, especially if they have no children, or none locally. An older woman with sons has at least fulfilled one of her main functions. If the widow is young she is also constrained by the risk of local gossip, and dare not be seen talking to men; if she has unwelcome advances from men, the community will blame her. If she continues to go out to work she may find the restrictions irksome, particularly if she does not share in the beliefs and attitudes of the older members of the community. The restrictions can be so severe that she returns to her family if they will have her back.

Just as the death throws the wife into the role of the widow, so the role of the eldest son, or in some cases the nearest son or a daughter, is changed by the death, since they now have to take responsibility for a parent and, if they are still at home, younger siblings. The dynamics of the extended family, even when people are not living under one roof, is likely to alter far more after the death of a parent than in the more fragmented nuclear family system where it is expected that adult members will get on with their own lives from an early age. Some younger widows remain in their home with their children; if they are already living with their in-laws they may experience anger and resentment over the husband's death. Older widows, if they are not already living with one of their children, may move in with their son's family, or more rarely, a daughter's and may find satisfaction in caring for their grandchildren and, where appropriate, helping with the family business. Sometimes, however, there is little room or a welcome in a small nuclear household. If the mother-in-law does move in and the two women are not accustomed to living together, there can be tension between them, especially if the widow is from a very traditional background and the daughter-in-law is westernized. One professional couple had always lived on their own but when the father died the son felt he ought to have his mother live with him. However, she and his wife did not get along very well, so she remained in her old home for much of the time. The periods when the older woman moved in with the family, such as when she was unwell, created a lot of tension. The younger woman came from a different religious tradition and was much more westernised in her outlook towards child care and diet. The young man's problems were compounded by anxiety that people would talk about them: 'My mother lives alone and that is not the accepted Indian culture. They'd say to her, why are you living alone? I keep an eye on her, even though she's not living with me, and do everything for her, but when she dies there will be a lot more guilt, because I'm her only son here.'

An advantage of living in Britain is the economic cushion provided by the welfare state, which enables some widows to live independently without interference from their children or daughters-in-law, and there may be opportunities for work in local factories or sweat shops which provide company as well as a small income.

REMARRIAGE IN BRITAIN

Attitudes to remarriage are similar to those in India among similar class and caste groups. Brahmin widows are normally not allowed to remarry, but some other castes, such as the Lohanas, Prajapati Kumhars and Darjis are allowed to remarry if they are young; the latter after one and a half to two years. At a recent Lohana conference in Britain it was decided to get younger widows remarried as soon as possible, 'so that they could get on with their lives, although it is much harder to approach a widow with remarriage in view'. Many of these marriages seem to be to younger brothers, and a number of reasons are given for this. The woman herself might wish to remain in the family because of her attachment to her in-laws, and there may be pressure from both her parents and the husband's parents to stay, especially if there are children and property considerations, as the in-laws would not want the dowry or inherited property to go out of the family. Some of my informants also felt that once a girl was given in *kanyadana*, no one else would want her, although it was conceded that a widow with property might be an attractive proposition to a widower.

Second marriages may be legitimated by a registry wedding, but are not considered 'true shastric (scriptural) marriages', which can only occur once with the *saptapadi* (seven steps around the sacred fire), although this is not always performed, even in first marriages. As in India, different castes have their own traditions to confirm such 'secondary marriages', of which a few are mentioned here. A Panjabi Brahman, while stressing that Brahmins, 'never remarry', described the *chador*, referred to above, for other castes, and others knew of Brahmin remarriages. In a Lohana marriage the sister-in-law of the groom placed a *thali* (tray) in front of the bride and groom, filled it with water, and told them to look into it. When they did so, she pushed their heads together as a symbol of their union. A Kumhar widow married someone outside the deceased husband's family. She had returned to her parents after her first husband's suicide, because she felt that his death had been brought on by his family's problems around their business. The new husband was a forty-nine-year-old bachelor who wanted to marry a rich wife, and was prepared to take her son, whom he also adopted informally so that he would eventually perform the step-father's death rites. After the civil ceremony the parents of the new groom left an empty pot outside their house. The prospective bride had to indicate her willingness to marry by filling the pot with water and carrying it into the house, where a few prayers were said by the pandit. The deceased man's parents were outraged, as they had already outcast their other son for marrying an English woman. Because they were now estranged from their daughter-in-law they went to court to establish visiting rights for their grandson.

Among the older women there are some who were widowed as children before the marriage was consummated, although the hand clasp contact at the wedding means they are still considered married. As 'virgin widows', they are very much revered if they have had the virtuous life of a *sannyasini*. One such Panjabi Khatri woman had been widowed at thirteen. She was called 'Rani', princess, because she had been 'clean and pure' all her life, and honoured as the leader of the clan.

CONCLUSION

The concept of *stri-dharma* is still potent in British Hindu culture, often reinforced by older women. Part of its power lies in the inextricable link to karma and the next life, which is determined, both for herself and her husband, by a woman's observation of her *dharma*. In such a role a woman is in an ambiguous position, powerful, yet at the same time, potentially weak, inauspicious and impure, a view strongly reinforced by society, literature and myth (Kakar, 1981, pp. 56 ff). If her primary purpose was to serve her husband as a god and bear him sons to perpetuate the lineage biologically and by the performance of ancestral rituals, her failure to keep her husband safe was both a source of blame by his family, and internalized guilt for her own supposed part in his death. However, for many women there is also a positive view of marriage as a religious and spiritual union, in which they have invested all their emotional and spiritual resources, so that when the husband dies, satihood, in the Gandhian sense, is what they choose as the most satisfactory way of life.

Life in Britain challenges many of these traditional attitudes to marriage, womanhood and widowhood because young women (and men) are being educated and work alongside British young people with strong ideas about individualism and choice of partners, for good or ill, and economic opportunities allow for greater independence. Many younger educated women are also reacting against a patriarchal view of women seen primarily as means to an end; that of ensuring their husbands' spiritual welfare both by their piety and by producing sons (cf. Knott, 1996). Widows may be able to make more choices than was possible hitherto, not least because the state provides housing and social security which allows for considerable independence. It would be naive, however, to assume that the changes are all positive. The nuclear household may relieve some of the more difficult pressures of the joint one, but can also lead to a loss of support and cohesion. There may not be room, or a welcome for an older widow, who can experience great loneliness. Mistaken assumptions may be made by medical and social work professionals that the Hindu community takes care of all its members, whereas some individuals may be isolated and depressed. There is also the danger that in rejecting those aspects of a culture which are seen as unsatisfactory, some of the more positive values, such as loyalty and commitment to the family as a whole, can be lost. It could also be argued that although western ideas about the value of the individual may seem to be desirable, the models of cohabiting relationships and serial marriages which are now common in Britain leave much to be desired from a Hindu perspective, and new models, within a religious framework, will need to evolve, which will also provide a secure basis for widows. Research such as Menski's (1984) into Hindu marriage, Nesbitt's (1993) into the way in which religious and cultural values are passed on to Hindu children, and my own (1994, 1997) into the ways British Hindus approach death and bereavement, suggests that a vigorous process of adaptation is taking place, maintained by a strong umbilical link to India.

NOTES

1. This chapter is based on observations I made while engaged in research into the ways in which Hindus approach death, dying and bereavement in a British coastal city, Westmouth (a pseudonym), as well as three months in India.
2. For convenience 'suttee' is used for the act of widow-burning, whether voluntary or involuntary. '*Sati*' refers to the woman who ascends the pyre and is declared to be possessed by the goddess, as Roop Kanwar was. One becomes a *sati*. Not all widows who were immolated were regarded as *satis*.
3. Suttee occurred largely in Rajasthan and Bengal, with some evidence in Vijayanagar, and usually, but not exclusively, among upper caste women. See Harlan, pp. 79 ff.; and the debates by Embree, pp. 151 ff and Oldenburg, pp. 159 ff.; and Nandy, pp. 131 ff. in Hawley, 1994.
4. Dubois, 1906, p. 361; Kane, 1973, p. 604; Leslie, 1987/88, 1989, 1991a; Sharma *et al.*, 1988; Parry, 1994.
5. This was condemned by Manusmrti 9.64–66. Later commentators said that this was permitted in earlier times but forbidden in the Kali age (Dermot Killingley, personal communication). See Saraswati, 1988, p. 71; Altekar, 1956, pp. 143 ff.
6. Stevenson, 1920, p. 204; cf Padfield, 1908, p. 205; Dubois, 1906, p. 353; Leslie, 1991b, pp. 8–9.
7. Singh and Singh, 1989, p. 57.
8. Gandhi, M.K. (1958) *Women*, Ahmedabad: Navajivan Publishing House, pp. 80–1, cited in Singh and Singh, 1989, p. 57.
9. Leslie, 1991b, p. 2; 1987/88, pp. 18–19; 1991b, p. 6.
10. Leslie, 1991a, p. 181, citing Badhwar cf Mishra, 1989, pp. 51–2.
11. Pandey, 1969, pp. 214–15; Chadha, 1978, p. 155.
12. Legally recognized marriages include the *Pat* marriage, in which the wife is 'looked upon as a wife, with a wife's duties, responsibilities and privileges' (Ningu v. Sadashiv, AIR Bom 30), the *karewa* (levirate) marriage in the

Panjab, and the *Chandar-andazi*, in which a sheet or shawl is held over the couple, as the expression of 'intention by the parties to live together as man and wife . . . a contracted union . . . an indication of their mutual willingness to live as husband and wife', legitimated by the cohabitation of the couple (Diwan, 1984, pp. 69–70).

13.   Arya Samaj, founded by Dayananda Saraswati (1824–83), attempted to return to true Vedic teaching and rejected the use of images, dependence on Brahmin priests and the stress on purity and impurity. Pushtimarg (Pushtimarga) was founded by Vallabhacharya (1479–1531). Popular in Gujarat, followers worship the infant Krishna. Swaminarayan, an ascetic reform movement popular among Gujaratis, was founded by Sahajanand Swami (1781–1830), who came to be known as Swami Narayan, a name for Vishnu. My informants followed one branch, Akshar Purushottam Sanstha, under Pramukh Swami. Sanatan Dharm (Sanatana Dharma), the eternal dharma, is the term used by Hindus for 'mainstream' or traditional religion.

14.   Polygamously married wives were permitted to come to Britain prior to the 1988 Immigration Act, provided the marriage was legal in India.

15.   At the beginning of my fieldwork Gujarati women did not attend any of the funerals I observed in Westmouth, but a number of younger women go now. The reverse appears to be the case in Leicester, as some temple committees have discouraged the practice because the women 'cannot take the strain'. British Panjabi informants attended cremations in Delhi and other cities in India, and go the crematorium here as a matter of course.

16.   The period of death impurity, according to the texts, varies according to class, *varna*. For Brahmins it is ten days, twelve for Ksatryas, fifteen for Vaisyas, and a month for Sudras (Manusmrti, 583), but there are caste variations. The mourning period, *Soka*, is longer, especially for a young man, or that of a widow for her husband.

Section 3
The Second Generation:
Gender and Change

6 South Asian Women and Arranged Marriages in East London
Kalwant Bhopal

This chapter examines the position of South Asian women within the family and household, with particular reference to arranged marriages. It will also examine the influence of education and how this affects whether South Asian women participate in arranged marriages. The chapter is based upon research carried out in East London.

Arranged marriages have been customary for centuries among South Asian people. They are considered to be a ritual and a sacramental union. Previous research examined the arranged marriage system in India and indicated that the arranged marriage reveals no significant departure from the traditional method of mate selection. The Indian family system is maintaining its basic character and adhering to traditional patterns of life (Kalra, 1980).

Research has shown, (Bhachu, 1985) that the traditional criteria of spouse selection and kinship organization of South Asians in the UK follows much the same pattern as that in India (Pocock, 1972). Arranged marriages take place in one's own caste; inter-caste marriage is rare (Macleod, 1976). Caste endogamy is a basic criterion of marriage arrangement in the UK, as it is in India (Rao and Rao, 1982).

Research in the UK on arranged marriages has indicated there are profound differences between the western notions of marriage and the arranged marriage (Khan, 1979). One of these differences is that in the West individuals have the right to autonomy and independence. However, South Asian youth are not socialized into the rituals and mechanisms of finding a marriage partner for themselves (Brah, 1978). Within the South Asian tradition, Hindu, Sikh and Moslem marriages differ critically in some precepts and customs. For example, the groups from which a partner is drawn may differ. Muslims may marry within the kin group, Hindus and Sikhs may not do so, but are more likely to marry within the caste or occupational group (Anwar, 1981). For Hindus and Sikhs, the importance of marriage is primarily based upon a sacramental union, whereas for Moslems it is primarily a contractual union, which indicates that attitudes to re-marriage and divorce are different. But the similarities between the three groups in terms of the relationship of the individual to the family, the social and economic importance attached to marriage, the family structure and the possibilities for mate selection are important (Wilson, 1978).

Recent research by Stopes-Roe and Cochrane (1990) however, has suggested a typology of arranged marriages among Asian groups. In the '*traditional*' pattern, the parents and elders of the family select and choose a spouse for their children. In the '*modified traditional*' pattern, the young person has an effective power to decide the outcome, although only from the selection made by the parents, but the final choice does rest with the young person. In families following a '*cooperative traditional*' pattern, either the parent or the young person may make the selection depending on the timing of events, the eventual decision is a cooperative matter, but one in which the agreement of the parents is an essential part. The research has also shown that South Asians are likely to want to marry someone from their own ethnic group and do not want to break away from the arranged marriage system, but want some modifications of the system (Stopes-Roe and Cochrane, 1988, 1990). However, more recent research (Office of National Statistics 1996) has revealed that some Asian men and women do marry out of the community.

Such research has provided us with a detailed understanding of the processes involved in the arranged marriage and its importance. However, some of the research is dated and has not examined women's recent experiences of arranged marriages. Are arranged marriages oppressive for South Asian women? To what extent does education make a significant difference to South Asian women's participation in arranged marriages? Has there been any significant change in South Asian women's perception of arranged marriages?

THE RESEARCH AND THE SAMPLE

This chapter presents data from in-depth interviews with South Asian women living in East London, in order to assess the effect of patriarchal household arrangements on their lives (Bhopal, 1996). The sample was made up of women who were born in the UK, but whose parents had originated from the Indian sub-continent: India, Pakistan and Bangladesh. The ages of the women ranged from 25 to 30 years. Three groups were investigated to examine the impact of religious difference, consisting of women who defined themselves as Hindu, Sikh and Moslem. Twenty women from each group were interviewed. Ten interviews were conducted in Punjabi and all others in English. The interviews were tape-recorded and subsequently transcribed. The sampling method used was the snowball sample.

The marital status of respondents varied considerably. Half of the respondents were married and had an arranged marriage. Of the respondents 38 per cent (23 out of 60) were living with their partners (but were not married to them) and 12 per cent of respondents (7 out of 60) defined themselves as single (some who were with partners and some who were without). There were no respondents in the study who were married and had a non-arranged marriage.

Respondents were from different educational backgrounds. Some respondents had 'O' levels (27 per cent), and a number had an undergraduate degree (27 per cent) or a masters degree (15 per cent). Others had 'A' levels (6 per cent), BTEC/HND (10 per cent), CSEs (3 per cent) or no formal qualifications (12 per cent).

THE FINDINGS: THE ARRANGED MARRIAGE

Respondents were asked various questions on arranged marriages: how did they define an arranged marriage? How did parents influence the arranged marriage? What type of contact did married respondents have with their prospective partners and how important did they feel the arranged marriage was? The following sections will examine these issues.

Definition of an Arranged Marriage: How Does it Operate?

As we have seen, arranged marriages are a long-standing tradition for South Asian people and are considered to be the norm. They are customary practices which influence the social standing of parents in the community. Respondents were asked how they would define an arranged marriage. Arranged marriages were defined by half the women in the sample as the parents choosing a partner for their daughter to marry.

> it's when they [parents] find someone for you and they tell you they want you to get married to them ... if you're lucky you might be able to meet them.

when the parents tell you that you have to marry someone and you don't have any choice in who it is and you have to do it...because they make you do it.

Other respondents (37 per cent) said it was the parents *and the relatives* who chose a partner for their daughter to marry.

all the parents and the aunts and uncles get together and they all start looking for someone and then they get you married.

your mum and dad and all the other people in the big family, all sit down and discuss your life, then they start to look for someone for you...they all do it together.

Here the role of the extended family was important. Members of the extended family played a significant part in selecting a partner for the young. Since they were blood related members of the family, they too were able to contribute in selection. The influence and opinions of family members, (both nuclear and extended), are fundamental to the arranged marriage. Women's choices are made not only by their parents, but by the extended family.

A small number of respondents said it was a 'middleperson' (8 per cent) or the father (5 per cent) who chose a partner for their daughter to marry.

they go and ask someone they know in the community...they get someone who we call a 'middleperson' to do it...that person isn't always related to you, he can be, or he can just know you in the community.

we're very strict in our families and we all leave things like that to the head of the family...our dads are the ones who go and find someone for us to get married to...he's the head of the family and so he chooses who he wants us to marry.

Arranged marriages were seen as an arrangement between two families rather than between two individuals. They were based upon a contract where both sides had to fulfil their obligations. Once a decision had been made, there was an emphasis upon fulfilling the contract. Not to do so would result in a threat of damage to the *izzat* (family pride and honour) for male family members. This would bring *sharam* (shame) upon the whole extended family. The emphasis was placed upon another person, (other than the bride or groom), seeking a partner on behalf of the parents. However, it was a very close relationship.

The research suggested that arranged marriages differ for women and men. Women had less control and influence over the arranged marriage than men. Women were unable to refuse a prospective partner, while men were able to be more selective.

> if a girls says no, it's really considered a bad thing... but not for boys, they can say no as much as they like and people just think they're being careful, if we [women] do it, they say we're being fussy and think we're too good for them [the men].

> just because you're a woman you have to feel grateful that someone wants to marry you and you have to just go along with it... if you didn't there would be just hell to pay from your parents and all your relatives... it all depends on what the parents say to you... if they like the boy, they just say yes for you.

Parental power may be modified by allowing the young person the right to refuse, but this right was more likely to exist for males than females. For women, this right remains more of a principle than an effective practice, since duty towards the family and respect for the parent's wisdom and authority are deeply laid down. Women are under pressure to comply, since the good name of the whole family and its individual members will be put into question by repeated refusals of eligible spouses. Moreover, it was the parents who made the ultimate decision.

> they [parents] say you have a choice, but you don't... at the end of the day, they tell you who they want you to marry, and they don't even listen to your feelings.

> I think most parents would say they want their daughters to be happy and so in the end they will choose someone they think will make you happy... but that is different to what you want... *what your parents want for you and what you want are two different things* ... and because they're your parents they have the final say.

In this sense, obedience to parents and family members is important. It indicates a concern with family values rather than individualistic ones. Getting the young person married is seen to be the main responsibility of parents. Family reputation is considered to be of utmost concern. However, it is women who are ultimately responsible for the *izzat*. A daughter's reputation must be guarded at all costs and if a daughter steps out of line (by refusing too many proposals), she not only jeopardizes her own chances of marriage and respect from the community, but also her parents' social standing in the community and furthermore the chances of her siblings for entering into an arranged marriage. Hence, her actions may determine the actions of her immediate family and the extended family.

Many women accept the arranged marriage, because they believe in the principles on which it is based. They have grown up with the values of respect, obedience, filial duty and parental obligation; with a knowledge of the supreme importance of the family, its position and honour within the community; with a strong sense of tradition and a self-definition in terms of family role rather than personal individuality.

> for us it's very different, the reason why we have arranged marriages is because it's something we have been brought up with, something we have to accept because we always know that it's going to happen ... and so you know it's something you have to do ... you sort of know you'll have an arranged marriage from a young age.

> I just accepted it all because I sort of was expecting it to happen and I always knew I would have to have an arranged marriage; it's what we just know is going to happen ... we learn about marriage when we're very young and so you're going to accept it anyway, it's like it's inbred in us and so we accept.13

In addition, as the family is the primary support system individuals must expect to give support to all family members; particularly parents and siblings should expect to consider family interests before their own. The prime responsibility is towards family welfare rather than personal development, together with concern for the family's reputation and proper attention to what is due to elders and those in authority.

Parental Influence on Arranged Marriages

Parents had the ultimate control over arranged marriages, as well as relatives who were able to influence the parents' decisions. Relatives tell the parents which people they think are suitable, the parents then making the final choice.

Respondents were asked in what ways they felt parents influenced the arranged marriage. Of respondents, 48 per cent said parents had the power and control to make all the decisions conveying the arranged marriage. They selected suitable partners and (in some cases) decided *who* they wanted their daughter to marry, *when* they wanted the marriage to take place and *where* the marriage would take place.

they [parents] are the ones who decide on everything . . . they control it all and you just have to do what they tell you and you have no choice . . . you cannot question it.

you aren't allowed to do anything and you can't decide anything, as soon as the engagement takes place all the arrangements are made and you are told when you will be getting married . . . it just happens very quickly.

In some cases, where respondents did not have a very good relationship with their parents, they felt parents wanted them to be married as quickly as possible to the first eligible partner they found.

I think it's a shame, because I know with my sister, she was a bit wild and she didn't listen to them [parents] and so they got her married off to the first guy that came along and he was awful . . . but with my older sister they [parents] didn't do that, they let her see some guys first.

it's hard because if you have one person in the family who does what they want, then it just gets hard for the younger sisters . . . my cousin ran away from home a year ago and her younger sister was married when she was only 16; I think her parents were worried she would be doing the same thing and it would bring shame to them.

However, close extended family members also played an influential part in the process.

the parents get in touch with all the other uncles and aunts and they sit down and decide if the family's okay and if they think we should get involved with them.

one thing that's very important to us is our family members, all my mum and dad's family live near us and so if we do anything, they will know about it . . . they have so much influence over my dad and he always listens to them . . . if my uncle said he didn't want me to marry someone, then my dad would listen to him . . . so in a way, we also have to think about the rest of the family as well as our own parents.

The pressure of the extended family indicates parents, too, must conform to behaviour that is expected of them, by their family and the community. This in turn means the daughters must conform. If they do not, they are punished by many people; their parents, their relatives and ultimately the whole South Asian community. They may even risk being ostracized by their family and community.

It is important for men to control the women in their family to preserve the *izzat* of male members. If the *izzat* of male members is shattered, the family becomes the focus of gossip and scandal, and loses status in the community.

Thus the arranged marriage means considerable loss of personal autonomy on the part of women. Duty towards and respect for the family is firmly laid down, and daughters have to rely on their parent's wisdom and authority in selecting a suitable boy.

Type of Contact

During the process of selecting a suitable boy for their daughter, parents allow little or no prior contact between the prospective partners, as this would be considered breaking community rules. Respondents who had an arranged marriage (50 per cent) were asked the type of contact they had with their prospective partners before marriage. The range of contact varied from meeting their partner on the one occasion and then getting married to them, telephoning their partner, writing letters to their partner or actually dating their partner.

A total of 43 per cent of married respondents (13 out of 30), had met their partner on the one occasion and had then married them.

> I only met my husband once for about 20 minutes...we talked and then he said yes and we got married about 6 months later and I didn't see him until then.

> I was only allowed to meet my husband once, and even then I wasn't even going to be allowed to do that...then we met once at a family function, but I wasn't allowed to talk to him and after that we got married.

Other respondents (10 out of 30) were allowed to telephone their prospective partners.

> we were allowed to phone each other...that was considered to be safe because I lived in Bradford and he lived in London and when we chatted, my parents were in the same room.

> my husband would phone me, but I was never allowed to phone him ...and they [parents] didn't mind really, we needed to get to know each other.

Some respondents (5 out of 30) wrote to their prospective partners and a small minority (2 out of 30) had dated their prospective partners.

I was living in Pakistan then and so we wrote to each other all the time, that was allowed...because it was so far and they [parents] knew it was only letters...we couldn't meet, it was too far away.

I went out with my husband before I got married to him, but nobody knew about that, if they did, they would have gone mad and things would have got nasty...but we just made sure nobody saw us and we went to places that were safe, where we wouldn't see people we knew...it was fun then.

Women were not allowed to have too much contact with their prospective partners as it might damage the *izzat*. Also here was the danger they might not get on and the marriage would be called off.

they [parents] don't allow us to meet, because they think we may not get on and then refuse to get married...that would just put the parents to too much shame and humilation.

parents don't want their daughters to meet their husbands before they get married, they get scared...you may see what he's really like and then just run away and say you don't want to marry him.

The lack of contact between the two partners demonstrates the degree of control parents posses over the marriage relationship. Daughters were kept at a distance from their future family and partner. Once the marriage ceremony had taken place and the daughter's future was secure she was able to mix freely with her husband's extended family. Love therefore came after the marriage, not before.

Arranged marriages are linked to strict moral codes. Premarital celibacy is considered a great virtue for girls. Moreover, women are constantly under pressure to please others; their parents, the extended family and the community. If they refuse a man, they disappoint many people. If they marry, their parents achieve respect and status in the community. Again, family power is evident. It is used to direct women to comply with community values and acceptable standards of behaviour.

Importance of Arranged Marriages

Respondents were asked if they felt arranged marriages were important in South Asian society. A total of 55 per cent of respondents said arranged marriages were important and gave a variety of reasons for this. Many women highlighted cultural expectations as important. Arranged marriages were considered to be part of the distinct cultural identity of South Asian people.

> they are very important and mainly because it's the identity... especially for us women... it's part of our lives and our parents and the people before us all did it and we have to follow in their footsteps.

> they are part of the culture and the people believe in them and it's the people who want to stick to the culture, it's like it's their identity to have an arranged marriage.

My respondents emphasized that women were the ones who particularly felt they had to hold on to their identity.

> it's different for women, we have to have arranged marriages more than men; if they [men] don't have arranged marriages they will still be accepted and people will think he is going through a hard time and doesn't know what he wants, and it would be accepted. But if that was a woman, it would be a different story, she would be kicked out... and nobody would talk to her parents and they would be blamed and seen as being really bad parents.

> if a woman said she didn't want to have an arranged marriage and did her own thing, people would say bad things to her and say she was a slag and they would give her parents a hard time, they probably wouldn't talk to them... but if it was a man, they would turn a blind eye and accept what he did.

Entering into an arranged marriage was part of the process of being identified as an *Asian* woman. Strong cultural forces define South Asian women's position in society. Within South Asian communities, women have traditionally been portrayed as obedient and submissive.

However, 45 per cent of women (27 out of 60) did not consider arranged marriages so important. Most of these women felt it was the community pressure which made individuals *think* arranged marriages were important.

> it's the pressure from the people in the community and also the culture itself... the parents make you think arranged marriages are the only thing you have and so they pressurize you... because people are pressuring them... that's only because they have to think of their good name in the community... that's the only thing they care about.

people make you think arranged marriages are important because they come with the culture and so everyone has to have them...they don't want to be the ones who'll be talked about...and so won't ever change.

Arranged marriages were, once again, linked by my respondents to achieving respectable status within South Asian communities:

you have to make sure you have a good clean reputation and a good *izzat* and so you want all your children especially your daughters to have an arranged marriage...and you do what has to be done to make sure that happens.

if parents had a bad reputation that would be so bad; once you have lost your *izzat* it's hard to get it back and so parents have to make sure it stays clean and people see them in a good way.

The importance attached to adhering to cultural standards of behaviour indicates the ways in which individuals wish to retain their South Asian identity. One of the ways this identity is maintained is through the continuation of arranged marriages, so that individuals are accepted in the community. It can be argued that there are powerful forces pressuring women to conform to accept cultural practices as a way of conserving their place in South Asian communities and reaffirming their South Asian identities. However, not all women conform despite these pressures.

'Deviant' Women

A total of 38 per cent of respondents (23 out of 60) in the study were living with their partners and were highly educated. These women had made a conscious decision to reject an arranged marriage and felt arranged marriages were degrading for women and indicated the lack of power women had in South Asian communities.

if women have arranged marriages, they are the ones who are seen to be inferior to men and men are the ones who have the power over women, they [arranged marriages] put women down and make them look cheap...like pieces of meat.

in our culture, there are different rules for men and for women and men can more or less do what they want...if you're a woman you can't say no to an arranged marriage and if you do people say bad things to you.

As these women had broken the rules of the community, they were no longer respected and were regarded as being sexually loose.

> when Asian women decide they don't want to follow the culture, the culture just punishes them...instead of trying to understand the reasons for living alone and being independent, they immediately think you want to sleep around...they don't understand and don't bother to understand and make too many assumptions.

> they think we just want to sleep around, but that's so stupid, we want to make our own choices and do our own thing, and not be forced to do what *they* want us to do.

These women were also seen as having ruined the *izzat* of the family and bringing *sharam* upon the whole extended family.

> if women want to do what they want, they are not seen as being strong women, but they are seen as having ruined the family name ...everything depends on other people...the Asian culture is very selfish, it doesn't allow people to be themselves...they have to please their parents first and they have to satisfy the *izzat*.

> once you've left home, that's it, there's no going back, people have found out and your dad's reputation is ruined and he'll probably never forgive you for that.

Furthermore, these women did not want their own daughters to have arranged marriages.

> I don't want my daughters to have arranged marriages, they just make women look inferior and they humiliate women, because women don't have a choice and women are the ones who are worse off than men...I think they degrade women in a bad way.

> I want my children to make their own decisions and they can choose who they want to marry...they should be able to do that, it's their life, let them live it how they want to live it...nobody should decide who you're going to marry, that should be the one decision you should be able to make by yourself.

These women had made a hard decision to leave their families, since they had been ostracized. They regretted hurting their parents and suffered immense guilt and pain. But they had felt unable to accept marriage with someone they hardly knew. Even though these women appear very strong and courageous, they were not seen in this way by their communities. Ironically, they were seen as being weak and as sexually promiscuous. This was considered the main reason why they wished to leave home. As married respondents indicated:

> If they don't do what they are told, what do they expect? They are just women who want to sleep with different men and they want the culture to approve...that will never happen and all the men will see them like they see prostitutes and they will get used by them.

> all they want to do is what the white women do and they expect us to accept that and say it's ok...they are just selfish and want too much and end up ruining everyone else's life...just for their own pleasures.

Single, independent women in South Asian communities are considered as 'deviant' women.

Many South Asian women felt, because the arranged marriage was part of their socialization, they were unable to reject it and were afraid of rejecting it, as they in turn would be rejected from the community. Those women who rejected the arranged marriage had paid a high price for their own freedom and no longer had the respect afforded to women who participated in an arranged marriage. The idea of keeping things as they were was important to these groups and many in the communities fear changes, especially as they may weaken men's traditional authority in the family.

If women have become independent they are punished for having broken the rules and having rejected cultural norms and values. In turn, the extended family and the community may punish the family, by criticizing the lack of control they have over the women in their family. Parents through fear, then may place stronger demands on their remaining daughters. When women rebel, the family must come to terms with conflict and change.

For many South Asian people, the arranged marriage is part of their childhood socialization and is something they grow up to expect. Socialization plays a great part in dictating the roles women must follow. To deviate from these roles is considered wrong and women have a high price to pay if they do so.

TWO CASE STUDIES

Parmjit[1]

Parmjit is 26 years old. She is a Sikh Punjabi woman who lives in East London with her husband and his parents. She had an arranged marriage when she was 19. She came from Birmingham to live in London when she married her husband. She has two children, a daughter aged 4 and a son aged 2. At the age of 18, Parmjit was told by her mother that she would have to leave school as her father was keen to get her married. During this time, Parmjit was very disappointed since she wanted to continue with her studies, but felt pressurized to conform.

> I didn't really want to get married then, but because all my cousins at my age were getting married, I think that influenced my father a lot and because I was a girl, he felt it was the right age.

Parmjit however, was allowed to meet her prospective husband.

> I was very nervous. We went to my uncle's house and I had to go and give the tea, you know the same old thing... so they can look at you... it was pretty awful and I just didn't want to let my parents down.

About a year after this, they were married and Parmjit went to live with her husband and his parents in their home in East London. Initially she found it difficult to adapt to her new life and did not get on well with her in-laws.

> it was very hard for me, I was so used to doing what I wanted at home and it was so easy with my own parents... and now I had to do what my mother-in-law wanted me to do and that was very depressing. At times I would just cry and tell my husband.

However, after suffering periods of depression and even thinking about suicide, Parmjit is now content with her life. She is no longer living with her in-laws and the birth of her children has bought immense pleasure and joy into her life.

> It's taken me a long time, but I feel happier now and I think that's because of my children. They make me happy and I sort of live for them and look forward to them growing up.

Parmjit strongly believes in the tradition of arranged marriages and wants her own children to have them.

> I think it's part of us and who we are... we will never be white and so it's important that we keep our own identity and that means if we have arranged marriages we are doing that and also because they do work... well, most of the time they do.

She also believes in the importance of the community and the support they provide for the family.

> for us the community is always there and everyone just wants to be accepted. They want the community to like them and I can understand that ... the community do a lot for us, they are our society.

Parmjit also emphasizes the future behaviour of her children and its significance in maintaining the *izzat* of the whole family.

> if my daughter ran away from home, the community would think it was my fault and they would say things about us [me and my husband] and they would also say things about my mother and father-in-law and that would bring too much shame to our family ... so I want my daughter to be respected. If she does what we tell her to do, then we'll all be respected ... including her.

Nasreen[1]

On the other hand, Nasreen is typical of women who have rebelled. Nasreen is also 26 years old. She is a Moslem Punjabi and lives in East London with her white partner. She works as a personnel officer in the city and is studying part-time for a masters degree. She left Bradford to study for a degree at a university in London, where she met her partner. Since then she has decided to stay in London.

> When I started my degree, I didn't think I would never go home and then I met Julian and we just wanted to be together ... my parents don't know about him, but I think they have an idea ... they would never accept him, my father would just disown me.

Nasreen's parents and family constantly pressure her into having an arranged marriage.

> Because I can just say to them that I have to finish my course, they can't say anything, but then when I finish I don't know what they will say to me.

Nasreen does not believe in the principle of arranged marriages, she feels they disadvantage women.

> I think arranged marriages were designed *by* men *for* men [respondent's emphasis], because as women we just lose out and we always have to do what the community wants us to do, and that is very stressful.

Nasreen herself would like to have children, but feels she would not continue the tradition of arranged marriages.

> When I have my own children, I don't want them to feel they have to do things for me or for anyone else, I want my daughters to be able to be independent and make a life for themselves... not constantly thinking they have to please the community and worry about what other people say.

As Nasreen is the only daughter (she has 3 brothers) she feels there is great pressure upon her to have an arranged marriage.

> I think it's because all my brothers are older than me and they have all had arranged marriages and so my father just wants me to get married now, so that he doesn't have to worry anymore... and because I'm the only daughter, he's more protective towards me... and he always will be.

Nasreen would eventually like to marry Julian, but she told me,

> Even if I was single and didn't meet Julian I still would not want to have an arranged marriage, because I don't agree with them and I think they are wrong... they degrade women.

THE SIGNIFICANCE OF EDUCATION

The educational background of respondents made a significant difference to their views regarding arranged marriages. All respondents who had a high level of education (those who had a BA or MA) perceived arranged marriages in terms of family control and believed that arranged marriages trapped, degraded and controlled women. These women I would define as 'independent' women. However, those women who had a lower level of education (those who had 'O' levels or no formal qualifications) perceived arranged marriages as acceptable because they indicated the respect individuals had for their parents and demonstrated women's identity as an *Asian* woman. These women I define as 'traditional' women.

Traditional women held conformist attitudes towards arranged marriages. They saw arranged marriages as being positive and advantageous for women and had agreed to an arranged marriage. By contrast, independent women held non-conformist attitudes towards arranged marriages and saw them as being oppressive for women. They were living with their partners and did not intend to have an arranged marriage.

CONCLUSIONS: SOUTH ASIAN WOMEN, ARRANGED MARRIAGES AND SOCIAL CHANGE

Arranged marriages are customary practices which have existed for generations in South Asian communities. Opinions and practices on arranged marriages are divided. Some respondents felt arranged marriages were positive for women, while others felt arranged marriages degraded women.

Level of education affected women's attitudes to arranged marriages. Highly educated women did not agree with the practice of arranged marriages and had no intention of having an arranged marriage. They saw arranged marriages as being oppressive for women and held liberal attitudes towards arranged marriages. These women become educated, decide they do not want to have an arranged marriage and become employed, which results in them being more self-sufficient. They may use their education and employment opportunities to break away from the oppressive nature of arranged marriages. Traditional women however, do not have the opportunity or are unable to become educated. They have fewer choices available to them and are more likely to have an arranged marriage.

When selecting a partner for their daughters, parents consider the moral and personal qualities of the prospective relatives. A good family is defined by the absence of scandals and incorrect marriages, stressing the importance of previous marriage relations in determining the background of families. 'Deviant' marriages are not tolerated and may hurt the pride of all the individual members of the extended family. Women's lives are closely controlled by male members of the community; fathers, brothers, uncles and husbands. Men's power over women reinforces their position as one of submission and having to be controlled by men. It is through marriage that women are able to achieve respect and status in South Asian communities. Single women are stigmatized and regarded as having failed the community. Thus, I would argue, South Asian women's identity is achieved through the men in their communities. Women are only respected if they belong to a man. Male respect is central to South Asian communities and female respect is achieved through male respect. Conformity for women is considered to be fundamental to women's status and identity.

To conclude, I am arguing that arranged marriages can be seen as a form of social control for 'traditional' women. It is through the system of arranged marriages that women's lives are closely monitored. Women's identity and social roles are structured to meet society and men's needs. Women's behaviour has to be controlled in accordance with traditional practices in South Asian communities. Through arranged marriages, male control is reinforced, which reproduces solidarities and maintains cohesion through social relations within the particular group. The marriage relationship confines 'traditional' South Asian women to the private sphere of the household and oppresses them. Traditional women have a dependent relationship in marriage and so are unequal to men. Arranged marriages are used to keep women powerless and controlled by men. However, as some 'independent' South Asian women become highly educated, they are moving out of households, rejecting arranged marriages and making their own choices in life.

ACKNOWLEDGEMENTS

I would like to thank Sylvia Walby, Martin Myers and the editors for reading earlier drafts of this chapter and providing very useful comments. I would also like to thank all those who participated at the *Ethnicity, Gender and Social Change Conference* (September 1995, University of Bristol) where an earlier version of this chapter was presented.

NOTE

1.   These are pseudonyms.

7 Cultural Diversity and Religious Conformity: Dimensions of Social Change Among Second-generation Muslim Women
Charlotte Butler

The arrival of New Commonwealth migrants into postwar Britain init-
iated public disputes and media debates about the future of these
'minority groups', and the extent to which they were likely to become
assimilated into British society. By the late 1960s the assimilation model
was becoming increasingly questioned. Evidently not all migrants were
shedding their cultural allegiances in favour of British norms and values,
as some had predicted or expected. There was a conscious desire on the
part of some migrants and their descendants to retain many elements of
their 'original' cultures, modifying them only marginally, and sometimes
emphasizing them even more actively with the passage of time. It
became evident, therefore, that cultural allegiances warranted special
attention. Some research examined the distinguishing cultural features of
selected groups of New Commonwealth migrants, charting the ways in
which these groups differed in such things as language, religion, core
values and social attitudes, kinship patterns, diet and routine life styles.
This research fed a growing concern with ethnicity, as opposed to 'race
relations'.

This chapter focuses on the concept of ethnicity and its specific application to the lives of second-generation Asian Muslim women in Britain. The main argument is that the concept of ethnicity cannot alone
account for changes occurring within the various Muslim communities
in Britain. The notion of an 'ethnic group' fuses too many cultural characteristics together, such as language, religion, diet, dress and nationality, and may not allow adequately for diversity and change. Yet it is

evident that change is occurring within the Muslim population. Thus it becomes necessary to unpick the notion of ethnicity.

From my own research based on interviews with second-generation Pakistani and Bangladeshi Muslim women it is clear that they are maintaining their commitment to Islam but modifying and adapting many of their parents' traditions and customs. Religion would seem to be the key to this process. These women are using religion as a guide to adopt a new role for themselves in British society, one which gives them more freedom and choice, yet at the same time, supports and strengthens their commitment to Islam. However, the development of this new role can not be seen as merely a consequence of their experience of two contrasting cultural systems. 'Race', class and gender are also crucial to this process of cultural redefinition, as their cultural beliefs necessarily reflect the structural determinants that affect their lives. The intersection of 'race', class and gender locates individuals in their social positions and subsequently generates social considerations of beliefs and identities.

The chapter begins by examining some of the theories of ethnicity that have become prominent in Britain over the last few decades, focusing particularly on the issue of the second generation. The aim is to highlight some of the familiar preoccupations with this approach, as well as to outline the various conceptual difficulties that they face. The second part uses empirical material to explore some of these difficulties, as well as highlighting the significance of structural determinants such as 'race', class and gender. The chapter concludes by suggesting the way in which a more complex representation of culture can be adopted; one that allows for change and the influence of structural forces such as racism, class and gender, yet at the same time acknowledges that some individuals wish to maintain a sense of common 'identity' and cultural exclusion.

ETHNICITY IN THEORY AND PRACTICE

An 'ethnic group' has been defined by Yinger (1981, p. 250) as

> a segment of a larger society whose members are thought, by themselves and/or by others, to share a common origin and to share important segments of a common culture, and who, in addition, participate in shared activities in which the common origin and cultures are significant ingredients.

The most familiar examples of ethnic groups are usually considered to be based on nations, territorial units, religious codes, common language, and kinship. Some writers have further suggested that 'race' is another likely source of 'ethnicity' so that one might expect the boundaries between 'racial' and ethnic groups to coincide. Lyon (1972), however, argues that a clear distinction can be made between a 'racial category' and an 'ethnic group'. First, he argues, an ethnic group is defined culturally, whereas a racial group is physically defined. Second, he states that an ethnic group is an inclusive category whereas a racial group is a category of exclusion. Third, Lyon argues that ethnic groups display a sense of solidarity that provides a substantial capacity for mobilization of their collective interests, whereas racial groups can only be considered to constitute 'residual categories' with little or no prospects for collective action.

According to Miles (1982), Lyon has clearly taken the notion of boundary and ethnic group from Barth's work; but his analysis differs from that of Barth in two fundamental ways. First, Lyon states that social boundaries can be established and maintained both internally and externally. Second, he claims that social boundaries that are established and maintained externally can be formed only through the identity of phenotypical criteria. However, Miles argues, in this way Lyon ignores the most innovative characteristics of Barth's analysis, that is, his claim that ethnic groups are defined by the process of boundary maintenance and not by the fact of cultural difference *per se*. Lyon's conceptualization represents an attempt to sort out important terms and avoid confusion, but ultimately it fails to establish a clear distinction. For example, there is no convincing reason why a racial group cannot be 'self-defined', possessing a positive sense of its own identity and purpose, and displaying considerable potential for political and social mobilization. The experience of racism itself may help to produce a unifying cultural 'identity'. Moreover, members of a racial group tend to live in the same areas and grow to share the same economic and social experiences, and from this a common culture may develop. Consequently, the separation of 'race' and 'ethnic group' cannot be sustained.

Jeffery's work (1976), one of the earliest in using ethnicity, marks a return to Barth's analysis, by focusing on the social processes involved in non-assimilation and the maintenance of ethnic boundaries. Like Barth, she argues that cultural differences and similarities are not necessarily compatible with the way social relationships are patterned, and it is therefore necessary to concentrate on the structural aspects of the situation. It is the social structural processes that enable distinct ethnic groups to co-exist through time, even when they do not occupy the same territory and when their members have social relationships not only within the ethnic group but also with members of other groups. Thus for Jeffery, an important factor for Pakistanis in Britain is the links which extend outside Britain to the sending country. Such elements, previously ignored by ethnographic studies, encourage Pakistanis to maintain their culture as their desire is to eventually return home. However, while Jeffery feels that Barth has made an important contribution to the study of 'ethnic relations' and the ways in which social factors help to maintain cultural differences, she believes that he deals only superficially with the factor of power. Thus in her view, maintaining an ethnic identity may for some individuals merely represent a poor substitute to their unfulfilled desire to be accepted by the wider society. However, she states that this particular 'drawback' to Barth's analysis is not crucial for her Muslim informants since they wish to maintain their separation from British people, and do not want to be merged with them.

Jeffery's work, like many others of the period, was predominantly concerned with the first generation of New Commonwealth migrants. However, an important area of concern for studies of ethnicity is the changing nature of ethnic affiliations over time, and so a great deal of attention has been paid to the second generation: the British born, or at least British educated, children of migrant parents. These young people have been exposed to socialization in two very different cultures, at home and at school. Thus, attempts have been made to assess the extent to which they preserve the traditional culture of their parents, and the degree to which they have adopted more 'Western' cultural values. Earlier commentators pointed to the Asian youngsters' devotion to their culture and country of origin (Brown, 1970; Evans, 1971); while later writers have highlighted the many difficulties faced by these young people who have found themselves caught between two cultures (Thompson, 1974; Taylor, 1976; Watson, 1977; CRC, 1978). According to the Community Relations Commission (CRC, 1978), exposure to British norms and values undermines the parent's traditional authority and leads the second generation to question their parent's culture.

In addition, several commentators have pointed to the crucial importance of 'push factors' such as prejudice and discrimination, in determining the decisions which the second generation are making (James, 1974; Anwar, 1982; Ballard, 1979; Robinson, 1980; Hiro, 1991). Thus, despite the fact that they have lived most or all of their lives in, and are thoroughly familiar with, British society, young Asians are constantly aware of being 'different' and of being treated as 'inferior' because of the colour of their skin. Such racial hostility, it is argued, plays a major role in causing these young people to reassert or hold fast to this 'ethnic identity'. As Watson (1977) points out, very few of the first generation of South Asian migrants had any interest, hope or intention of becoming British in a cultural sense. Thus it cannot be said that the maintenance of culture is linked to social rebuff or rejection on the part of white people. For the second generation, however, the fact that they continued to maintain a degree of cultural distinctiveness, despite pressures on the contrary, is highly significant. According to Watson, racism has precipitated a 'reactive pride' in their separate 'ethnic identity'.

Watson (1977), in his edited book, *Between Two Cultures*, takes what he calls the 'political approach' to ethnicity, found in the work of Cohen (1969). Cohen argues that alliances based on ethnicity function like 'informal interest groups' and should, therefore, be seen as political entities which operate through the identity of shared 'culture'. According to Watson, ethnicity in this context only has meaning when two or more groups are competing for control over scarce resources. He, like Wallman (1979, 1986), believes that ethnicity can change and be modified according to political and economic circumstances. However, Watson states that one of the limitations of the studies of ethnicity to date is their inability to sort out the interconnections between class and ethnicity, and he admits that the contributions to *Between Two Cultures* are no exception. Thus, like Jeffery, Watson feels that studies of ethnicity have failed to address issues of power, oppression and exploitation.

Saifullah-Khan (1982) attempts to deal with the question of power in her later work, arguing that the relationship between dominant and subordinate ethnic groups is a relationship of power which is manifest and maintained by the economic and social order. Thus Saifullah-Khan (1982, p. 197) defines culture as: 'a system of shared meanings developed in a social and economic context which has a particular historical and political background'. Culture only has reality within the social context from which it is derived and which it helps to structure. What is of interest for Saifullah-Khan is not the fact of cultural difference, but the process by which, for example, migrants from the Indian sub-continent become aware of their difference once in social contact with sections of the majority population. She uses ethnicity, therefore, to refer to the development and maintenance of ethnic awareness and identity. Thus, according to Saifullah-Khan, one cannot speak of 'Pakistani ethnicity' in any meaningful sense because migrants from Pakistan rarely consider themselves as sharing common characteristics. Rather, their sense of difference from the majority population in Britain is perceived in relation to their family and fellow villagers from the same region. This subjective component refracts the considerable social differentiation within the population of Pakistanis in Britain.

For Saifullah-Khan, therefore, the main focus should be on the perception of difference which is dependent on how individuals and groups define a system: what the main components of culture are and how they relate to the social environment and the economy. It is the lack of fit between these two notions that to Saifullah-Khan is of prime importance to ethnicity. However, having stressed the importance of structural determinants in the process of 'ethnic identity', she still focuses on culture as her prime concern. Hence she talks about majority/minority relations in terms of the influence of the 'dominant culture' on the 'social interaction' of 'ethnic groups'. The existence of racism is acknowledged, but only in its cultural form. As Lawrence (1982) argues, what seems to go unnoticed is the fact that the communities that 'ethnic minorities' live in and the culture they operate under, are subject to conditions which are not of their own making. Thus the problem for Saifullah-Khan and for studies of ethnicity as a whole is that they tend to obscure the relationships of power and treat it as a meeting of cultures on equal terms.

Ballard's (1994) edited collection *Desh Pardesh* represents one of the most recent attempts to focus on issues which relate to ethnicity. He attempts to locate common strategies used to create *Desh Pardesh* ('home from home' or 'at home abroad') among 'ethnic minorities' generally. With reference to the second generation, he argues, there are two important factors to consider: first, they employ a similar strategy to rejecting assimilation by relying on their own meaning for creating *Desh Pardesh*; second, each group has its own specific human and cultural resources. Hence each community is different, the overall result being 'steady progress and ever-growing diversity'. According to Ballard, the second generation participate more fully in the wider social order and are therefore subject to different moral and cultural conventions. As a result they are skilled 'cultural navigators'. For Ballard, the problem with the notion of 'culture conflict' stemmed from the mistaken notion that culture is the comprehensive determinant of behaviour. Instead, Ballard conceives of culture as codes, and individuals possess the ability to switch from one code to another. In conclusion, Ballard states that the second generation are well aware of differences between the majority society and their parents, and therefore are strongly committed to ordering their own lives on their own terms; yet their commitment to *Desh Pardesh* remains. Ballard's work represents an important contribution to the analysis of culture, and to an understanding of the way in which individuals make sense of different and often competing cultural systems. However, what Ballard fails to explain is why it is that the second generation continue to build a 'home from home', and the factors that influence this phenomenon.

A CRITIQUE OF ETHNICITY

The preceding ethnographies by no means exhaust the entire repertoire of available studies, but they do illustrate the general direction and familiar preoccupations of this approach. According to Miles (1982), the framework of assumptions involved in such studies in many ways represents a breaking of the mould of 'race relations' research. The essential problem with theories of 'race relations' lies in the fact that it is not possible to analyse the situation in terms of how people of different 'races' interact as scientific evidence shows that permanent and distinct 'racial types' do not exist. Racial differences, therefore, should be understood as physical variations which are seen by the members of a community or society as significant. 'Race' is therefore nothing more than an ideological construction operating within specific historical and material contexts (Phizacklea and Miles 1980).

One of the major contributions of ethnicity as a concept, therefore, is that it avoids this 'reification' of 'race'. By acknowledging the social construction of 'race' it draws attention to the fact that real phenotypical difference only has social 'effects' when some social significance is attributed to that difference. Consequently, the focus of study must concentrate on how 'race' is socially constructed. In this way, it also takes account of ethnic groups whose physical appearance is very similar to the majority population (for example, the Irish, Poles, Greeks, and so on). Such groups, although possessing similar phenotypical characteristics to the majority of the population, have experienced a degree of ideological, political and economic exclusion similar to that faced by New Commonwealth migrants. This, according to Miles (1982, p. 64), would clearly seem to support the notion that, 'skin colour or any other phenotypical characteristic is not itself an active determinant of social conflict, but such differences can serve as a focus for, or symbol of, conflict which has an origin in other, quite distinct characteristics'. Thus, where a group possesses no distinct phenotypical differences, other, cultural characteristics may be given social significance to mark off that group from the majority population. Consequently, Miles argues, what is of prime importance is the way in which phenotypical difference is perceived and given significance rather than the actual characteristics of that difference.

However, for Miles this advance in the study of ethnicity also points to its theoretical limitations. For although the social construction of 'race' is identified, the process by which such categorization has occurred is ignored. Thus studies of ethnicity sometimes fail to explain why, for example, 'race' has been constructed only in specific contexts and at specific points in history. Such an analysis cannot be achieved by focusing on the 'attribution of meaning to phenotypical difference', but in identifying the structural determinants operating within society that allow the attribution of meaning to take place.

The difficulties which studies of ethnicity have in accounting for the influence of social structure has also led to another criticism; they are seen as attaching ultimate 'blame' (for relative disadvantages) to the minority ethnic groups themselves. It is argued that these studies, by focusing their attention on the migrants' cultural distinctiveness from the 'indigenous' British population, tend to emphasize the 'pathological' or 'inappropriate' nature of these cultures. For example, crime among West Indians is seen as resulting from their 'weak' family structures rather than their depressed position in society; the disadvantaged position of Asian women in the employment market is attributed to their traditionally 'subordinate' role rather than from the exploitation of their labour in Britain (Phizacklea, 1990). The predominant emphasis on ethnic cultures deflects attention away from the racism endemic in British society. 'Race' problems are subsequently framed in terms of 'mutual misunderstandings' and the solutions are posited along the tame lines of 'multicultural education' and 'cultural pluralism'. Bourne (1980, p. 346), criticizes ethnicity theorists, who, she argues, by freezing the dynamics of race struggle in culture and ethnicity, subserve the interests of the state.

Another criticism of studies of ethnicity is that they often exaggerate the differences between ethnic groups. Clearly, these differences are sometimes clear-cut (as in the case of religious belief-systems), but more frequently they involve subtle variations in emphasis, and in many respects the ethnic minorities subscribe to the same values as the majority culture. Part of the problem, according to Phoenix (1988), is the use of narrow definitions of culture. She states that such explanations are unsatisfactory because they serve to reinforce the notion that black people are deviants from the norms of white British behaviour. Phoenix (1988, p. 153) argues that:

Concentration on cultural differences between black people and white people has frequently obscured the fact that cultural beliefs, identities, and practices necessarily embody the structural forces that affect people's lives, and that culture itself is dynamic rather than static.

Phoenix thus rejects cultural explanations of early motherhood among Afro-Caribbean women as resulting primarily from the cultural traditions of specific regions of the Caribbean, and instead attributes it to the class forces operating in British society, class forces which also impress upon the lives of young white women.

It is the influence of racism, class and gender that studies of ethnicity as a whole have, at times, ignored. For many researchers, what is of prime importance is not 'racially defined groups' and the effects of racism and discrimination, but 'ethnic groups' who are self-defined and whose attitudes and values have to be assessed in terms of their distinct culture. Thus their cultural distinctiveness becomes the primary object of inquiry. However, as Barth (1969) argues, cultural characteristics cannot be considered adequate signifiers of an ethnic group, for such cultural traits are not fixed and impermeable but are constantly being changed and modified by the group itself. It is therefore impossible, Barth argues, to define an ethnic group and explain its separate status by the cultural characteristics it displays, as those characteristics are likely to change over time. Instead, he argues, it is necessary to examine the power relationships between different ethnic groups and the factors which help in the maintenance (or loss) of cultural characteristics.

Thus one of the major inadequacies of studies of ethnicity is its insufficient concern with making connections at the structural level. There is a tendency to see 'culture' as a distinct entity, unconnected with other social processes. The effect of this, according to Lawrence (1982), is to produce a static and idealized vision of migrant cultures which cannot account for class, caste or regional differences and which cannot explain the changes that have occurred within these cultures. Thus, for many commentators (Miles 1982; Phizacklea 1984, Gilroy 1987), the underlying problems are structural ones of power and conflict, and these issues can not be tackled by abstract debates about 'culture'. Racial disadvantage, it is argued, is not the 'natural' outcome of a multicultural society in which some ethnic groups cling to cultural values: it is the structural outcome of an exploitative oppressive society which can only be transformed through radical change.

MUSLIM WOMEN IN BRITAIN

The aim of my own research is to examine the experiences and attitudes of second-generation Pakistani and Bangladeshi Muslim women in Britain. It is concerned specifically with the way in which these women come to terms with, and accommodate, the various cultural and structural forces that necessarily influence their lives. The aim, therefore, is to examine the method by which factors such as religion, gender and ethnicity are experienced and utilized to form and transform the lives of these women in British society.

One of the most significant findings of the research was the continuing commitment of all of the Muslim women interviewed to their religion. For some, being Muslim was the most fundamental aspect of their lives. All of the young women felt that Islam was very important to them; and the majority responded with a straight forward statement of orthodoxy, which was justified, if at all, in terms of providing the individual with the basics of life. The following quote is typical of many of the responses:

> I think that whatever I do, that it [Islam] influences everything I do, every decision I make. I think Islam is not just a religion, it's more like a code of life for Muslims. That's the way I feel about it anyway.

Several of the respondents stated that they had drifted away from Islam in their teens, but had since come back to it, and they believed that their faith was now stronger as a result. Some had begun to take more of an interest in Islam when they were studying at college, and mixing with other Muslims of their own age. As one woman commented:

> I've realized that this life is just a test, and like before I never used to wear a headscarf, it was only once I started going to Poly that I wore one and it's really here that I joined an Islamic society group and started attending that and I realized that my religion's the most important thing.

However, although there was a strong identification with being Muslim, very few identified with being Pakistani or Bangladeshi. Furthermore, many of the young Muslims were critical of Asian culture generally because they felt that much of it was not directly related to their religion, and some of it went against Islamic law. Many of the women interviewed argued that customs to do with the marriage system, the giving of dowries, and caste segregation were aspects of Bangladeshi and Pakistani culture that had been taken directly from Hindu and Sikh culture, and represented traditions that were totally adverse to Islam. One of the informants expressed her views on the issue of traditional culture:

> Well I think there's a problem in England, well among the Muslims anyway, a lot of culture they say it's part of the religion but really it's not. The culture's totally different from the religion and unfortunately some people bring the culture into the religion. Like, for example, some girls in my family have been forced to have an arranged marriage, that's just part of the culture, it's not the religion at all. So I think it should go.

Furthermore, it was believed that many of these traditional customs were aspects of Asian culture dating back to the 1960s. Several of the informants pointed out that one of the major problems in the relationship between the first and second generation was that the Muslims who originally came over to Britain were still maintaining the traditions and views of Pakistan from thirty years ago. Pakistan, on the other hand, has moved forward, modifying and adapting many of the old traditions and customs. As one of the women stated:

> What's happened over here is that when the parents came over here twenty or thirty years ago, they came here bringing the traditions and culture that were present at the time, when they were living there; and they've held on to these traditions and cultures for fear of losing their identity or whatever. But what's happening in countries back home is that in their effort to become more westernized they sort of dropped all these old traditions, moved forward, and when you go back you realize just how backward we are living in this country, compared to the people in Pakistan and India.

Thus many of the women interviewed felt that what needed to be addressed by the second generation was not all of Asian culture but those aspects that they felt were outdated and inappropriate not only to themselves as Muslims, but also as Muslim women living in British society. This latter point is significant in that many of these women felt that although certain traditions had been modified and updated in Pakistan and Bangladesh, these were not necessarily appropriate to Asian Muslim women living in Britain. Generally the informants believed that Muslim women in Britain displayed contrasting lifestyles to women in the Indian subcontinent. They felt that Muslim women in Britain wanted more of a lifestyle outside the home; they wanted to go on to further and higher education and to seek employment in more varied careers.

In Pakistan, on the other hand, they felt that women were generally more content to stay in the home.

These differences between the first and second generation reflect the different cultural and social experiences which the two generations have experienced. Growing up in a western society and western culture it is inevitable that the Muslim women will have been influenced by their surroundings. Nevertheless, it is clear that the second generation are not abandoning their parents' way of life in favour of British culture; nor does it seem that they are finding themselves 'torn between two cultures', as previous commentators have suggested. It would appear that the second generation are adept enough to adapt to both cultures, to gain a deeper understanding of their religion and to tailor their own culture around it. As one of the informants commented: 'People are accepting more now the fact that Islam's the Quran rather than all these other laws that humanity has created along the way, so those have been eroded more and more'. The women interviewed are seeking to conduct their lives on more Islamic lines, rather than unquestioningly adopting all aspects of Pakistani or Bangladeshi culture. For many this requires a process of separating religion from culture, leaving them free to form a relatively new culture of their own, one which can fit more easily into the British way of life, while at the same time allowing them to maintain and strengthen their commitment to Islam.

But is religious affiliation enough by itself to constitute ethnic allegiance? Can second-generation Asian Muslims be regarded as an 'ethnic group' at all? Is it useful to conceive of them in this way? If for ethnicity theorists the concept of an ethnic group encompasses such things as language, dress and family patterns, as well as religious belief systems, then we might want to question whether the second generation can be perceived in this way. This highlights one of the problems of research into ethnicity; the concept of an 'ethnic group' fuses too many cultural characteristics together and makes it impossible to account for changes taking place within the various 'ethnic' communities. In addition, it tends to lead to the misleading view that the Pakistani population can in some way be considered homogeneous.

According to Raza (1991), the Pakistani community in Britain is far from uniform. Not only does it display ethnic divisions inherited from Pakistan, but the inability of the second generation to identify with their parents' country of origin, for which they have little or no first hand knowledge, means that they have taken on an Islamic or secular identity. In this way, Raza argues, the Pakistani community can be seen as exhibiting three broad trends of cultural behaviour: 'ethnic, Islamic and secular'. With reference to my own research, there is clear evidence from the Muslim women interviewed of a move to a more Islamic identity. They are seeking a new role for themselves based on the knowledge of their religion. These women are using Islam as a tool to question traditional culture and to eliminate features which they feel are not strictly proscribed by Islam. These women, therefore, are not finding themselves 'torn between two cultures', for they have the principles of Islam to help them find a workable middle course between British and Pakistani/Asian culture. Nor is it a case of rejecting one culture over another, but merely taking the parts from each culture which they feel appropriate for themselves as Muslims in Britain.

What it is important to emphasize here, is that this process of cultural redefinition is not simply a case of individuals choosing one cultural model over another, or indeed, selecting elements from several cultural models. In order to understand why one set of cultural norms triumphs over another it is necessary to analyse the structural constraints and historical circumstances within which such cultural models compete for supremacy. Factors such as 'race', class and gender inevitably affect the choices that individuals make. The interaction of 'race', class and gender affects all members of society as it locates individuals in their social positions and subsequently generates social considerations of beliefs and identities. It is, therefore, crucial to examine the way in which individuals perceive and respond to these forces in order to understand the way in which they maintain and transform their own identity.

THE INFLUENCE OF 'RACE', CLASS AND GENDER

Any decisions that the second generation may choose to take concerning their identity and position in society not only involve their relationship to their community in Britain but also to the wider society. Each individual still has to choose a workable middle course between a culture whose totality he or she has never experienced and a culture which ultimately rejects them as unwanted outsiders. It is important to point out here that although all of the Muslim women interviewed considered their Muslim identity to be most important to them, the majority also identified with being Asian. This allegiance to an Asian identity had as much to do with factors such as prejudice and discrimination as it did with contradictory experiences of two cultures. Although a majority of the interviewees regarded Britain as their home, very few considered themselves to be British. As one woman commented:

> Britain is my whole life, I haven't really experienced any other life. I was born and bred here. But I don't see myself as British though, but to me Britain is my whole life, if you see what I mean.

Thus, in general there was an acceptance of British nationality, but a rejection of 'a sense of belonging' to British society. Thus, although they have grown up in Britain, and feel 'at home' here, they were very much aware of being treated as 'different' by the majority population. This allegiance to an over-arching Asian category, therefore, is a clear indication of the impact of racism in their lives. The category 'Asian' cannot be considered an ethnic group, as the Asian population is far from homogenous, but instead must be seen as a racialized group. This is not to say that many do not feel genuine pride in being Asian and in certain aspects of Asian culture. However, the fact that they are likely to be labelled as Asian by outsiders, whether or not they regard themselves as such, is a significant factor.

The influence of class background can also be seen quite clearly in the research. If one takes the view that ethnic affiliation is a matter of straightforward choice, then we would expect the most socially advantaged to show greatest resistance to change, since they would have the greatest resources within which to protect and pursue traditional values. However, as Raza (1991) points out, middle-class status in the British context, predominantly acquired through income and education, has led many Asian Muslims into following 'Westernized' lifestyles and 'Western' value systems. He goes on to argue (1991, p. 9):

> The poor Muslims have more faith in Islam than the status-elites. Few Muslims from the latter take their religion seriously. They may not be anti-Islamic but apart from rendering lip-service to Islam, they are more seriously engaged in accumulating money to be able to afford the status symbols and indulge in conspicuous consumption.

The young Muslims interviewed confirmed this view arguing that religious and cultural conformity was far stronger in inner-city areas where there was a large Muslim, or at least Asian 'working-class' population. However, the extent to which this 'conformity' can be attributed to class relations and the extent to which it may be explained by the influence of living in a predominantly Muslim-based community needs further examination. Nevertheless, it would seem to imply that the predominance of large numbers of Muslims in inner-city areas may have more to do with structural factors than it does with cultural 'choice'.

Gender can also be seen to have a significant influence on the lives of Muslim women, for, as several of the women argued, all cultures are predominantly 'men-made' phenomena, employed by men to sustain their own position in society. Thus, many felt that it was not the laws of Islam that were responsible for the subjugation of Asian Muslim women, but culture. The women interviewed pointed out that it was not Islam but traditional customs that confined women to the home and discouraged them from seeking employment or going on to further and higher education. Such restrictions were not laid down in the Quran, but in aspects of Asian culture which had become infused with the Muslim way of life in countries such as Pakistan and Bangladesh. As one of the interviewees commented:

> Islam's not to blame for women being kept in the house, covered up 24 hours a day, it's the menfolk that do this. It's not Islam, Islam doesn't impose and say you've got to do this. And covering your hair, it's not important, or covering your legs and so forth, it's not that important as obeying Islam and following Islam. To follow is more important than to wear clothes and so forth, and dress in a certain manner. If your heart follows Islam then you follow Islam, and clothing's got nothing to do with it, or culture. Cultures are man's invention I suppose.

The majority of the women interviewed believed that the inequality that existed between men and women in the Asian Muslim communities in Britain had come about as a direct result of certain aspects of Asian culture, and not through Islam. Far from being part of their religion, some of the informants considered these customs to go against the Islamic notion of equality between men and women.

Gender is especially significant for Asian Muslim women as they are having to confront not only the sexist assumptions from within their own communities and from Asian culture, but also from British society as a whole. Thus, although their parents' culture may place restrictions on their life styles, the sexist and racist stereotypes that exist in British society restrict them even further. Standing up for their rights as women means challenging traditional gender relations within Pakistani and Bangladeshi culture, but it also means fighting against their image as exploited and oppressed 'victims' which pervade British 'common sense' notions of Muslim women in general.

For the women interviewed, religion would seem to provide the answer. Adherence to Islam enables them to construct roles that give them more freedom and choice. It also offers them a positive sense of self identity. This latter point is particularly important. Several of the women argued that by gaining a better education, by making themselves more aware of their rights, and having the confidence of that knowledge, Muslim women could bring about change within their own communities as well as within wider British society. As one women commented:

> I think having an education, knowing all about Islam as well, so that you do not get opposition from the male members of the community, you can stand up and say, 'Well Islam says I can do this and you have no right to stop me'. So if they're informed about the facts then I think they've got more of a case to do that.

Thus Muslim women are in a process of sifting those cultural traditions, both British and Asian, which formerly restricted them, and expanding their role in society by a more conscious adherence to the beliefs and practices of Islam.

CONCLUSION

It would be useful here to return to Raza's argument, that there exist within the Pakistani population in Britain three visible trends: Pakistani, Islamic and secular. A similar analogy can also be made of the Bangladeshi population. From research carried out among the first generation, it is clear that there are many Muslims who are actively seeking to maintain their Pakistani or Bangladeshi identity in Britain. In addition, it is also possible to confirm that some Asian Muslims, particularly from the second generation are seeking to follow a more secular lifestyle; although in many cases I would suggest that their sense of 'self' is more likely to stem from a positive assertion of their Asian and/or black identity, rather than a British one. With reference to my own research, I would argue that the Muslim women interviewed are actively seeking to follow a more Islamic framework. If we accept the existence of these three separate trends, then the concept of an ethnic group becomes difficult to maintain.

However, although we might want to question the usefulness or accuracy of studies of ethnicity, this does not mean that culture as a whole is irrelevant to the study of 'ethnic and racial minorities' in Britain. The existence of culture and of a sense of common identity among groups of people who wish to reinforce and maintain their cultural characteristics in relation to others must be recognized; for this process has real political, economic and social effects for the groups concerned. Yet, equally, it must be acknowledged that these individuals are members of the society as a whole and subsequently dominated by the processes of 'race', class and gender which operate in that society. Thus, as Gilroy (1987) and Phoenix (1988) argue, what is needed is a more sophisticated theory of culture, one which embodies the structural influences of class, gender and 'race'. Culture should not be seen as a 'fixed and impermeable feature of social relations', but, instead, the active, dynamic aspects of cultural life should be emphasized.

This call for a redefinition of culture needs to reach beyond the description of relevant belief systems towards a search for the social factors which shape and condition those beliefs. Cultural beliefs cannot be seen as 'given' or simply 'there'. Instead we must acknowledge that a society's 'culture' (its network of attitudes, values, meanings and ideologies) is connected in complex and intricate ways with its 'structure' (its productive arrangements, power relationships and social institutions). In this way, culture can be seen to refer to the processes, categories and knowledges through which communities are defined, that is, the way in which they are rendered specific and differentiated. An emphasis on the social construction of 'race', as well as that of gender and class, acknowledges the fact that individuals play an active role in the creation and maintenance of meaning. Nevertheless, this activity takes place within particular historical and structural contexts which tend to limit people's choices and make certain behaviour and cultural responses more likely than others. The sociology of 'race and ethnicity' or 'racialized relations', therefore, entails the study of social consciousness, of intergroup behaviour and of social structure.

8 Negotiating Marriage : Young Punjabi Women's Assessment of Their Individual and Family Interests
Hannah Bradby

INTRODUCTION

This chapter is about what marriage means to the daughters of migrants from the Indian subcontinent, who are familiar with the choices available to majority ethnicity women and also schooled to appreciate the central role that marriage plays in the subcontinent's social systems, particularly the system of honour and reputation. Drawing upon conversations with young women in Glasgow, the chapter considers how they evaluated their elders' model of family-contracted marriage, which they called 'arranged'. Where drawbacks of arranged marriage were identified, the strategies that these women employed to mitigate the drawbacks will be described, and the balance that young women draw between their own interests and those of their patriliny will be explored.

Ethnographies of South Asian migrants to Britain have shown the centrality of links with the sending society, established and maintained through marriages (Jeffery, 1976). Marriages are preceded and accompanied by rituals of gift-giving which continue after the wedding as a means of cementing social relationships (Werbner, 1990). The network of kin and non-kin linked by gift-giving and marriage is referred to as the *biradari*. The closeness of the links within this network was seen as important in explaining the relative paucity of links with the majority ethnic group (Jeffery, 1976; Anwar, 1979). An ethnography that included informants who had arrived in Britain as children rather than as adults, or were British born, indicated that negotiations with the older generation over how marriages were to be contracted, constituted a pivotal moment in shaping the future of South Asians in Britain (Shaw, 1988). The marriage system of the Indian subcontinent which forms the model for the older generation, was likely to undergo some changes after migration in the British context.

According to the 1991 census there are 21,715 people of South Asian ethnicity in the Strathclyde Region which amounts to approximately 1 per cent of the total population (Scotland, 1993, p. 887). The population of South Asian origin is concentrated in Glasgow where it represents approximately 2 per cent of the population (Avan, 1995, p. 7). This clustering is explained by the presence of exploitable economic niches in the city which attracted many of the pioneer migrants. Some of these arrived directly from the subcontinent, and others came via England and Wales, attracted north by the myth of the lack of racism in Scotland (Dunlop and Miles, 1990), and the availability of work in Scotland at a time when workforces in England and Wales were being laid-off in the face of recession (Maan, 1992, p. 162).

In the rural Indian subcontinent, from where most migrants to Britain have come, marriage is almost universal for women, and happens at a young age (Brown *et al.*, 1981; Mandelbaum, 1988; Ballard, 1990). It is contracted by representatives of the woman's patriliny who negotiate the transfer of a daughter to the care, control and responsibility of another patriliny. It is the older generation and not the daughters who contract this marriage. In the rural northern subcontinent women have very few alternatives apart from marriage, as a means of graduating to adulthood while keeping their patriliny's honour intact. Honour rests upon the judgements of others and in a subcontinent village mundane activities take place out of doors, and the community is small, so most actions are subject to the scrutiny of the community. By contrast, in urban Britain anonymity is the norm. Housing is closed to the public view so that daily activities are carried out in private. On leaving their homes South Asians are surrounded by strangers and so are not subject to the scrutiny of others of the same ethnic and religious background. So while in the rural subcontinent every member of the village might belong to the honour community, in the urban Scottish setting one's neighbours probably do not constitute the group who are making judgements about honour and shame. In the rural subcontinent the honour community largely overlaps with the *biradari* which is a network of people joined by kinship, marriage, caste, common locality and a system of gift giving and receiving. Due to the way family networks are confined to a single caste *biradari* is sometimes used as a pseudonym for caste and is also translated as 'brotherhood'.

In any urban setting, the membership of the honour community becomes more ambiguous. For South Asians in Glasgow, unlike in the rural subcontinent, there are many fora where judgements about honour are not made. There are areas that are private from the honour community, namely in the home. There are areas that are public to the scrutiny of the honour community, such as the temple and mosque, and there are areas that are neither private or public because they are inhabited by people who are not members of the honour community, for instance, supermarkets and public parks.

For young women the membership of the honour community was partly defined by generation because the older generation of kin, and their friends, were all likely to make honour judgements about young women. People of the same generation as young women had a more ambiguous relationship to the honour community. Depending on the space in which they met and their relationship with other people on a gossip network, other young people could affect discrimination on the basis of honour. However, young people were sometimes quite distant from the gossip networks central to the honour community, particularly if they were single, or if they were encountered in a place such as a university campus which was largely unoccupied by elders of the honour community. The honour community was largely limited to people of the same religion as oneself, but there was a certain amount of interchange of gossip between religious groups, through particular friendships or professional liaisons that rendered the religious boundaries semi-permeable. The boundaries of the honour community were not fixed, but were dependent upon context and time in combination with the social, and therefore labile, characteristics of those involved.

The universality of marriage for women in the subcontinent (Jeffery *et al.*, 1988) appears to remain the case for South Asian migrants to Britain (Bhachu, 1985; Williams *et al.*, 1993). Whether this will remain the case for the next generation is not yet clear. In comparison to the situation in the rural areas of the subcontinent, there are a wide range of options open to adult British urban women, of which only one is marriage. One of the crucial differences between the rural subcontinent and urban Britain is that it is possible for a single woman to become an independent householder and wage-earner, without the support of a husband, father or other male kin and without attracting opprobrium.

How marriages are contracted and with whom is crucial to defining the boundaries of ethnic groups and the roles prescribed for men and for women. Diagnosing the likely prospects for change to the ethnic group and to gender roles is therefore intimately entangled with understanding how marriage functions and relates to other social processes.

METHODS

The material in this chapter arises from a three-year study, based in Glasgow, of young women of South Asian origin, all Punjabi speakers. Thirty-two women were chosen at random from the 70 women aged between 20 and 30 and of South Asian ethnicity, registered at a general practice in the north side of Glasgow. They were interviewed twice, and all except three of these interviews were tape recorded and transcribed. The English language interviews were conducted by me, and, in the case of five women who preferred to be interviewed in Punjabi or Urdu, a colleague conducted the interview while I took notes. She also collaborated on the translation of the schedule and the transcripts. Interview material was interpreted in the light of extensive participant observation in the private and public fora of Punjabi life in Glasgow, including time spent at a mosque and at a Sikh temple.

The resulting body of transcripts and field notes were subjected to a qualitative analysis. In what follows, all statements are based on what respondents have reported or have been observed doing.

CHARACTERISTICS OF THE SAMPLE

The composition of the South Asian population of Glasgow, was reflected in the following way; most of the 32 women were Muslim (19) with about a third Sikh (ten) and a smaller minority of Hindus (three). Of these women, 21 were born in the British Isles, nine in the Indian subcontinent and three in East Africa. Seven of those who were not British born received most or all of their education in Britain, after arriving as children. Of the women, 20 were married at the time of the first interview and of these most were living with their husband and children with just two women occupying households with their husband's parents. All of the unmarried women were living with their parents either as spinsters or as fiancées awaiting the arrival of their future husband from Pakistan. The majority of the sample were not in paid employment, but judging by their husbands' and fathers' occupations, the sample reflected the South Asian population of Glasgow by being overwhelmingly involved in small family owned business. Ownership of small grocery shops or take-away foods, or working in restaurants owned by other families accounted for the majority of husbands and fathers who were in paid employment. One husband was studying with a view to entering professional employment.

Although women reported that their caste affiliations were irrelevant to most intra-religious group interaction, marriage was the exception. Sikh and Muslim informants described how their religion emphasizes a brotherhood that overcomes caste differences. None the less, all respondents could name their own family's caste, even if they did not know the names of any other castes. The Sikh respondents reflected Glasgow's Sikh population in being either Jat (land-owning peasant) or Dakhan (carpenter, craftspeople, also known as Lakrian or Ramgharia), whereas the Muslims named a more numerous and wider range of caste groupings, some based on region (for example, Kashmiri, Mirpuri), but given the same status as more obviously caste-based groups such as Rajput, Zaminder and Arain. Jat respondents asserted their superiority over Dakhans and vice versa, and respondents from various of the Muslim caste affiliations explained that they were the 'top caste'. However, respondents' accounts of caste were relatively fragmentary and did not constitute a hierarchical structure. It was also widely agreed that caste differences had no effect on eating, socializing or working together, but only on inter-marrying.

While allowing for the possibility that young women will become more fully informed about caste considerations when they themselves come to contract marriages for younger women, (their own daughters for example), their version echoes analyses of caste from the subcontinent. Rigid hierarchy is not an accurate reflection of the caste system; two castes can claim superiority over one another in an apparent contradiction, yet everyone can agree that unequal caste prohibits inter-marriage (Quigley, 1993, p. 168). Despite the differences that women identified between their own and their mother's generation, the universality of marriage, albeit contracted at an older age, was not one of those differences. At the time of the first interview the 20 (out of a total of 32) respondents who were married all described their marriages as 'arranged', and the 12 who were not married, saw marriage in the near future as not only likely but also desirable. By the time interviewing was over another two women had married and two were engaged to be married. Women's criticism of their elders' marriage systems did not seek to undermine the institution altogether, but rather to modify how it was brought about.

What women described as 'arranged marriages' must, by definition be contracted by elders and a suitable husband is defined by strict rules concerning his background. He must be of the appropriate caste, religion, and age, and the comparison of his family's village of origin, with that of the bride's, is often crucial. The connection between marriage and honour means that there are strong sanctions against non-conformity that operate in terms of the reputation of the woman's family, and particularly the marriage prospects of single kin. In patrilineal systems sanctioned by honour, a woman's virtue and modesty is central to the good reputation of her family, and honour is a quality of the family, not the individual (Campbell, 1964; Lison-Tolosana, 1966). In discussing their experiences and expectations of marriage, women in Glasgow described the costs and benefits of conforming to the rules of a family contracted marriage. They differentiated between the benefits that they might forfeit as individuals by refusing an arranged marriage, and the hazards to their families if they did not enter an arranged marriage. In contrasting individual interests with those of their families, young women were challenging their traditional place within the honour system.

BENEFITS OF A FAMILY CONTRACTED MARRIAGE

For the Individual Woman

Almost all women's adult acquaintances and kin were in marriages that were arranged for them and, for the most part, they were said to be successful. It was suggested that young people lack the experience to make weighty decisions such as choosing a marriage partner and, therefore, parents' judgement should be trusted, particularly because they hold their children's happiness as a high priority.

Continued membership of the honour community of parents was the major reason for participating in a family-contracted marriage. Refusal of an arranged marriage would amount to a decision by the woman to abandon her parents' honour community and therefore her ethnic identity. As one woman put it, 'you're literally cutting yourself off from the whole Asian culture'. The choice could be a fairly stark one between, on the one hand, acquiescing in a family contracted marriage and staying in contact with Punjabi culture, or, on the other hand, refusing such a marriage and losing that contact for oneself and one's children, since damage done to reputation does not stop with one's own generation, but is passed on to the next.

For the Family Group

The principal benefit for the family of their young women entering into a family contracted marriage is the continued membership of the honour community, and its accompanying social alliances. An important feature of honour is that it extends through time. Thus, damage done to reputation does not stop with one's own generation, but is passed on to the next. Non-conformity to the rules of honourable marriage has implications for the children of the union. Even if the parents manage to overcome their differences and construct a harmonious life together, their children might not. It is suggested that the children would be pulled in 'different directions' and would not know to which group they belonged:

> The question would arise like if a child wanted to marry out of a caste, he would get married off. But when it came to their children one of them would go [to] the mother's caste or [would they go to] the father's caste? That's where the problem will arise... [with] the children. Otherwise they [the parents] could ex-communicate themselves, have a great happy life, but when it came to their children, that's where the problem would arise.

The problem was that the offspring of a marriage between two castes would belong to neither. Both groups, 'may say your caste is not right, not pure' and both might reject the child as a suitable marriage partner.

COSTS OF A FAMILY CONTRACTED MARRIAGE

Costs of the family contracted marriage were not considered to accrue to the family group, because this is the system that perpetuates lineages. In the rural subcontinent, costs of the process of entering a family contracted marriage for the individual woman are not enumerated because there are virtually no alternatives. To forfeit membership of the honour community is to relinquish the only possible social existence. The urban British context, however, offers young women, especially those with paid employment, the prospect of alternative social existences, out of the honour system, and also, a vision of different ways of contracting marriage. Although these alternatives were not being actively pursued by members of this sample, the individualism that characterizes much of the majority ethnic group's social organization was incorporated in young women's ways of thinking about the effects of the family contracted marriage system on their own lives. In thinking about themselves as individuals who can benefit in a distinct way compared to their family groups, women came to identify the costs of the process of family contracted marriages. These include lost occupational and educational opportunities, the personal costs of being subjected to assessment by strangers, and the possible future cost of having an unsuitable partner. Each of these will be considered in turn.

Women who had experienced pressure to marry when young expressed some regret that they had not been able to follow-up training and employment opportunities which had had to be relinquished when taking on the role of wife and mother.

The process involved in identifying a partner in family contracted marriages was felt to be personally costly in damaging self-esteem. A respondent described how her appearance had been criticized by the parents of prospective spouses, regardless of whether the young man, in her words, 'might look like the back end of a bus', but this was never considered during the negotiations. She, by contrast, said she had been rejected by families on grounds of her height (too short), moles on her cheeks (too many), and a problem she had with one leg. Other women described the process of being betrothed to someone after only a brief meeting as bewildering.

A major personal cost identified with arranged marriages was that they were suspected, particularly by those women who considered themselves to be 'westernized', of being a poor means of identifying a suitable partner. The brief meeting between the prospective spouses was not felt to be adequate to make an assessment of the man's character: 'marry someone that you've sort of spent, say 10 minutes talking with. You know it's very difficult'.

All that could be gathered from the meetings held prior to an arranged marriage was a man's appearance and occupation, which were not considered adequate for a judgement about his suitability as a partner:

> He could be gorgeous, OK, [have a] good job and everything, but how are we meant to tell his personality? How are you meant to know? He looks nice, he looks very westernized, oh yes he's got a good job.

Even the upper limit of contact that might be permitted by parents was felt to be insufficient:

> I mean, you spend a day talking. I mean I'm sure my mother wouldn't object [if I said] 'I want to go out with him for a week'. But I mean a week [she laughs]. What do you learn in a week? I could be nice to my worst enemy for a week [she laughs].

The penalties of failing to identify the right partner were divorce, or an abusive or adulterous husband and it was said that this might mean, 'being battered or abused really bad' or, 'the man having affairs right, left and centre', and then, 'you've got to live with it'.

Despite identifying these drawbacks, by the time of the second interview one woman had decided that she would ask her mother to contract her marriage. She explained that she had been in conversation with her close friend, also a Scottish woman of Punjabi origin, about their marital futures. Both had non-Sikh, non-Asian boyfriends in the past, but the respondent had recently followed her friend's example and broken off with hers. She explained that the boyfriend had been disrespectful towards Punjabi ways of life, such as food and dress. She valued her relationship with her mother very highly and mentioned watching Hindi movies on video together and cooking as activities that she would miss were she to marry someone who was not a Punjabi Sikh. Although her brother had a non-Asian partner whom her mother had met, the respondent felt the stakes were higher for her as a daughter, and that if she chose a non-Punjabi, non-Sikh partner her relationship with her mother would be jeopardized. In effect, this woman was balancing up a known and valued quantity – her bond with her mother – against an unknown quantity – an imagined relationship with a future husband. If she imagined her future husband to be non-Sikh she had to imagine losing her relationship with her mother, but if she imagined him to be someone chosen by her mother then there was no threat to the status quo with her mother.

Some women who had overcome the quandary that the last respondent described, and had married, were none the less strongly critical of family-contracted marriages. However this did not necessarily mean that they were dissatisfied with the outcome of the process in their own case.

STRATEGIES

There are clear advantages for young women to agree to a family contracted marriage, which relate to the benefits of belonging to a secure social network regulated by honour. There are also distinct disadvantages for individual women of the arranged marriage system, but the group-based advantages mean that the system is not likely to be abandoned, and therefore young women adopt strategies that keep them within the honour community while avoiding the highest of the costs. An ideal situation, where the woman did not have to pay any price to conform to her parents' wishes, was that of a respondent's friend who was said to be 'quite fortunate' because, 'she and her husband-to-be fancied each other, and both the parents were best friends and that, so it worked out very well, so I mean she's been very lucky'.

The women who were most explicit in describing the process of balancing out benefits to the group and to themselves were single, were wage-earners, and had resisted entering a family contracted marriage. As single women of independent means their activities represented a potential threat to the honour of their families. This threat consists of the increased opportunities that such women have for behaviour that is totally unmonitored by anyone of their community because they tend to work with people of the ethnic majority. Not only was a large proportion of their day spent out of the surveillance of the honour community, but the women were also accruing independent earnings that could facilitate behaviour that may not have been sanctioned by their parents.

Honour is safe-guarded not only by demonstrating the appropriate behaviour but also by being seen to avoid situations in which compromising behaviour would be possible. If a woman is constantly within the gaze of the honour community then no doubts can be raised over the propriety of her behaviour. Honour is regulated by gossip (Bailey, 1971) and gossip can have a damaging effect without being based on empirical fact, but just on the possibility of something having occurred.

It may have been significant that five of the single respondents who were most concerned to minimize the costs of arranged marriages to themselves personally, did not have fathers who were alive, and three did not have brothers living with them. Therefore, the traditional figurehead for the honour of the patriliny was absent, and the young women felt their behaviour consequently to be less constrained.

Despite the absence of figureheads, women reported strategies to contravene the constraints that operated. These included restricting activities that might be questionable to spheres of life that are not subject to the gaze of the honour community, and, more assertively, questioning the moral or religious rationale of constraining secular tradition.

AVOIDANCE OF THE HONOUR COMMUNITY

Even in the absence of both parents, and other Punjabi kith and kin, one woman maintained an elaborate pretence to hide an individually contracted marriage from the view of what she called, 'the community', by which she meant friends and acquaintances of her parents, most of whom she encountered at the temple. Two other women were equally careful in screening those aspects of their lives considered questionable from the view of their mothers' acquaintances. For instance, one woman had, for the previous 8 years had a non-Asian boyfriend, about whom her mother knew almost nothing. Another woman reached a compromise between her own and her mother's interests by confining her 'dishonourable' activities to a neighbouring city where she lodged during the week with a female colleague. Here, she had a non-Asian boyfriend and visited the pub and the cinema. Most weekends in Glasgow, when staying with her mother, she would wear Punjabi suits and stay at home to watch Hindi movies on video. Eventually she bought her own flat in the neighbouring city, but continued to stay with her mother at weekends. She suggested that her mother would be well-advised not to tell friends that she was living alone, so as to avoid the risk of gossip. Even in the neighbouring city, away from her mother's social network, she felt unable to visit restaurants run by other South Asians because of the, 'dirty looks' she got from men working there, which she assumed to be because she was seen to be unsuitably chaperoned. Thus, for this woman, Glasgow and the Indian restaurants of the neighbouring city constituted a space where honour and shame judgements were made. She therefore restricted her activities that were questionable in terms of honour, to the neighbouring cities, but avoided Indian restaurants.

APPLICATION OF RELIGIOUS VALUES TO SECULAR TRADITIONS

A powerful, but less often used, means of claiming legitimacy for one's behaviour was to point out the lack of religious rationale for the honour traditions. Two Sikh respondents criticized some of the rules about suitable marriage partners on the grounds that they were only secular traditions with no religious basis. One woman reported an argument with her mother over the lack of evidence in the holy book for a ban on co-villagers marrying:

> That's their tradition. That's what I quoted to my mum. I said, 'You tell me where it says in the Granth Sahib that I can't marry a person from the same village and then maybe I would, maybe, think twice about it', but they couldn't give me the answer 'cause they know it's not.

This line of reasoning attempts to divorce the moral power that a religious ruling holds from secular traditions of honour. If a woman succeeds in bringing about this cleavage to the satisfaction of her elders, she could, in theory, redefine her roles as a wife and daughter, without compromising the honour of her patriliny. Arguments in favour of women's rights framed in terms of the evidence from the holy text, or the meaning of the words of the Prophet or the Gurus, carry moral weight with elders, whereas framing these claims in the language of secular human rights, feminism or democracy carries little weight.

LONGER TERM STRATEGIES

The acceptance of the elders' marriage system, which is at times tacit, did not of necessity imply that women thought the system was appropriate for subsequent generations. Some women, who did not view arranged marriages as problematic for themselves, said that the system would be outdated by the time their daughters came to marry. They predicted that elders' power would weaken to the extent that their daughters would choose their partners unilaterally without considering anyone else's views

Discussions about marriage at women's meetings at a local mosque illustrated that conforming to the elders' marriage system did not necessarily imply approval of it. These meetings were held weekly and were ostensibly for the study of the Quran and of the Prophet's message. Both informal and formal discussion among the women covered a wide range of dilemmas facing the contemporary Muslim woman. The formal talks tended to prescribe appropriate behaviour and sometimes these lessons were illustrated by means of sketches or plays acted out by younger women at Eid parties. The meetings were conducted in English, with a Punjabi meeting held immediately afterwards in the same building. The English-language meeting was attended by the younger women, with their mothers and mothers-in-law going to the later one. Supportive, sisterly roles were often adopted in informal discussion by young women towards one another as they discussed their problems away from the hearing of the older women. Marriage and a wife's obligations to her kin and affines were often a topic of discussion because many of the women were in relatively new marriages in which roles were still being explored.

Arranged marriage was identified as a tradition that was not prescribed by the prophet, and the religious teachings on marriage that were emphasized by the meeting leaders were the mutual and reciprocal duties between spouses. It was emphasized that it was the role of Allah, and not humans, to judge whether others were fulfilling their duties properly. Therefore, wives were obliged to continue to act in accordance with their duties towards husbands, even if these were not reciprocated. In private conversations women said that marriage, and family contracted marriages in particular, were a lottery, and the odds of finding a good husband could be very slim. Yet women's religiously sanctioned duties to respect their elders, and husbands meant accepting the traditional system of marriage. Although not actively resisting the arranged marriage system, these women were not committed to retaining it for future generations.

CONCLUSION

The costs of non-conformity to the family contracted marriage system, both to their families and to themselves, were well-understood by young women. However, in the British urban context the benefits to individual women of remaining single were such that a number of strategies were identified by women, whereby marriage could be postponed, and the sanctions of the honour community avoided or attenuated. Women with education that led to professional employment, or with an ability to earn that was independent of their family business, were likely to be able to postpone entering a family contracted marriage in the name of gathering further qualifications or experience. Women whose fathers had died were also more likely to have been able to postpone entering a family contracted marriage, while minimizing the effects of sanctions on their mothers. Women felt their behaviour to be relatively unscrutinized, because their mothers were largely confined to their home and those women who had brothers did not feel that they had taken over as guardian of the family honour.

These women were not attempting to adopt the marriage patterns of the majority population, which were seen in a poor light, but rather, to remain within the same social world as their parents, yet with more autonomy than their mothers enjoyed. By postponing entry to a family contracted marriage, the system was not being rejected, but young women were attempting to reassess and renegotiate their role within it. By preventing their behaviour from coming to the attention of the honour community of their parents, it was possible to do things that would be defined as of questionable honour before entering an arranged marriage. Providing that her behaviour did not become the subject of gossip in 'the community', a woman could have an arranged marriage at a later date. By this time she could be in a position to stipulate certain conditions regarding her marriage, such as the extent of the obligations that she has towards her mother-in-law and, in particular, with whom she would share her marital home. Postponing a marriage in the name of education or a demanding career could increase the woman's ability to assert such conditions. Alternatively, the benefits of postponement might be so great that women might opt to continue unmarried indefinitely.

However, for this sample, this is purely speculative since the women who had postponed their marriages, had not yet contracted marriages and therefore the conditions to which they would agree, and the risk to which they would subject their mother's honour, were not yet apparent. Assuming that some young women manage to contract marriages that fulfil their own and their mother's needs for both honour and autonomy, the end of the institution of arranged marriages is not necessarily marked. There is anecdotal evidence of parents who contracted their own marriage against the will of their parents, but who none the less insist upon family contracted marriages for their own children.

The factors that seem likely to speed up the rate of change in the institution of family contracted marriage are those that have the effect of divorcing the attribution of dishonour from certain behaviours. Two places where the relationship between traditional married women's obligations and the allocation of honour may be re-worked are religious study groups such as the Muslim women's meeting in Glasgow and paid occupations not connected with the extended family. The women's meeting at the mosque was a forum where women could discuss their personal problems and where the lessons of the hadith and the Quran were applied in seeking a solution to everyday dilemmas. Depending upon the local leadership of such meetings, it is possible that an Islamic analysis of women's duties within marriage may develop that does not give credence to the subcontinent tradition of honour (Jacobson, 1997). This type of issue is being debated on an international level among Muslim women scholars and activists who are attempting to define a new role for themselves within Islam (Mernissi, 1985, 1991; Ahmed, 1992). It is the comparisons of women's roles between Islamic countries and with that prescribed by the Quran and hadith that forms the basis of such discussions.

Religion forms one source of honour that may be alternative to that regulated by elders, and employment, particularly professional employment, forms another alternative. In the rural subcontinent tradition an older woman's power and status often derived from her stake in contracting the marriages of younger members of her *biradari*. Although a young bride may dislike the duties that are seen to accompany her role, it may be in her interests to enforce them in later life. However, if women in urban Britain are increasingly participating in paid employment, this may represent an alternative source of prestige. It may also represent an alternative or additional route to participation in the community politics, as women qualified in medicine, law and social work are called upon to represent the interests of others of their ethnicity and/or religion in institutions such as regional councils, local councils, hospital trusts and health centres. The precise speed and direction of change in the contraction of marriage among Britons of South Asian origin is not yet clear. Assuming that women continue to attempt to accommodate their elders' wishes in their efforts to contract marriages that fulfil their own needs, then change is likely to be slow and piecemeal. However, the fact that change is underway should not be in doubt.

Section 4
Ethnicity, Identity and Narrative

9 Weaving New Lives From an Old Fleece: Gender and Ethnicity in Latvian Narrative
Vieda Skultans

> Who are those singing
> Without the sun in the evening?
> They are all orphan children
> Servants of a harsh master.
>
> (Latvian folk-song)

This chapter is based upon a year's fieldwork in Latvia between 1992 and 1993. It started out as an anthropological investigation of neurasthenia, one of the most common diagnoses in Soviet Latvia and, indeed, throughout the Soviet Union. However, once there, I found that Latvian informants themselves had strong feelings about what should be documented and about the shape of my research. The fieldwork outcome is, therefore, a compromise between my original formulation of goals and the needs and desires of my informants. Latvian men and women wanted their lives to bear witness to the wrongs that they had experienced and to the injustices of history. In the process of representing the past however, narrators shaped new selves. Informants dismissed medical diagnoses as irrelevant to an understanding of their past lives and I myself had no wish to medicalize their experience. Therefore, I address issues singled out by informants as important, namely, memory and identity and the ways in which these are underpinned by notions of ethnic belonging and gender.

My research method was also to some extent a response to informants' needs. Dialogue or narrative participation, to use a more weighty description, was an approach thrust upon me by my informants. They were preoccupied with testifying about the past and with the reconstruction of their biographies. In the course of these narrations they appealed to a mutual understanding of the Latvian national past. In this context, tape-recording and later transcribing many hours of narrative were not seen by my informants as a hindrance but as a due acknowledgement of the importance and seriousness of the subject matter. Altogether I recorded some two hundred hours of narrative experience. The great majority of my informants were women. My initial sample was drawn from two newspaper advertisements inviting neurasthenia sufferers to write to me which produced fifty letters, forty-one of them written by women, and of thirty-five further informants twenty are women. Although in Western Europe and America neurasthenia has been associated almost exclusively with women, in Latvia the gender link, though present, is not quite so strong. The preponderance of women writers may be linked to their greater readiness to discuss their lives. My analysis of neurasthenia sees it as a form of political protest. Lay aetiological theories put the responsibility for most illnesses, including neurasthenia, on state violence and political oppression, (Skultans, 1995). Women, perhaps because of their less complete integration into the public structures of Soviet society, are vociferous and articulate social critics.

AUTOBIOGRAPHICAL CONNECTIONS

My focus on narrative is also rooted in my own autobiography. My study led me to confront the implications of belonging to a textual community as well as to a matriarchal family. My own knowledge of Latvia had, until 1990 been entirely linguistic. I was born in Riga in spring 1944 to Latvian parents, but the Soviet occupation turned ours into a family of women. My grandfather had been killed during the first year of Soviet occupation and my father was killed some time in late autumn 1944. In October of that year when I was six months old my mother and grand-mother, along with some 10 per cent of the population, fled to the west. We left in a fishing boat from Kurzeme as communist troops tightened their grip on the country. We eventually arrived in England in January 1949, as part of the Westward Ho movement which brought some half a million east European political refugees to England, (Tannahill, 1958; Kay and Miles, 1992). The official grounds for admitting East Euro-peans were couched in the language of humanitarianism. However, refugees were restricted to work in hospitals, as domestic servants and as farm labourers. Refugee self-perceptions supported official govern-ment pronouncements: Latvians saw themselves not as immigrants but as political exiles seeking temporary asylum.

I give this brief historical and autobiographical account because it is connected with the importance which textuality came to have in my own construction of Latvian identity. My family and other Latvians saw flight as a temporary expedient. There were historical precedents for this. My grandparents, along with some 800000 other Latvians, sought refuge from the front which traversed Kurzeme during the World War I in Siberia. They ended up in Tomsk but returned in 1921 after an exile of some seven years. Indeed, the idea of Latvia as an independent state was largely a dream of exiles in St Petersburg. This feeling of impermanence was strong among exiles in England. Their children were groomed for a return to the homeland. Part of this grooming involved Latvian school at weekends.

I do not, therefore, have any personal memories of Latvia. I do, however, have a very clear and distinct picture of Latvia. It derives from my early reading of Latvian fiction and history. As a dutiful Sunday school attender the first language I read in was Latvian. However, equally powerful were the memories transmitted within the family. Coloured by pain and longing, they delineated a past of violence and dispossession which created a barrier between our family and the North Londoners among whom we lived. Latvians in exile defined themselves very much in relation to books. In the immediate postwar period in refugee camps throughout Germany émigré Latvians threw themselves into writing and publishing. An extraordinarily high level of literary activity continues to be characteristic of the exile community. This situation can be contrasted with that pertaining a century earlier. In the 1860s the growth of Latvian literature had played a central role in awakening a slumbering national identity. Many of the pastoral novels of the later decades of the nineteenth sought to enoble Latvian peasant identity. Folk songs were elevated to a scriptural status. However, whereas the literature of the nineteenth century sought to overcome emerging class differences and bind Latvians together in a unified pastoral identity, the exile literature served to preserve differences from their host country. It is in this sense that I use the term textual community of people who define their commonality in relation to texts which are elevated to a quasi-religious status.

My autobiographical experience also gave me a particular view of gender differences. In our family men made themselves felt by their absence. This had been true for many generations. My grandmother's two eldest children – both boys – had died in infancy: the eldest from exposure to the Siberian winter, the second from cholera on the month long train journey back to Riga in 1921. My grandfather had been killed during the first wave of arrests and deportations in June 1940. My father was killed as a soldier in the Latvian army in November or December

1944. Men were thus an elusive category who disappeared suddenly and left women to get on with the hard grind of living. I was, of course, aware that other families included men, but then other families had nicer furniture and houses. As far as I was concerned men were a luxury and my view found support in the fact that male family members seemed like weak appendages – themselves in need of support rather than supporting others. That my view of men was not purely idiosyncratic finds support in a recent monument erected near the station in Koknese. It shows three figures: the surfaces of the two smaller figures, a mother and child, are raised, the larger, presumably male, figure in the background is hollowed out. Mother and child are represented in relief as physically real, but the father is present by a shape which suggests where he should be: in other words, by his absence. My childish perspective is encapsulated in a personal memory of a historical event. I was seven when George VI died in the spring of 1952 and I remember loudly proclaiming to all and sundry, 'I'm glad the king's dead!' thus further jeopardizing our already uncertain standing within our local working class and intensely patriotic community. My act of bravura was, of course, a shaky cover-up for a deeply felt sense of loss. However, it created consternation and perplexity for my anxious mother and grandmother.

The relevance of my autobiography and this early history of the exile community to my research in Latvia is that my knowledge of the country had been through narratives which were familiar both to me and to my older informants. In other words, we belonged to the same textual community. This explains in part, perhaps, why I got on best with older informants, women of my mother's and, in a few cases, of my grandmother's generation. However, other oral historians have also found that older women are the best informants. (See, for example, Pahl and Thompson 1994.)

HISTORICAL BACKGROUND

Latvian history and memory are difficult to prise apart. Autobiographical memory both draws upon and challenges official historical accounts. Thus individual narratives are influenced by shared accounts of history learned in childhood. For example, living memory of labour camps reverberates with earlier historical accounts of physical oppression and violence against Latvian serfs. Siberian exile during the Stalinist period reiterates other earlier periods of exile under the czars. Accounts of forest partisans draw upon the idiom of earlier revolutionary exploits. The importance of land and the farmstead in living memory draws also upon nineteenth-century tales of the land hunger of freed serfs. The role of women in articulating experience, especially pain and sorrow, follows a long tradition in which they wove and sang during the long years their menfolk spent conscripted into the czarist armies. Latvian ideas of gender and ethnicity have been shaped by historical events and they draw emotive power as they are recycled and recontextualized through memory.

Much of this history is reflected in folk songs. Like the Transylvanians described by Gail Kligman (1988, p. 15), Latvians are familiar with this genre and folk texts appear on celebratory and ritual occasions. They have come to be seen as the collective voice of the people, carriers both of folk history and identity. Their importance lies not only in their explicit use as gender, ethnic and national self-representations, but in their more subtle uses. They are the 'cultural fleece' from which Latvians weave their own texts of experience and identity. (I have borrowed the phrase from Anthony Cohen, 1996, p. 29.) For example, the peasant hatred of their German masters finds a voice in song which has come to stand for all forms of political oppression.

> A black snake is grinding flour
> In the middle of the sea on a stone
> Let it be eaten by those masters
> Who force us to work without the sun.

Folk songs also attest to the duration of peasant military service in the eighteenth century, but the separation of men and women through war also speaks to later experience.

> Going to war
> I left my sister in the cradle;
> Coming back from the war
> I found a great weaver.
> I asked mother
> Who is that weaver?
> That my son is your little sister
> Whom you left in the cradle.

Serfdom persisted until the nineteenth century but it left an impact on memory and identity long afterwards.[1] When serfdom was abolished the liberation left the peasants landless and the lives of peasants actually worsened.[2] These events gave rise to a passionate and unrelenting peasant longing for land.[3] Much of Latvian literature is pastoral and revolves around the meaning of land to the Latvian peasant. Ethnic identity and nationalism were forged in the context of hunger, famine and dispossession. Love and careful husbanding of one's own small piece of land are core elements of Latvian national identity. So too is a dignified vision of peasant life, one which reverses a centuries-old tradition of denigration and humiliation.

The cutting of feudal ties and the precarious relationship to the land contributed to the national awakening of the 1860s. Latvian nationalism faced the formidable task of transforming a derogatory peasant identity into a shared national identity which could encompass all elements of an increasingly differentiated society: the majority of country people, the growing urban industrial workers as well as the small but important class of intellegentsia.[4] It did so by transforming an oral tradition of folk singing into a literary canon. In this way folk memory was used as the basis of Latvian ethnic and gender identities as well as putting flesh on the bones of nationalist history. Collection on a grand and systematic scale was undertaken by Krisjans Barons. Altogether more than 200000 songs were collected.[5] Although the authors of these songs can no longer be identified, the majority are composed in the feminine voice, thus confirming women in their role as keepers of memory. (See, Andrups and Kalve, 1954)

The history of the twentieth century lies within living memory. Bloodshed and military sacrifice are core elements of both individual memory and historical accounts and, as many historians have noted, are among the most potent weapons for building nationalism. The revolution of 1905 spread to the Latvian countryside where peasant anger had a particularly radical edge.[6] The target of anger was baronial property but it was countered by physical punishment, exile and killings on a massive scale (see Ezergailis, 1974). Following the revolution many people went into hiding in forests and others were exiled. The Latvian revolutionary spirit was forged by these events of 1905 which provided it with symbols and martyrs. The outbreak of the World War I thus drew upon painful memories of revenge exacted by the punitive expeditions. The Christmas battles of 1916 to defend Riga in which all but a handful survived have become part of national martyrology. Contemporary ethnic and gender identities have their roots in the bloodshed and sacrificial deaths of young men and contribute to the idea of men as both brave and vulnerable.

On 18 November 1918 independence was declared with Karlis Ulmanis head of the peasant party as president.[7] Between 1914 and 1920

Latvia had lost one quarter of its population. Vast areas of the country-side were devastated and its industry had been dismantled. Some 8000 inhabitants of Riga died of famine in 1918. Latvia existed as an Independent state between 1918 and 1939. It is remembered by older people, almost without exception, as a golden age. Such memories are rooted in the economic and social progress of those decades. Despite political instability, the consensus of historians is that the brief independence period was marked by economic success and certainly that is how most older Latvians remember it, (Smith, 1994). The reforms appeased the land hunger but did not extinguish the love of land.[8] The independence period consolidated a particular pastoral version of Latvian national identity.[9]

The independence period came to an end in 1939, with the establishment of a Soviet military base.[10] Soviet decrees concerning nationalization of land and property were immediately passed. The appropriation of land struck at the heart of Latvian ethnic identity and reversed the gains of centuries of longing and struggle. The subsequent destruction and censorship of a literature which celebrated the land consolidated the attack.

During the first year of occupation Soviet forces targeted professionals, administrators, business people, but also county elders, teachers and farmers. Torture and week-long interrogations were routine. Many went into hiding in the forests or lived itinerant lives of the hunted following a tradition established in 1905. During this first year of occupation some 35 000 people were killed and deported, (Misiunas and Taagepera, 1993, p. 42). Nearly half these deportations – some 15000 – occurred on the night of 13 to 14 June. Among the Latvians deported during that first year of Soviet occupation were some 5000 Jews (ibid, p. 64).

The immediate postwar period is referred to by Latvians as *juku laiki* or the time of chaos. Massive population losses – some 25 per cent of the prewar population disappeared or were killed – affected nearly every family in Latvia. Homes had been expropriated or destroyed. Agriculture met with disaster and hunger prevailed. There was a scarcity of consumer goods. The history of the war and conscription of Latvians into both the German and subsequently the Soviet armies created fear and distrust between people. Guerilla activity was widespread in the countryside creating the feeling that the war was not yet over. Local country people who supported the partisans with food and medicaments were killed or deported for doing so. Land and property were redistributed. On 25 March 1949 some 50000 country people, men, women and children, were deported from Latvia. They constituted one-tenth of all farmers. Those who survived deportation and exile often had no homes to return to. The deportations had the desired effect of speeding collect-ivization. By the end of 1951 more than 98 per cent of all Latvian farms were collectivized.

Soviet repression in Latvia constituted a powerful assault on ethnic identity but in some ways reinforced gender identities. The war and later Soviet killings left a matriarchal society robbed of its men. Precise fig-ures are not available but about four-fifths of those sent to Siberian labour camps were men. Women were left without husbands and children without fathers.

SOCIAL MEMORY

The particularity of lived experience invests history both recent and remote with meaning and emotion. Certain historical events and images have become mythologized. In the process they transfigure personal experience. Thus accounts of the remote past may give shape to experi-ences in the present, but conversely present experience draws upon the past in selective ways to suit its own needs. This creates a two-way traffic between history and memory and has implications for ethnic and gender identities. My approach draws upon two, in my view needlessly, polar-ized views of identity. There is the nineteenth-century view associated principally with Herder which sees national identity as the expression of a distinctive character and experience. Although such ideas have little academic currency they continue to influence popular thought. In con-trast the view associated with writers such as Anderson (1992) sees national identity as artificially constructed and related to the needs of modernity. However, I would argue that just as memory and history mutually influence each other, so too gender and ethnic identities draw both upon past experience and present exigencies.

Physical oppression and martyrdom run like veins through Latvian history. The vocabulary of serfdom and its many duties has been trans-ferred to the Soviet period and is used to describe deportation and col-lectivization. The nineteenth-century longing for one's own small piece of land acquires new meaning in the context of Siberian exile and home-sickness. Similarly, the personal experience of death is shaped by accounts read and heard of earlier deaths. Decades-long military service is commemorated in folk songs like the one quoted earlier. These songs describe sons, bridegrooms and brothers going to war and leaving behind women who weep and wait. Such powerful images transcend centuries and gather additional meanings. Early-twentieth-century accounts emphasize the needlessness of death and martyrdom. For example, companies of schoolboy soldiers from Cesis who fought the Germans in 1917 have become central to national mythology. Thus history offers narrators certain cultural paradigms for expressing grief and coping with bereavement. Thus Lidija recounted the arrest and death of her husband and her son's much later death from a heart attack without crying. However, she wept as she described an earlier death – that of the medieval hero Nameijs.

As several historians have argued, societies are good at commemorating a particular kind of death: that of young soldiers fighting for their country. Catherine Merridale (1996, p. 11) writing about death in twentieth century Russia points out that certain types of victim are left unmourned. In Latvia oral accounts emphasize the fact that children, the old and the infirm were also arrested and deported. Sites of commemoration are railway stations from where those arrested were transported eastwards in cattle trucks. Here large unhewn rocks rather than statues of men or women are used. Nevertheless historical paradigms as well as the actual course of recent history do influence the way in which men and women remember Siberia.

On the night of 15 June 1941, 7000 men, 5000 women and 3000 children were arrested. The men were imprisoned or sent to labour camps whereas women and children were sent into Siberian exile thereby reversing a centuries old pattern of departing men and waiting women. However, about four-fifths of the men died whereas the majority of women survived. These mortality figures arising from the different circumstances in which men and women found themselves help to support old ideas about their role in the course of history. They also reinforce Latvian gender stereotypes of women as patient and enduring and men as brave but vulnerable. Precise figures are not available for the numbers of men and women deported in 1949 but greater numbers of men were both deported and died. The killings paved the way for a new social order, but in the process they resuscitated centuries old feelings and ideas. Paul Connerton (1989, p. 12) puts this particularly well, 'The attempt to break definitively with an older social order encounters a kind of historical deposit and threatens to founder upon it'. Thus history and folk memory interlink. The homeland viewed from exile remembered has a feminine face. For example, the motto of *Via Dolorosa* a book of recollections of labour camps and exile, has as its motto, 'Only the homeland and the mother' (1990, p. 6). Thus exiles long for mother Latvia whereas soldiers defended and fought for the land of their fathers. Nationalism and ethnicity draw selectively upon images of Latvian masculinity and femininity depending upon context.

A practical consequence of the greater mortality of men is that surviving memory is largely that of women. Thus the majority of contributors to *Via Dolorosa* are women. Their memories clearly have a social component. However, the workings of Latvian social memory do not readily support theoretical writings on the subject. Halbwachs's ([1950], 1981) claim that all personal memories are sustained by group interest clearly does not fit the countries of the former Soviet Union where memories were silenced and seldom voiced even within the family. Similarly Paul Connerton's (1989) linking of social memory with commemorative practices although it has much to tell us about the post-independence shaping of memory, leaves a question mark over the survival of personal memory during the Soviet period.

The writing on social memory is particularly relevant to my material in its emphasis on the way in which memory can break free of the raw experiences of the past. When men and women reflect upon their personal past, individual chronicles of experience are selectively drawn upon and transformed into tales with a moral. In these cases truth follows fiction. The way we remember our lives is shaped by the stories we have heard and read. When libraries are physically destroyed, as happened in postwar Latvia, this restricts the possibilities of giving a coherent and meaningful account of the personal past. A lack of textual belonging helps to account for the difficulties of some informants in bringing coherence into their lives. Memories of the most terrible events try to break free of the original experience and seek allegiances with other texts. Thus memory is embedded not only in present experience (Fentress and Wickham, 1992) but also in the past and the memories of others.

FORM AND CONTENT

My attention to narrative form of memory is influenced by the *Writing Culture* debate: the important idea that form and style of ethnographic writing are not superficial decorative elements but betray deep-seated attitudes and content, (Clifford and Marcus, 1986). There is a contrasting approach exemplified by psychoanalysis which perceives truth as hidden at the core, only to be reached after many verbal circumambulations in the cathartic moment of revelation. My initial allegiance to this approach was disastrous. In preparation for the early interviews I would have an informal chat before turning on the tape-recorder. These preparatory dialogues captured internally rehearsed narrative truth which did not permit repetition. To repeat precious phrases would have destroyed the illusion of spontaneity. Thus my attempts to repeat rehearsals and develop the narrative met with reproaches that I had not listened and understood properly and were therefore, failures. In the course of my work I found that emotional truth is not buried deep in discourse, but is to be read in each phrase and gesture.

My work has a pronounced feminine provenance. Some of the reasons for this have been discussed. Latvian history and the mortality of men are partly responsible. The folk song about the brother who leaves his baby sister and returns to find her weaving refers to more than the long military service under the czars. The etymology of the word suggests that weaving was perhaps the peasant forerunner of writing. The earlier meaning of the Latvian verb *rakstīt* was to weave; its current meaning is to write. Weaving was an elaborate affair with intricately patterned symbolic motifs. Women wove the clothes for their soldier husbands while they waited for their husbands to return. Thus both to weave and to write involves the symbolic transformation of experience.

This accounts for the relative ease with which women both participate in the narratives of others and construct their own. The authority and compelling nature of Latvian narratives derive from personal experience and agreed cultural truths. The fusion of personal experience with fictive writings produces narratives that compel respect and attention. Why should men be less likely to produce such narratives? Or, to put it more bluntly, why do some men, particularly those who have lived lives of extraordinary heroism and endurance, give monosyllabic accounts of their lives? The answers lie in a particular and well known version of Latvian masculinity. Masculinity is achieved through the control of emotion, especially fear. Folk songs attest to this masculine attitude:

> Going to war
> I locked my heart in a stone
> The light comes, the sun rises
> The stone splits open singing.

When I interviewed a particular kind of delivery signalled the achievement of this script, characterized by a tone and pitch more suited to a large auditorium. Such masculine narratives seek to derive authority from their appeal to historical facts and texts. Feminine narratives by contrast appeal to experience, but do so in ways which implicitly incorporate textual understandings. Thus Latvian women are both the critics of society and the preservers of cultural meanings.

Implicit in this discussion of Latvian gender differences are two basic approaches to narrative which inform theoretical writing as well as the understandings of men and women narrators. They are the representational and ontological view of narrative, often taken to be mutually exclusive. The representational approach, associated with earlier life history studies, was interested in narrative as a means of acquiring a window on little known, often deviant worlds. By contrast, the more recent ontological view does not see narrative as instrumental. Narrative is itself an interesting social reality through which individuals position themselves in their social world. The dualisms of self and society are avoided through narrative which in the process of constructing experience and identity encompasses both.

These two distinctive approaches to the analysis of narrative are also to be found in the attitudes of narrators themselves. Latvian men tend to adopt the representational approach. Women, more than men, use narrative both to represent the past and to describe the personal meaning of those past experiences. Their style of narrative is closer to my own approach which has tried to maintain a hold both of the representational and the ontological view of narrative. Many narratives were given in the spirit of testimonies and to ignore their representational purpose would be to invalidate the narrators. Their eye-witness status was conveyed by a reversion to the present tense, in reminders of their physical presence at certain events and in claims about the impossibility of putting certain experiences into words. And yet, of course, many narrators do succeed in finding words for the most violent and terrible of experiences and in doing so they enter a shared world of cultural understandings which succeed in breaking down the uniqueness of the experiences described.

This brings us to the ontological aspects of narrative: its social, collective and fictive nature. Young (1988) writes of the unease which attending to the literary form of Holocaust narratives can evoke: as though literary form denies the full magnitude and horror of the experience. However, Young suggests that attending to form is one way of understanding how human beings cope with the unthinkable. This is not to claim that all experiences can be put into neat, celebratory stories. The threshold of individual vulnerability is enormously elastic. I would not wish to query Langer's (1991, p. xi) claim that, 'oral Holocaust testimonies are doomed on one level to remain disrupted narratives'. There are problems in translating knowing into telling, (White, 1987, p. 1). However, narrators do employ various literary and metaphorical devices in order to circumvent these problems. Well known literary themes are intertwined with personal recollections to produce a habitable past. The result is that many Latvian narrators who recall imprisonment, labour camps and physical deterioration do so through a celebration which fuses individual experience with cultural symbols. I found this fusion in the oral narratives which were recounted to me. It appears more systematically in published memoirs of survivors. During the last six years, starting with *Via Dolorosa* several hundred narrative accounts of deportation have been published. They are largely written by educated and articulate people and they follow a formulaic tradition which focuses on the preservation of a distinctive cultural identity. The publication of such memoirs in the pre- and post-independence period is not coincidental. It points to the central role which deportations have come to occupy in the quest for national identity.

There is a view of narrative which suggests that stories about the past are really about the present: more specifically the form in which narratives are cast depends upon the narrator's present social circumstances. Such an analysis casts some light on Latvian narratives although it does not give the whole story. My interviews began shortly after the declaration of independence when there was widespread optimism in Latvia and euphoria among ethnic Latvians. There was an appeal to a joint destiny and nationality which united Latvia's Latvians and exiled Latvians. In other words, my research was carried out before the harsh economic realities had begun to bite. I am sure that were I conducting my research now I would get a less open response and a very different attitude to the past. The celebration of the past was also a celebration of independence achieved. The publication of survivors' memoirs facilitated the translation of private memory into collective memory and the linking of past and present.

Part of the fascination of narrative lies precisely in this ambivalent relationship to reality. It reaches out to the past and yet in the process itself constitutes a new reality. Language comes in pre-assembled parts, to use Barbara Herrenstein's apt term, and these parts carry shared meanings. And so it is that the recurring literary themes of Latvian personal narratives connect with the building blocks of Latvian ethnic identity. The Latvian farmstead, young shepherds, and expelled orphans are iconic symbols which help fuse individual and national destiny.

GENDER DIFFERENCES

What then are the differences in the way in which men and women use narrative? There are certain well aired differences between men's and women's use of language which apply to the Latvian material. Deborah Tannen (1991) has shown that women's conversational style differs from men's in the emphasis they put upon empathy and solidarity as opposed to men's emphasis on information. In autobiographical writings women, it is argued, put more emphasis on the development of relationships, men on the development of autonomy, (Gergen and Gergen, 1993, pp. 28–54). These distinctions fit the Latvian narratives: Latvian men aspire to the authority of facts and women to the authority of inner truth or experience. The importance which women attach to empathy and relationships and their disregard for autonomy makes them more ready to articulate and share their personal experiences.

I looked for gender differences in social memory based on the ideas of Halbwachs (1981, p. 23), arguing for the collective nature of memory: 'Our memories remain collective, however, and are recalled to us through others even though only we were participants in the events or saw the things concerned. In reality we are never alone. Other men need not be physically present, since we always carry within us and in us a number of distinct persons'. This memorable claim, 'We are never alone', is true of situations where we might not expect it to apply and yet it fails to reflect the experience of some others.

Men intertwine their childhood memories with grand history in a way that women do not. They place their narrative literally at the centre of events. Miervaldis situates his childhood at the very heart of Latvia:

> My childhood was spent exactly in Riga's centre. I lived in old Riga and because of that I knew the history of old Riga and all the old buildings – I was very familiar with them.

Uldis describes his birthday as occurring just before Ulmanis' decisive coup:

> I was born on 11 May and I looked around and I saw that there was no order after all and then I ordered Karlis Ulmanis to make a coup on 15 May [laughing]. And that's what he did.

Talis who as a boy was link person for the forest partisans remembers his childhood in mythological terms:

I dreamt much about history. In my young days I dreamt of what my mother and father taught me about my ancestors about the formation of the Latvian state.

Women's childhood memories, by contrast, centre on family celebrations and recurring rituals, birthdays, namedays and Christmases:

And I am enormously grateful to my parents that they encouraged precisely that...Despite everything spiritual values are the most important in life. And I remember that, when there were celebrations, my favourite present was a book – nothing else.

Women's childhood narratives have a timeless quality, which men's aspirations to historical agency deny them. These divergent narrative styles serve women better when it comes to recalling the experience of exile and extreme physical hardship. The need to cast narrative in a heroic and historical mode presents men with a difficult and painful task. Not surprisingly, therefore, women in extreme situations appeared to find more solace in memory than did men. By contrast men's factual narratives convey a disconnectedness and an inner solitude which makes them difficult to listen to. Narratives recount situations where social structures have been smashed and individual lives dislocated. In these situations it seems, that women's memory plays an important role as the preserver of shared culture and individual identity.

In discussions of imprisonment and internment in labour camps it was generally acknowledged that women fared better. They were more likely to survive physically than men and less likely to experience a moral disintegration. Men's death rates were linked to the harsher working conditions. Women were more likely to be given indoor work. Deaths were also linked to diet and the fact that men, though physically bigger, did not necessarily receive larger food rations. Health was also linked to cigarette smoking and the fact that men were more likely to exchange food for a cigarette. However, beyond these very important physical differences in the circumstances of men and women prisoners, there were also differences in the relative ability of men and women to maintain a sense of personal morale. Men, it was suggested, are less able to withstand humiliation. Here is Ilze who had spent ten years of her young adulthood in a prison camp, talking about her first meeting with her husband to be and the men in the camp generally:

I looked and I saw [laughing] there was this man sitting there behind the table. He didn't look like a Russian. He was wearing...you know in my youth men wore such windcheaters. Well, it wasn't from nylon, but a kind of cloth. And underneath there was sewn a white collar, like an officer. Oh, I thought... Because men there looked pitiable. Those that I sometimes saw in the camp. In our women's camp they brought brigades of workers, carpenters and electricians. Sometimes they were brought in from neighbouring zones. The men had to mend something and then leave. Then we saw them. They had let themselves go completely. We women would curl our hair in little scraps of rags, trying to look decent. From some old rags we would sew ourselves collars and fix them to the prisoners uniform so that we'd look a little better. But not the men – no. They suffered terribly. And even now they are much more traumatized than we women. Because they can no longer find a place for themselves in life. We women settled back sooner. Perhaps it was because we were the ones who set up hearth and home here.'

I wanted to know more precisely why men found the experiences so much more difficult.

That's men's nature. In difficult circumstances women are more enduring, more patient. It's not for nothing that women are the ones who give birth. A man would not be able to endure childbirth. You know I am a nurse. If a man has something wrong, he thinks it's a global event, if he has a cold or a cough or a splinter. It's crazy, men can go to war. That's a place where only men go. But in times of peace men are very fragile, without endurance. And even spiritually they are without endurance. Well and then I think because they'd been to war, they'd been at the front, they'd endured those long years in the ice in Russia. And after that they'd been in very bad circumstances in prison camps. They were treated much more mercilessly. They were also beaten. And the norm was the same, both for men and for women. The so called norm. Norm, yes it's a good word, food, a portion. But a man wants to eat more. Afterwards when I spoke to my husband I learned that we'd both had more or less the same to eat.

Ilze's views represent the views of many other narrators, both men and women. Her views support George Mosse's analysis of stereotypes of masculinity and their dependence on warfare (1996, pp. 107–32), and yet they identify a new arena – the gulag – in which qualities of manliness prove insufficient and break down. Stereotypical gender differences are reflected in mortality statistics and in differences in narrative style. Men and women draw upon the resources of memory in different ways. For women exchanging memories is a way of giving away something very

personal and thereby consolidating friendship. Here is Ilze again talking
about friendship.

> I was looking for friends with whom I had a spiritual closeness. I had
> one such – Yolande. She was a doctor from Uzbekhistan – I got to
> know her. And there were several with whom I still keep in touch,
> whom I phone. A close person was very important there, terribly
> important to celebrate a nameday, a birthday, we spoke about our
> childhood. Maybe one didn't talk about one's case. But one's child-
> hood, one's youth – one definitely described that. Because we had
> nothing else from the outside world. It was the only thing left – a close
> and sincere relationship. It was the only good thing left. Support from
> each other.

Thus memory becomes the only possession, the only thing left to
exchange. Since it is given away it needs to be good, to be worth giving.
One's case – the grounds of arrest – do not, of course, fulfil these
requirements. A pastoral vision of childhood does. In these circumstances
personal memories demand a cultural mould in the way that a true gift
requires proper wrapping. Women, more than men, linked their memories of an individual past to those of countless others. Women's greater
readiness to recount their autobiography in terms of relationships
means that their memories are more truly collective. Personal memories are retrieved and dressed in cultural symbols. Moreover, women are
more at home with self-disclosure than men. In this process memory is
transformed into a strategy of mutual support for women.
     In these extreme situations Latvian men found less solace in memory
as Miervaldis so well describes:

> We never spoke of those times when we lived well. Because we spoke
> about today, about what we would do because we each had our duties.
> Later when I was transferred to the mine, to the coal mine – then, of
> course, we only spoke about what had to be done and whether the
> plan was filled. Well, we might tell some jokes or pull each others legs.
> But specific memories about how things had been – that was very dif-
> ficult, very painful. Of course, I thought my own thoughts. Very often
> I walked Riga's streets, along the boulevard beneath the lime trees.
> There were dreams that perhaps one day we would succeed in return-
> ing. That was the hope and you see one could only survive with that
> hope. The alternative was death.

I draw this section to a close by letting Ilze talk about her courtship in
prison camp. Ilze met her future husband in the course of having her

personal possessions inventorized. In courting Ilze he presents himself as the shepherd, a well-known literary and national icon. In doing so he gains access to her memories as well as her affections.

> He asked me 'What are you going to hand over?' I said, 'My vest and spoon.' You can imagine and that's how it was. A vest and spoon. And then I went away and after a while I got a note from him thrown over the barbed wire with a little stone. And in it he wrote that he was very lonely and that he would like to correspond with me. That was the only way to correspond ... we couldn't ... And that's how we corresponded for about six weeks. We wrote every day. I've kept all my husband's letters. He writes ... he writes ... He had such beautiful handwriting. His uncle had been a writer. He himself had been a correspondent for a newspaper. And he wrote to me, 'I feel like a frozen shepherd, a little shepherd. I beg you to open the door and warm me, please open the door and give me shelter.' That was his first letter. I replied somehow or other and that's how it began. We began to write to each other.

Ilze's description of her meeting with her husband illustrates the principal theme of this chapter: namely, that situations which strip people of all material possessions direct people towards a revaluation of their cultural capital. Women are the preservers of this capital and, as the letter shows, this role is recognized.

I am not, of course, insisting upon absolute distinctions in the way that men and women narrate the past. However, my sample testifies to Latvian women's greater readiness to give a personal account of the past and statistics demonstrate their greater aptitude for survival.

DISCUSSION

In many of these narratives women occupy the centre stage. They are the heroines of their own lives, in a way which is not at all characteristic of women's autobiographical writing. For example, Shari Benstock (1986, p. 20) writes of the decentering, subservience or even disappearance of the textual self in women's autobiographical writing. It may be that the field-work situation, hours of questioning, listening and returning to listen further, promotes this kind of response. Perhaps it empowers women to become the prime movers of their life stories. It may also be that memories of extreme situations such as expropriation, separation from families, Siberian correction camps and exile encourage women to throw aside traditional restrictions of gender. Under such circumstances there may be a return to the classical traditions of auto-biography: 'a conscious awareness of the singularity of each individual life,' (Gusdorf, 1980, p. 29). This tradition has been attacked by femin-ists as gender biased: 'The model of a separate and unique selfhood ...establishes a critical bias that leads to the misreading and margin-alization of autobiographical texts by women and minorities in the process of canon formation,' (Stanford-Friedman, 1986, p. 34). However, it seems that the autobiographical narratives of Latvian women override gender restrictions.

Both older women and older men use literary and biblical paradigms to structure their individual lives. What kinds of structures and para-digms are at issue here? The narrator as heroine of her own life story is supported by the paradigm of the quest, which structures both men's and women's narratives. The elements of the traditional quest story are well known. They involve a hero of low birth, exile, the threat of terrible dangers and moral evils, the hero's victory over them, and a reward which transforms the social standing of the hero. Many Latvian accounts of imprisonment and peregrination through Siberia are mod-elled on the quest paradigm. However, there is a specifically Latvian version of the quest tale which is to be found in Latvian fairy tales and in personal narratives. The best known literary version is that of Anna Brig-adere's fairy tale play for children called *Spriditis*, after its hero. Spridi-tis is an orphan. As such he is immediately set up as a national symbol, since Latvians are referred to as an orphan nation in folk literature. There are several words in Latvian for an orphan. Among them is *serdi-enis* a word which refers both to children without parents and to peoples subjected to a foreign power. Thus references to orphans act as a bridge between personal and collective experience and this bridge can be crossed either way. References to political oppression draw upon the emotional resonances of a motherless child. Conversely, the child orphan serves as an image of servitude. There are many hundreds of folk songs about orphans and Brigadere's play draws upon this folk tradi-tion. Spriditis is banished from the farmstead by his wicked step-mother. In the forest he meets a king whose arrogant daughter is threatened by the devil. Spriditis overcomes the devil with the help of a magical whistle and stick given to him by the forest deities mother wind and mother for-est. In what seems to be a specifically local twist to the plot, Spriditis rejects the offer of marriage with the cold and haughty princess and returns home to the farmstead.

Parts of this very well known story are encapsulated almost verbatim in some personal narratives. One informant refers specifically to Spriditis as giving him moral courage at a time when he was very dispirited. However, elements of this story form the backbone of most narratives. There are the obvious parallels of being orphaned and banished. The Siberian landscape is remembered as morally chaotic. The iconic farmstead and forest are the symbolic equivalents of the magical whistle and stick, around which narrators weave their accounts of an idyllic childhood and from which they draw magical powers of endurance. And finally, there is the homecoming to the humble farmstead. Through this story women throw aside gender restrictions and affirm ethnic belonging. It may be that ethnicity comes to the fore at certain critical points in history and in lives, (Allen, 1994). Since the narrative I is a fusion of past and present selves, it also draws together two historical epochs both of them major historical turning points. During the 1940s and 1950s there is the trauma of mass population losses through violent deaths and deportations. In August 1991 there was the declaration of independence. Deportations contributed to the development of nationalism in this recent period in important ways. Indeed, as Roberts Kilis (1996) has pointed out, the first openly anti-Soviet demonstration on 14 June 1987 was simultaneously a commemoration of the deportations on that same day in 1941.

Thus Latvian ethnicity and gender-identity are born of particular historical circumstances.[11] Serfdom, lack of land and loss of men through war and political repression are of paramount importance in shaping such categories. These historical events have been transmitted through song and thus preserved in folk memory. Enshrined in folk memory and canonized as the literary expression of the Latvian soul, narratives of Latvian ethnicity and gender have continued to shape individual experience under Soviet rule. New, unanticipated sufferings rework the plots of earlier times. Old symbols drawn from the period of Baltic serfdom have acquired a new home in the Soviet gulag. Men and women both draw upon the emotive power of the symbolic farmstead, the shepherd and the orphan. However, gender differences established over centuries and reinforced by experience have produced divergent versions of the past. Suffering and pain can either isolate and break down structures of thought, or it can be used to create a community of suffering, (Das, 1987). The Latvian experience of suffering is strongly gendered. In articulating their experience women are continuing a literary tradition in which they speak for the family and community. Latvian men have also followed tradition. However, the attributes of their traditional hero, the bearslayer of superhuman strength and courage, are no longer appropriate. I was told, 'He didn't help us when we needed him.' They have instead locked their hearts in stone.

ACKNOWLEDGEMENT

I want to thank Harriet Bradley for encouraging me to write this chapter and for her many critical readings of it.

NOTES

1. Garlieb Merkel is responsible for bringing revolutionary ideas to this part of the Baltic. His book *Die Letten am Ende des Philsophischen Jahrhunderts* was published in 1797 and paints a grim picture of peasant life.
2. Serfdom was abolished in the province of Kurzeme in 1817, in 1819 in the province of Vidzeme and in 1861 in the eastern province of Latgale.
3. Janis Purapuke (1864–1902) wrote *One's Own Small Piece of Land* about the plight of landless labourers. It was published in 1898.
4. Latvian nationalists were sons of peasants able to take advantage of newly acquired freedoms. Among them were Krisjans Valdemars (1825–88) Juris Alunans (1832–64) and Atis Kronvalds (1837–75). They saw themselves as actively rediscovering and reshaping a slumbering national identity and they were referred to themselves and were known as the New Latvians (Jaunlatviesi).
5. Krisjans Barons (1835–1923) studied at Tartu university. He started collecting and categorizing folk songs or dainas from all parts of Latvia in the 1870s. Six volumes were published between 1894 and 1915.
6. The Streilnieki were Latvian riflemen who also contributed to the success of the bolshevik revolution. (See, for example, Ezergailis, 1974).
7. Ulmanis's coup of 1934 brought parliamentary democracy to an end. However, in an era of dictatorships, that of Ulmanis was mild. However, the weakness of Ulmanis's government lay in his relationship to other political parties both of the extreme right and left. By outlawing such parties he strenthened their opposition.
8. Radical land reforms between 1920 and 1924 transformed the nature of Latvian society. As a result of the reforms big landowners were expropriated, not being allowed to keep more than fifty hectares. Although the reforms appeared to have a disquieting resemblance to bolshevik practices, they constituted 'an effective barrier to the spread of communism through the creation of a landowning peasantry'. (Hiden and Salmon, 1991, p. 80) Some 70000 farmsteads were created in this way. These new farmsteads were small. Contrary to expectations the rural economy flourished in Latvia and Britain became the chief importer of Latvian timber and dairy products.
9. Compulsory summer farmwork was introduced for city schoolchildren by Ulmanis. This educational policy was designed to strengthen the attachment to land and respect for farmers and created symbols and sentiments which cut across social classes.

10. The secret clause of the notorious Molotov-Ribbentrop pact signed on 23 August 1939 had assigned Poland and Lithuania to the German sphere of influence and Estonia and Latvia to the Soviet sphere of influence. Belated attempts at cooperation between the three Baltic states came too late.

11. I refer to both national and ethnic identity in this chapter. In the nineteenth-century context and during the period of independence the relevant term is clearly national identity. However, contemporary narratives recalling deportation and exile are not concerned with national issues so much as ethnic belonging. Ethnicity is, of course, defined in relation to other ethnic groups and yet Latvian narratives are distinguished by the absence of such references. Other ethnic groups, particularly Russians, are alluded to rather than being directly represented.

10 A Creative Discourse: Gender Roles in Ethnic Minority Fiction

Helen Kanitkar

In a recently published paper, Homi Bhabha reveals the tensions of the presenting cultural dichotomy that migrants must somehow reconcile to realize the potential of their new experience. He sees their emergent construct as, 'partial culture', a 'contaminated yet connective tissue between cultures . . . bafflingly both alike and different.'[1]

Thrusting their way through the shifting mists of this bafflement come the ever-growing number of writers from the ethnic minorities of modern Britain. They are establishing a discourse which articulates challenge to both the majority culture and the cultural norms, often dearly clung to by members of the minority communities, who see the new as too threatening, too sudden, a demoralizing force which destroys without pause, without evaluation, without regard or question. Penetrating among these challenges are the voices of black women writers, who question the role-creating stereotypes which have confined and compartmentalized women, especially, perhaps, black women through history, confined to activities that express the boundaries set by male hegemony. Carole Boyce-Davies,[2] has debated the attempt by some black women authors to speak only from the perspective of 'blackness', ignoring 'femaleness'. Blackness is indeed 'marginalized, overdetermined, and made stereotypic'; but femaleness is as powerful a force, restricting or liberating, and inextricably enmeshes with blackness in the experience of assailment. Davies maintains:

> it is the additional identity of femaleness which interferes with seamless Black identity and is therefore either ignored, erased, or 'spoken for'. One still finds some women trying to say that they want to speak only as an African or as a 'Black', and not as a woman, as if it were possible to divest oneself of one's gender and stand as neutered within the context of palpable and visible historical, gendered and racialized identities.

A dominant theme in the work of the American Nobel laureate, Toni Morrison, is the recreation of female black identity.[3] She questions the equation of womanhood/motherhood, the 'earth mother' presentation which insidiously perpetuates the 'male is to female as culture is to nature' dichotomy suggested, as an analytical tool for much social research. This paradoxically reinforces women's culturally devalued status even as it attempts to explain and contradict it. Motherhood is an integral part of womanhood, but it is not the whole. In *Beloved*, Morrison tries to delineate the process of negotiation a woman may go through in attempting to accommodate the emotive demands of her culturally patterned role as mother with her independent, individual selfhood. In her latest novel, *Paradise*, (Morrison, 1998), she sees the whole concept of paradise as it is envisaged in the human mind as a socio-literary construct. Representation of paradise will, nay must, change according to its referent time and community. Gender values and representations are likewise constructs, and black women novelists are agents, revealers, mediators of change. Among them, the two writers whose work forms the illustrative core of this chapter, have their own spaces where they can create a selfhood that is dependent on neither past nor present values, but is a new and assertive creation emerging from a discourse of both.

It is only comparatively recently that social researchers have followed their literary colleagues and turned to these writings as sources of information and as aids to understanding other cultures, as well as their own.[4] Those who have, have been strongly supportive of the social value of such literatures; for example, George Marcus and Michael Fischer write:

> Such literatures offer not only expressions of indigenous experience, unavailable in any other form, but also constitute, as similar literatures do in our own society, indigenous commentaries as a form of auto-ethnography that in particular concerns itself with the expression of experience.[5]

The power of literature to carry and convey the traditional values which inspire its creation, as well as the challenge of change in a new environment, has been theoretically and practically illustrated, not least, indeed, by the anthropologist Bronislaw Malinowski. He notes how, during fieldwork, he would withdraw into his tent and, tying up the flaps, retreat into a novel-induced state of self-reaffirmation when he sensed he was losing his cultural identity under the pressure of the encapsulating social values of the Trobriand Islands.

THE NOVELS

It is certainly no kind of retreat that I am proposing here; rather the reverse. I shall focus on the novel as a means of communication with an 'other' self, who presents, as writer, a creative perception of an individual emigrant ethnicity and the effects of challenges to it emergent from that world of interaction outside the tent flaps. I have chosen to focus on the novel since it is a literary genre that has proved to be particularly suited to critical social portrayal, to the development of character through the challenge of change both chosen and involuntary, and through which social statements are subtly and persuasively made. They are persuasive because of the entertainment value of novel-reading, and subtle, since a reader, when relaxed and agreeably disposed is most effectively under the writer's influence. The novel is a literary form that is popular and well-represented among the body of writers I am dealing with here, a form through which they have chosen to speak out, and communicate the mental and physical stresses of migration and the processes through which they have tried to achieve a new cultural equilibrium.

These novels are written in English, which is usually the 'mother-tongue' of the writers, and they are a major contribution to twentieth-century literature in English. Since the writers have an experiential approach to their subject-matter, their work forms a distinctive genre. I have termed this either 'British-Indian', or 'British-Black' literature, to indicate that the authors have cultural links either, on their own account or through their parents, with the Indian sub-continent, or the Caribbean, or Africa, although they now live in Britain. In this way 'British-Indian' literature, for example, differs from what is called 'Indo-Anglian', which is literature in English written in India.

CONTRIBUTIONS TO SOCIAL RESEARCH

I have deliberately chosen to illustrate my theme through writings by women novelists, since they are often concerned with women's issues, and gender relations as they affect women of the migrant communities – two themes prominent in recent social investigation of minority groups. It is also true that women writers are among the most outspoken and critical, and therefore lively and exciting, of those emerging from these communities in Britain. They challenge not only the situation in which they now find themselves, but also their social position as laid down in traditional values. Frequently they adopt, and manipulate for their purposes, the familiar 'stream of consciousness' approach, and the tales are often told in the first person, making the experience more immediate, involving and effective for the reader.

For the social scientist, the writer is no less an informant than an interviewee seated face-to-face on a village bench, in a board room, or gently rocking her grandchild while sorting through rice-grains for the family meal. But there are major differences which call for wariness. The reader is not an interviewer; questions for clarification cannot be asked; there are no opportunities for cross-checking statements and it is impossible to follow-up points of particular interest unless the writer is cooperative enough to do this independently. In addition, the writer's purpose is not that of a social investigator. She does not record detail for future analysis and interpretation, neither will she describe events sequentially, or necessarily in relation to the same social sub-group interacting synchronically in time and place.

The novelist is a participant observer in society, but her aim, and method of presenting her accumulated impressions, are very different. She creates characters, rather than records informants. Out of keen observation and activity in varied contexts she constructs an experiential amalgam, or composite character, who passes through the filter of the author's perception to act out those socially and culturally determined interactions which reveal the tensions and cooperations that are the generators of the social organization that is germane to social research.

Besides being a participant observer, a writer is truly an insider of the group of which she writes as informant, and is therefore bound up with its internal hierarchies, social values and responsibilities, sectarian and status divisions, whatever the bases may be – gender, class, education, occupation or caste. On the other hand, the novelist is likely to be a member of an elite, educated group, and may already have internalized outsider, or 'occidentalist' values[6] which can hamper or distort a representation of the traditional. Awareness of these limitations is essential to a social scientist using fictional material in analysis, but, that said, the value of the inside observer's voice in providing for a deeper understanding of the motivations of the 'other' is becoming more widely recognized, since it provides a further important channel of communication between observer and observed.

All creative writers draw from observation and experience, and on internalized impressions determined by their own perceptions. The composite, created characters who people their work move in situations within which interpersonal relations of dispute, anger, argument, celebration or affection are played out. Such situations are likewise purposefully created, and experientially composite. More than a social scientist, whose attention is focussed on a region or community, writers can reflect the variations to be observed within and between social groupings, while nevertheless showing underlying unifying values and structural elements. Their purpose is to reveal, rather than record and analyse, the norms by which their subjects operate. While a social investigator attempts to record actions and events meticulously (for who knows what may be useful later), the creative writer picks selectively from a plethora of varied internalized experiences, so that little case histories emerge throughout the text, each scene adding to the reader's understanding of what makes the characters and their social setting adapt, develop, change, or maintain a familiar relationship structure.

But here again a note of caution must be sounded, for novels are not systemic social analyses. After all; it is not only things as they *are* that are being conveyed, but, perhaps, as the novelist *would like them to be* and this very fact can add a useful perspective to a researcher's contemporary view, by providing a pointer to possibilities of social change. The selected small dramas the novelist describes can reveal, say, the processes of extended family living more memorably and often more intimately than a formal, analytical account; as long as a researcher remembers that the novel is, after all, fiction.

AMRITVELA

It is now appropriate to analyse the methods by which women writers of the diasporas reveal the distinctive experiences to which their racial, economic and gendered marginalities expose them, and the ways by which they accommodate to altered scenarios of activity, and maximize the opportunities available to them.

I turn first to a remarkably revelatory and communicative British Indian novel by Leena Dhingra, *Amritvela*. Meera, a young woman born and brought up in north India, is now living in Britain. She has married an Englishman, Martin, and has a young daughter, Maya – an interesting choice of name in the circumstances, with its connotation of a transitory illusion. Martin has had to live apart from his family on account of his work, and it emerges that the couple are growing apart, so that Meera decides to visit her relatives in Delhi to try to 'find herself', find out where 'home' is to be for her and Maya. She is returning to her 'roots', starting again from the beginning, for she feels that India holds what she is looking for, and that the two areas of her existence are incompatible and force a choice upon her. She is presented as being in a classic 'in-between' situation, which is physically exemplified by the opening of the book on a plane bearing Meera from Heathrow to Delhi and her elderly aunts, with whom she is to stay. 'If I feel myself to be suspended between two cultures, then this is where I belong, the halfway mark. Here in the middle of nowhere ... is my space.'[7]

From this 'nowhere' Meera lands in Delhi, and from her first day there begins to develop a consciousness of social and spatial encapsulations that mark out and determine interactions – the residential colonies that are enclosed and withdrawn into themselves, within which it is safe for ladies to walk, to sit in their gardens and chat undisturbed; the caste barriers that exist even within the same house, making it shocking to Minoo, the untouchable child-servant, to be asked by Meera to bring her the obligatory early morning tea, though it is quite acceptable for the bath-water to be prepared by the child.

Such restrictions at this early stage in the narrative are greeted with tolerant amusement by Meera; her joy at being again in India is so great that there are no niggling irritations to bother her, except the memory of her husband and daughter walking away from her at the airport, complete in their companionship, making *her* feel the rejected one. No direct questions are forthcoming from the aunts about their absence; only gentle insinuations about divorce cases known to them, which they hope will prompt Meera to confide her problems – for they are sure there must be problems, otherwise why did the little family not come together?

Dhingra uses the literary device of the letter confidante to expose Meera's confusions of thought and their slow resolution as the tale continues. Approximately every third chapter takes the form of a letter written in her 'letter book', which she addresses as 'dear friend'; an adaptation of the 'dear diary' of earlier writers. This works well, giving the reader a deeper understanding of Meera and the happy, as well as traumatic, childhood experiences, that have made her the woman she is, with the needs that she has to define before finding satisfaction and 'wholeness'.

Cultural patternings and expectations that have become internalized by Meera during her absence from India begin to catch her involuntarily at an early stage of her trip, in spite of the anticipatory delight she feels on arrival – 'This morning I woke up in India! It's wonderful to be here!' Irritation over Indian casualness about pre-arranged plans and time-keeping begins to show on the second day: Meera wants to post a parcel, and this emerges as a complex procedure which her aunts feel she is ill-prepared to undertake. Her Aunt Pushpa has to be waited for, as 'she will know exactly what to do'.

> By lunchtime Aunt Pushpa has still not come and I am dismayed. Time, which felt so comfortably suspended yesterday, now begins to feel irritatingly slow as I sense my well-planned day slipping by.[8]

In the event the younger aunt, Daya, knows how to prepare a parcel for posting, but it is not her place to make preparations as long as there is a possibility of the elder sister giving her opinion. This hierarchy within the joint family structure is constantly operative, even in the smallest matters; Pushpa and Daya are driving with Meera when a cow is seen sitting in the middle of the road. Clearly no violence is possible, yet the car has to pass. Necessarily Pushpa takes the lead, sounds the horn, moves her car forward threateningly, revs the engine, shouts, all with no response; only then does the gentle Daya step out with spinach taken from the shopping and tempts the animal successfully to the roadside. Pushpa, in her turn, is restrained by Meera's great-aunt Bibiji, eldest woman of the extended family, when she attempts to voice the suspicions of the gossips about the strains Meera's marriage is going through: '"She's one of our girls. If anybody talks, you should stop them." . . . "Yes, yes, Aunty, you're quite right. No, no, we've heard nothing." My aunt is suitably chastened.'[9] Even Great-Aunt Bibiji's authority is bounded. She may be the oldest member of the extended family, but she is not its head, for she is a woman, so, although her advice may be sought, decisions are left to the oldest male, who is considerably younger than Bibiji. Meera herself is soon made to learn her place in the family. Attempting to make a statement about the inadequacy of reporting of Indian news in Britain, she encounters the ill-informed convictions of her elder cousin's wife, and is made to accept that it is *her* inattention and lack of effort that makes her miss out on what is happening in India, and not neglect by the British media.

Such 'little case histories' illustrate entertainingly and memorably the hierarchical checks and balances that maintain extended family equilibrium, ensuring its survival as a shelter to which the threatened may return, as, indeed, Meera does.

In her wisdom, Bibiji encourages Meera to meet with younger members of the family, to learn of contemporary India, its social life, economic pressures and political structure. From the younger generation she feels even more isolated; they have changed faster than she has, and in very different directions. They are well-to-do, successful in their professions and their businesses, and circulate within a narrow and repetitive elite which is concerned with new cars, servant problems, the cost of living in the style they feel essential to them, and the best places to obtain even the smallest necessaries of life, be they sandals or sweets. Wherever she goes among family and friends, Meera is given the temporary status of 'visitor'; her stay is a 'visit'. Her peers cannot visualize her as part of India, and are made more convinced of her difference by her outspoken awareness of surrounding poverty and hard labour:

> 'My God, Meera, you're just now speaking like one of these simplistic visitors!' Her cousin's wife is shocked by her appreciation of the building workers. 'They aren't the builders. They just carry out the work. Fetch and carry. If they didn't do it, donkeys would do it ... they are very grateful to have the work to do and to get a square meal a day.'[10]

Although her contemporaries in the family appear to live modern and sophisticated lives, Meera is surprised at their continued observance of religious rituals, festivals, fasts and prayers, which she has abandoned, though she is still paradoxically spellbound by the moral tales of deities and holy persons that her aunts continue to tell, often at her request. It is one of these stories, about the metamorphosis of clay into a receptacle for holy water, that finally helps to give Meera insight into her in-between situation. Daya narrates how it is only through the buffetings, blows, moulding of interaction with others throughout life that human beings, like the dirt that forms potters' clay, can achieve a form worthy of presentation before God. *All* experiences help to make our 'selves', so Meera should not need to select, but accept, in order to reach her full potential.

Throughout her tale, Dhingra has referred to the dust that is everywhere in India. It floats in the sunlight, it gathers ceaselessly, noiselessly on the floor. It is everywhere, like the deities, the festivals, the fasts and prayers, the legends and scriptural tales. Even on the first morning, Minoo, the sweeper-child, reminds Meera that she has to sweep and wash the floors twice a day because 'there's so much dust'. As Buddha says, dust is the quintessence of creation, it exists in all things, as does the 'ram, ram' that Bibiji constantly writes in her diaries, covering every page of her life with the name of God. It is Daya's story that brings all this together for Meera, and it is Daya who presents her finally with her mother's and grandmother's very special shawl, the *shahtus*, a family heirloom that is hers by right, and which she must keep for her daughter, Maya. This is all she takes away from India for herself, and yet it is everything. By wrapping its warmth around her in the aircraft, she experiences the wholeness of her life's experience in herself, and finds her place in the *amritvela*, the time of nectar just before dawn, a time which holds both what has gone before and what is yet to come. It is significant that, for Meera, this discovery of a new selfhood can only be expressed in Sanskrit through a traditionally Indian image.

Hence the meaning of this book, which Dhingra holds until the end. The vivid metaphor of completeness and hope that is the *amritvela* promotes an important empathic understanding of the 'in-betweens' of the Hindu diaspora, an understanding that can be usefully gained from these experiential novels which speak from within communities studied.

Complementary to, but very different from *Amritvela* in presentation, ethnic setting and thematic content is *Waiting in the Twilight*, by Jamaican-born Joan Riley. Through rich and powerful imagery, notably meta-phor, simile and pathetic fallacy, the author improves her readers' comprehension of the high hopes with which immigrants set out and arrive, followed by a gradual dispiriting down-curve in achievement in spite of hard and often depressing work attracting low remuneration. The 'glass ceiling' so often quoted as representing the unseen barrier to promotion in women's world of work becomes a 'white glass ceiling' for far too many black workers of both sexes, but it is especially real, and painfully hard on impact, to black women. As is clear from her dedication to her book, Joan Riley has chosen to speak for them, for 'the forgotten and unglamorous section of my people' who came to Britain as to a mother-country, only to encounter barriers of both overt and concealed, or partially veiled, racism which gradually wore down the self-value and individual pride of skilled workpeople. She goes further. Her main char-acter, Adella Johnson, is a woman who is thus subject not only to the prevailing racist reactions of, at best, a cold hostile reserve, at worst, open hostility, but also sexist discrimination from the men of her own community. She suffers a stroke when in her fifties. Since this is a dis-ablement associated with old age, she is classified as such, and the disad-vantages of ageism and the all-too-common reaction to any kind of observable physical challenge are added to her burdens:

> There were only five jobs, and eight women waiting. She saw the way they looked at her, how they dismissed her when they saw her crippled side . . . Only the desperate need to get a job kept her where she was, the humiliation of her other interviews still alive in her memory . . . She got the job! . . . She did not even notice the contempt on the reception-ist's face, the way the porter let the door swing back at her'[11]

Even Adella's husband reacts with scorn:

> "A get a jab, Stanton," she said . . . "A jab?" he repeated, as if he could not quite believe he had heard her right. "Whe you get jab fram?"[12]

Although Stanton has never ceased to complain about how heavy a financial burden has been placed on his shoulders since Adella was forced to stop working, paradoxically he is not pleased by her success, which is perceived as a threat to his new-found authority as husband, and a means of greater independence for her. She knows only too well that Stanton, a qualified carpenter, has lost confidence in his abilities since coming to England, where he has been unable to practise his trade, and his jealousy for her ability to save out of the little she earns, so that she manages the down-payment on a house, has impelled him to seek another woman who can bolster his ego. To restore him to an amenable mood Adella is forced to play down her success, to make it seem a small thing in her husband's eyes, even though she so badly wants some congratulation and praise:

> she saw the near anger in his eyes, the resentment he felt at her announcement. 'Is nuting big,' she said hastily. 'Is jus a cleaning jab in a big office . . . De pay no good, but it will tek de burden off yu if a working too'.[13]

Adjustment to wives' slowly growing economic power, and the greater independence that comes from it, is something that some husbands within the black community, and outside it, find hard to achieve, and Riley shows her readers a progressive marriage breakdown at the basis of which is Stanton's weakening self-image of himself as husband and father and the resentment arising from this, coupled with Adella's expectation of some regard and consideration for her efforts and hard-won achievements. That this is not a rare scenario is clear from women's conversations throughout the book. Adella's worsening situation has a universal relevance to women and effects a cross-cultural appeal to readers' sympathies.

THE MESSAGE OF METAPHOR

Riley is a powerful writer, and her imagery – metaphor, simile, personification, pathetic fallacy – reiterates messages of darkness, cold, rottenness, bitterness and dirt, which force us to descend into the increasing despair of Adella's experience, until we wonder how she can continue to drag her enduring disablements around any longer. A skilled needle-woman, she loses this rewarding job after the stroke; this is when she takes up office cleaning. In Jamaica, and at first in England when her hopes were high, she could embroider a colourful pattern for her life; but later, the figurative reflection of her life and daily treatment by society is only too evident in her cleaner's bucket:

> She stared into the murky depths of the scum-ringed bucket... The contents looked revolting, grey darkness of floor dirt blending with ash from carelessly discarded cigarette butts. Adella's lips thinned as she looked at the small mound of fruit peelings, sweet-wrappers and anything else that needed disposing. They used her as a mobile rubbish tip, the rust-streaked silver bucket like a magnet, attracting litter wherever it came to rest.[14]

Adella's humiliation is not only symbolic; she suffers insolence, both active and verbal, from young office-workers who have no sympathy for her disability or respect for her age:

> 'Johnson!'... 'Yes, mam' she said aloud, turning to see a young white girl no more than seventeen years old. Her feet had left a fresh trail of mud... This one had been working less than six months and already she had learnt how to treat the cleaning staff. 'I hope you emptied the ashtrays this morning,' the girl said coldly. 'We had to do them ourselves for the last three days and I certainly don't get paid to be a cleaner.'[15]

The racist cold and bitterness, like the 'trail of mud' emanating from individual comment exemplified above, is also imaged in the climate; and Adella's defencelessness is made almost tangible to the reader through her inadequate clothing:

> The wind blew icily against the thin canvas coat as she let herself out into the grey January day. It found all the holes and patches, pouring in through her clothes... The wind hit her as she turned into the gloomy street, pushing icy fingers down her neck and through gaps where buttons had fallen from her coat... She could feel the cold seeping into her shoes, through the places where the plastic had split, and the stitches had unravelled at the seams'[16]

Only memories of her upbringing in Jamaica preserve Adella's self-image, her pride in herself. At least she has such memories; young black folk born in Britain do not have such positive experiential support, and have to build up a personal prestige inch by painful inch. Adella perceives the difference in self-confidence between her son brought up in London and the boy reared in Jamaica. The latter has positive ambitions, though he may never have the opportunities to achieve them, while the former does not look further than what white society deems to be an 'acceptable' job for a black man, that of a tube train driver. Later in the novel Riley shows the very different reactions of Adella's two highly educated daughters, who have the confidence and confrontational skills to challenge the hierarchies of white society when they see it necessary to do so. To compete within a class society, they have abandoned Jamaican grammatical structures and vocabulary, and habitually use received pronunciation English between themselves and in conversation with their mother and her friends, who always use London Jamaican. Riley divides the generations, especially women, educationally, occupationally, linguistically. Young black women challenge institutional racism to maximize opportunities. They question doctors, welfare officers, council officials; they know, or investigate, their rights as citizens, while the older generation, though upset or unhappy, maintains the stoic silence of an imposed insecurity, just as Adella and Stanton endure the sales talk of an estate agent who shows them round what all three know to be a sub-standard, rotten and leaking house. The agent drops his keys; immediately Stanton, 'hurried forward, half-running up the stairs to pick up the keys for the agent. Adella felt sick as she watched the deference in his face'.[17]

How pleased she is later, when her daughters take her to a specialist, to hear them ask the doctor for further explanation of her condition – they will not be put off by a routine, uninformative statement. 'Respeck' is Adella's constant theme; 'respeck' for parents, for the elderly, that she saw in Jamaica, but never in England.

It is always this 'respeck' that she searches for that continually eludes her, and makes her adopted surroundings seem cold, lifeless, unresponsive, just like the house they are forced to buy because in pleasanter areas, 'some people are funny about just who they sell their houses to'.

> Adella felt the dampness of the place fold around around her and seep into her clothes... Her fingers met solid wall, slid into furry coat of spongy dampness... The smell of junjo rose to her nose. It was like a bad dream and she peered around suspiciously, half-expecting to glimpse something rotting in a hidden corner.[18]

Adella's physical disablement mirrors a social one. Her husband, disillusioned by Britain and Adella's inability, as he sees it, to give him sons, leaves her for her cousin. This brings shame, depression, a lasting sorrow and loneliness from which Adella never fully recovers. She never remarries, but remains determined to prove her fidelity by awaiting Stanton's return, while living with her youngest daughters. This down-turn of her fortunes is reflected in the loss of the house for which she saved and worked so hard, which was a symbol of her independence, an attempt to put her roots down in Britain, to belong, to gain the 'respeck' due to a householder. Her physical independence, too, grows less as her disability increases. Her house quite literally begins to fall down around her, like her ambitions and dreams; her family scattering, her days stretching blankly ahead with mainly the television, the dog and the cat as companions. The warmth, the light, the colours of Jamaica fill her memory, and, above all, the supportive network of women she always found there, whether in her natal village or the bleak yard she inhabited near Kingston waterfront as an unmarried mother:

> Kingston hot, and de man dem dress sharp and de woman dem have fashion. Dem ride in tram car, it have a lot a noise where de Higgla dem come down from de hills to sell dem fruit and grun provision. Plenty rich people live dere. Buckra, and high yellow people, wid servant and posh car.[19]

As the tale progresses, images of Jamaica brighten, while those of England grow duller – there is no likelihood of an improvement, and Adella's twilight moves ever nearer to night. Riley's story concludes with Adella being rushed to hospital on account of her final stroke. Even here she is in a twilight zone, for there is no bed for her, and she sees out her life in England on a trolley in the hospital corridor, still on the periphery of acceptability. For the longed-for 'respeck' she has to wait till her next existence, where she sees her family from Jamaica, as well as her long-awaited errant husband, awaiting her:

> Everybody was there, and they were not condemning her... She heard him call her name again. Softly, in the secret way that was just between the two of them. Stanton had come back, just like she knew he would ... She had fulfilled her promise to herself and she knew in her bones that they would keep a Binkie for her like Mada Beck and Granny Dee. 'All dat respeck,' she murmured to herself, and this time her eyes smiled as they closed.[20]

Although Adella may die content, the reader is left with a bitter frustration in that all that work, all that struggling, scrimping and saving, all that thwarted ambition rests finally on a hospital trolley, excluded in death as in life from the 'respeck' she sought.

CONCLUSION

These two books, *Amritvela* and *Waiting in the Twilight*, are very different in many ways: stylistically, thematically, ethnically, and in their conclusions. Nevertheless, they are unified in showing only too distinctly
how migrants, particularly women distanced from the strengths of their
gender-based support networks, can suffer not only material deprivation but also emotional and psychological challenges to identity. It is not
only the cultural and experiential information provided by the novelist
that is of value to the social scientist; it is the choice of characters, the
way they are portrayed, which of them takes centre stage, which of them
speaks, why and how. All these factors are revealing, as much about the
writers as their stories. For Meera it is not only her traditional heritage
as an Indian woman which presents a challenge. Her adopted life-style, in
which her husband and daughter are so much at home, proves an uncomfortable shape into which she has moved, not grown. She is a re-potted
shrub; her roots coil around unprofitably, seeking a purchase from
which she can spread, develop. Which challenge will prove the greater,
we may ask. Dhingra, however, chooses to end *Amritvela* on a positive
note: Meera has found herself, found her place; for her it is the beginning of a new day.

In Adella's case, the new environment is a challenge for her and for
her whole family. Here is another plant-pot which cannot contain what
it holds, and the surrounding atmosphere is full of many threatening
elements to which the old plant cannot adapt. Riley, then, chooses a
downbeat conclusion – Adella sees herself as a non-achiever in spite of
others telling her she has succeeded. The only positive aspects are the
achievements of two of her daughters, but their stories are not Adella's,
and events rarely stray far from her personal involvement. Although she
finds peace at last it is in spite of her migration experience, rather than
because of it. Those figures who greet her as her eyes close are of Jamaica,
not London. It is as if the intervening cold, isolating, depressing years
had never been. Changes in role are not internalized, and the status, the
'respeck' she values are based on older, deeper criteria. We may agree
with Marcus and Fischer, quoted earlier, that these literatures offer,
'expressions of indigenous experience, unavailable in any other form'. If
this is so, they are a valuable background to social research.

Earlier in this chapter we found Malinowski reasserting his normative
ethnicity through textual injections of the familiar on an alien shore.
The interest of his lonely figure lies in its witness to the power creative
writing has to evoke cultural patternings and make them rationally and

relevantly live, even at a distance. By turning to novels that represent cultures other than our own we open up the flaps of our ethnic purdah-tents, our cultural compounds, if you like, to a broad perspective within which figures move and draw nearer to us, preparing us for the reality of personal communication, through which alone interpersonal under-standing lives.

NOTES

1. Bhabha (1994) p. 54.
2. Boyce-Davies (1994) p. 8.
3. For a fuller, more detailed discussion of this point see Boyce-Davies (1994) p. 136.
4. Three recent articles by Kanitkar (1991, 1994, 1996) illustrate this devel-opment. Reference may also be made to a new book discussing the Afri-can novel as an effective medium of cross-cultural communication between writer and reader, Gikandi (1987).
5. Marcus and Fisher (1986) p. 84.
6. A useful discussion of this concept may be found in Nadel-Klein (1995).
7. Dhingra (1988) p. 1.
8. Ibid., p. 25.
9. Ibid., pp. 17–18.
10. Ibid., p. 92.
11. Riley (1987) p. 87.
12. Ibid., p. 88.
13. Ibid., p. 89.
14. Ibid., p. 1.
15. Ibid., p. 2.
16. Ibid., pp. 5–6.
17. Ibid., p. 17.
18. Ibid., p. 17.
19. Ibid., p. 35.
20. Ibid., p. 165.

11 When the Mirror Speaks: The Poetics and Problematics of Identity Construction for Métisse Women in Bristol
Jayne Ifekwunigwe

We can try to deprive ourselves of our realities but in the darkest hour of the night, when no one else is around and we have gone to the loo to spend a penny, we must look in the mirror. Eventually that moment comes when we look in the mirror and we see a Black woman ...

Sharon

Sharon is a woman in her thirties who grew up in racial isolation in care in the north of England without either her White English mother or her Black Ghanaian father. In an English society which codes its citizens on the basis of their colour, Sharon must reconcile the psychic split between a genealogical sense of herself which is Ghanaian and English and a racialized self which is Black and White. As her statement reveals, the psychological struggle begins when she realizes that bi-racialized[1] English society dictates that she embrace her Blackness and deny her Whiteness.

Her sentiments reflect the profound existential paradox facing individuals whose lineages historically situate them as grandchildren of both the colonizers and the colonized. I refer to such individuals as *métis(se)*. In England, the multiplicity of terms in circulation to describe individuals who straddle Black and White racial borders drove me in search of a new formulation. More often than not, received terminology either privileges presumed 'racial' differences ('mixed race') or obscures the complex ways in which being *métis(se)* involves both the negotiation of constructed 'Black'/'White' racial categories as well as the celebration of converging cultures, continuities of generations and overlapping historical traditions. The lack of consensus as to which term to use as well as the limitations of this discursive privileging of 'race' at the expense of generational, ethnic, and cultural concerns, led me to *métis(se)* and *métissage*.

In the French African (Senegalese) context, in its conventional masculine (*métis*) and feminine *(métisse)* forms, *métis(se)* refers to someone who, by virtue of parentage, embodies two or more world views, for example, French mother and Black Senegalese father (Diop, 1992; Koubaka, 1993). However, it is not exclusively a 'racial' term used to differentiate individuals with one Black parent and one White parent from those with two Black or White parents. *Métis(se)* also pertains to people with parents from different ethnic/cultural groups within a country, for example in Nigeria, Ibo and Yoruba, or in Britain, Scottish and English. By extension, *métissage* is a mind set or a shorthand way to describe the theorizing associated with *métis(se)* subjectivities: oscillation, contradiction, paradox, hybridity, polyethnicities, multiple reference points, 'belonging nowhere and everywhere'. *Métissage* also signals the process of opening up hybrid spaces and looking at the sociocultural dynamics of 'race', gender, ethnicity, nation, class, sexuality, and generation and their relationship to the mechanics of power.

Sharon is one of twenty five *métis(se)* individuals who were participants in my two-year-long ethnographic study based in Bristol, England.[2] Their individual and collective voices represent the significant part of a greater multigenerational whole comprising people in England with Black continental African or African Caribbean fathers and White British or European mothers. By virtue of the aforementioned contradictory bi-racialized classification in Britain, *métis(se)* individuals' narratives of self and identity both reflect the gender, generational, racial and ethnic tensions of English society and are located outside it in an imagined but not imaginary 'grey' space. That is, the ways in which the women and men I worked with tell their stories are as newfangled *griot(te)s*.[3] They simultaneously construct dual narratives, which embody individual and collective historical consciousness. They tell their own lived stories. At the same time, their memories preserve and reinterpret senses of past interwoven cultures. In his essay, 'The Choices of Identity,' Denis-Consant Martin talks about identity as narrative (1995, pp. 7–8):

> The narrative borrows from history as well as from fiction and treats the person as a character in a plot. The person as a character is not separable from its life experiences, but the plot allows for the re-organization of the events which provide the ground for the experiences of the person/character....Narrative identity, being at the same time

fictitious and real, leaves room for variations on the past – a plot can always be revised – and also for initiatives in the future.

These *métis(se)* narratives of identity provide scathing sociopolitical commentaries and cultural critiques of contemporary English African Diasporic[4] life and its manifest bi-racialized problematics.

However, the specific focus of this chapter is the differents ways in which cultural memories shape contradictory meanings of 'race',[5] self and identity for six women who by virtue of birth transgress boundaries and challenge essentialized constructions of self, identity, place and belonging. Their specific lived realities epitomize psychosocial struggles to make sense of explicit epistemological tensions between subjectivity and alterity. In particular, drawing on their testimonies, I will address the ways in which six *métisse* women confront problematic tensions between being *métisse* and becoming Black. English and Ghanaian philosopher Anthony Appiah (1992, p. 178) formulates an ethos of identities politics which reflects this complexity:

> identities are complex and multiple and grow out of a history of changing responses to economic, political, and cultural forces, almost always in opposition to other identities....that they flourish despite what I earlier called our 'misrecognition' of their origins; despite that is, their roots in myths and lies...there is, in consequence, no large place for reason in the construction – as opposed to the study and management of identities.

The principal narrators are: Similola who has a White German mother and a Black Tanzanian father and Ruby, whose mother is middle class White English and her father middle class Black Nigerian, both of whom were brought up in children's homes; Yemi and Bisi, who are sisters, grew up in a middle class family in Ibadan, Nigeria with both their White Northumberland English mother and their Black Yoruba-Nigerian father; and another set of sisters, Akousa and Sarah who came of age in a working class, predominantly Black African Caribbean community in Liverpool, with their orphaned White Irish mother and without their Black Bajan (from Barbados) father. Each woman's mother is at once White and Irish, English or German. Their fathers are both Black and either Bajan, Nigerian or Tanzanian.

Accordingly, as their stories reveal, most of their identities work concerns the management and negotiation of polyethnicity[6] in social and cultural contexts which frequently demand that they choose an essentialized Black identity. This is despite the fact that by virtue of lineage, they can and do situate themselves within at least two specific and yet over-lapping historical narratives.

SETTING THE STAGE

In *The Presentation of Self in Everyday Life* (1959), Jewish sociologist Erving Goffman's seminal work on self-formation and presentation as performance, he uses the analogy of the theatre to describe the ways in which individuals manage their identities in social milieux. Accordingly, there is 'front stage' behaviour and 'backstage' behaviour. In the equally important treatise *Black Skin, White Masks* (1967), Martinican psychiatrist Frantz Fanon exposes the psychic blurring of self and other as Black ('Negro') identities are distorted by the lenses of the White imperialist gaze. Similarly, in *Shadow and Act*, Ralph Ellison (1953, p. 47) describes the ways in which African American entertainers, 'in order to enact a symbolic role basic to the underlying drama of American society, assume a ritual mask'. Many years later English and Jamaican cultural historian Becky Hall (1996, p. 164) re-enacts a similar feminist psychodrama: 'Fascinated by the materiality of black skin and the discursive production of "race", it is through my own body that I investigate the fantasies of blackness and whiteness troubling the English cultural imagination that is also my own'. I incorporate all of these voices and argue that as social actresses the six *griottes* perform different dialectical dramas within the private domain among their immediate and extended polyethnic and polyracial families and in the realm of the public amid the essentializing and homogenizing gazes of society writ large.

IS ENGLISH SYNONYMOUS WITH ESSENTIAL WHITENESS?

While I was in the midst of conducting the initial research between 1990–92, there was an advertising campaign for the sweets 'Smarties'. Billboards and sweets wrappers read: 'Find out the real secret to the white Smarties.' The answer was: 'They are white all the way through ...they are made with white chocolate'. An analogous assumption would be that only people fitting the limited prototypic phenotypic description of a White person can be English. Everyone else will have to make do with British. In addition, the former is a citizen and the latter a mere subject. For example, artist and cultural critic Olu Oguibe (1994, p. xvii) states: 'That one is born in Hackney, London of parents born in

Hackney, London themselves, is never sufficient proof of belonging for people of African descent in Britain'.

In the same way as Black sons and daughters of the English-African Diaspora are denied English citizenship *métis(se)* people are denied access to an English identity which they can rightfully claim on the basis of ancestry. The ongoing and unresolved political debates are: first, should British-born Black people, *métis(se)* or with both parents from either continental Africa or the Caribbean, demand to be included under the pre-existing English umbrella? Alternatively, as children of a global African Diaspora, should we carve out a separate space wherein we acknowledge links and foster social, cultural and political allegiances with other Diasporic constituents in the United States, Canada, Brazil, the Caribbean among other points on the globe? From the vantage point of agency and not victimization, is there some way of reconciling our subjugated connections with former empire which will then enable us, whether *métis(se)* or not, to wear proudly the badge of belonging to/in England? Most importantly, are White English citizens prepared to redefine what it means to be English in order to include on equal footing both *métis(se)* as well as citizen children of so-called immigrant parents, whose natal origins are South Asian, Caribbean, or continental African? As we approach the year 2000, we as a nation have yet to crack these conundrums.

AKOUSA: IS BEING DARK-SKINNED THE PRIMARY CRITERION FOR ESSENTIAL BLACKNESS?

Akousa is Irish-Bajan and grew up in Liverpool amid a strong working class Black African Caribbean community and with her White Irish mother and her brother and sister. She is a Rasta[7] and yet not everyone sees her as a Rasta. She sees herself as a 'light-skinned' Black woman, and yet not everyone sees her as Black. In testimony number one, Akousa relives the psychological trauma brought on by the differential meanings and politicized rankings of skin colour in White and Black communities:

> when I was younger it hurt. I used to wish, God why didn't you make me darker? Why couldn't I have been dark like my sister? When I go out in the sun, I don't go dark like my sister, I go a nice golden brown. My sister goes dark. She goes black and there's me. It was a bad problem when I was in my late teens, middle twenties, tryin' to come to

terms with bein' a light-skinned Black person. Some people are goin' to point that fact out to me a lot more. I thought frigg it man, I am who I am. I am light, so what, look at Africa. From the North to the South, you're going to find people of many shades. We come in many shades. Some are sallow lookin', some are dark lookin', some are white like milk bottles. Whereas, Black people have different shades, why can't I be a different shade?

At the end of the day, I am who I am. That's the way Jah made me. Why should I try and change because people want to define who I am and what colour I should be? Now, I don't care. It doesn't bother me as it did. I think I've become stronger about who I am. As I get older, I get firmer. As I read more and gather more knowledge about myself, I become a lot stronger. If a White person starts tryin', I can answer them back.

If there's a Black person who has a problem with me being light-skinned, me I just raise my head up in the air, straighten my back up and I walk proudly down the street. I don't hang my head no more, which I used to do. Especially in the seventies when it went from bein' light is the in ting to bein' if you weren't as dark as ebony you had no chance bein' Black basically. It was goin' from one extreme to the other. There were other Black people where to them I was too light-lookin' and to them I was White. Also the fact that I had a White mother. I think with a lot of Black people who have both Black parents, in a sense you have to prove yourself that you are Black. That you are not, one, sittin' on the fence and two, don't think you are White. Once you get that across to them, Black people tend to accept you more because they then realize where you are comin' from.

I do know people myself who have one White parent and considered themselves to be White. I also know Black people who have both Black parents who considered themselves to be more White. I know other Black kids who were adopted into White families and consider themselves to be White. I think at the end of the day, when you look at it, Black is a state of consciousness. It's got nothing to do with how light or how dark your skin is. It's got to do with what you are inside, and that's what Blackness is about.

Akousa's commentary brings to the forefront what I refer to as the social chameleon phenomenon (Ifekwunigwe, forthcoming). *Métis(se)* people with so-called 'ambiguous' phenotypes, that is, very fair complexions; blue, green or hazel eyes; more 'pointed/sharp' facial features; light coloured or straight hair can 'change colour' from one social context to the next (Russell *et al.*, 1992; hooks, 1992). Here Akousa has described herself or has been described as *métis(se)*, White, and Black. Her testimony builds a strong case for a new theory of identities formation and transformation for *métis(se)* people which takes into account the frequently overlooked and infinitely complex impress of circumstances, for example, growing up in isolation, lived tensions between phenotype and genotype, growing-up with or without one's Black or White parent, and so on (Gilroy, 1992).

SARAH: NARRATIVES OF SPACE, PLACE, AND BELONGINGS

Irish-Bajan Sarah is Akousa's younger sister and her memories of her childhood and adolescence in Liverpool are remarkably different from Akousa's. Akousa frames her experiences in terms of the important people who passed through her life as well as the psychosocial and political trajectories she follows on the never-ending journey towards selfdefinition. On the other hand, Sarah's recollections of her life are interwoven with numerous vivid descriptions of the houses she and her family lived in and they become veritable sign posts along her journey:

> When I was small, I grew up in one house with my Mum and my sister and my brother. I have no real memories of that. But I remember me Mum talkin' bout that period. Saying that every Wednesday she used to have to decide what to spend the pennies on. Whether to go out and buy a few cigarettes or to buy a little extra food. She said that Wednesdays she used to always resort to makin' dumplins with flour and water and cookin' them on the fire. Then after that, we went to live with my Aunt and Uncle which wasn't far. I'm talkin' mainly about houses that we lived in. 'Cause this is the period of my kind of growin' up in Liverpool. I suppose we moved about five times from the time I was born until the time I was fourteen. So, those periods of movin' kind of brought in a lot of changes, and with each move, materially we became a lot better off as well. So, we went to live with my Auntie and Uncle. My Auntie and Uncle are from Guyana.
>
> I remember that Mama used to live over the road. She was from Jamaica. She used to smoke a pipe, and she used to wear a wig. But it was more like a hat, 'cause she used to wear it on the side of her head, like this. It was never on in the right way. She had chickens in the back yard. She was a big woman that's why everyone called her Mama. 'Cause that's what people used to call big women. She used to beat the

children with a strap. She had about seven children, and they were from babies up to twenty years old. She used to give them licks when they were bad, but we all used to get licks when we were bad. It wasn't a matter of, oh you don't beat your children. That's just what you did. You beat them when they were bad.

I could never understand her husband, 'cause he spoke in patois. And it was really strong. It was really difficult to understand when he used to talk to me. I think that was quite a nice time in my life. Just like runnin' and playin' with their children and comin' back and bein' in the house.

Most of the *griottes'* identity narratives are constructed in terms of turning points – leaving school, first love relationship, getting married, having children, and so on. However, in light of what I refer to as Additive Blackness[8] the awakening of Black consciousness is also a milestone that each of the women reaches at different stages and in remarkably different ways. How they articulate and contextualize their first encounters with Black consciousness is most significant.

In the case of the two sisters from Liverpool, Akousa links her own burgeoning politics to her struggle as 'a light-skinned Black person' to find a place in social contexts and political movements which, at times, seem to exclude her. Both Akousa and her sister point to both fictive Black African Caribbean kin in their community and two Black women, who functioned as cultural surrogates for them during their adolescence, as the major conduits for instilling positive cultural views about Blackness. Here Sarah talks about Akousa's sighting in their corner shop which triggered the beginnings of their emergent Black identity:

At home, Black Power was just comin' in and my sister went to the corner shop and seen her first afro and came home and said, 'Oh, I've seen some afros in the shop. Oh, they're really brilliant.' These group of women with afros, she's sayin' how brilliant they were. At home, we were startin' this awareness of Black power and Black identity. We always related to bein' Black, because all of the signals we got from when we were growin' up, we were nothin' else. We definitely were not White. Even when we were growin' up, my Mum would get angry with us, she always used to call us 'Black bastards'. It was always that we were 'Black' this or 'Black' that. When the Black Power started comin' along and all the positiveness that brought at that time was like brilliant. Like somethin' we could really feel good about.

RUBY: ACCEPTING BLACKNESS WHEN PRAYING DOESN'T
MAKE ONE WHITE

A 'race': 'a compact homogeneous population of one blood ancestry
and lineage' (Crummell, 1862). English Guyanese cultural theorist
Paul Gilroy (1993a, pp. 195–7) refers to 'race' as 'kinship where ... the family is the approved natural site where ethnicity and racial culture are
reproduced ... and in this authoritarian pastoral patriarch, women are
usually identified as the agents and means of this process of cultural
reproduction.' These two definitions serve my analytical purposes well
although operationalizing them within the familial contexts I researched
produces a major paradox: apparently, White English women are mother-
ing Black British children.

As previously mentioned, many factors influence the ways in which
women accomplish this task – for example, the circumstances surrounding the birth of the *métis(se)* child, the prevailing attitudes towards
mixed relationship, class background, and so on. Even though both her
birth mother and other blood relatives were alive, Ruby, who is Black
Nigerian and White English was brought up in a children's home outside London until she left at age sixteen. Their rationale for placing her
there was they wanted her to 'have a proper growing up experience'.
The overwhelming shame surrounding her birth – her father was married and Black continental African – made it impossible for both Ruby's
birth mother and grandmother to fully accept her. Here, Ruby recounts
some of the memories associated with growing up politically Black and
socially and culturally English in a White English children's home:

> In terms of 'race', gender and all that sort of thing, the home that I
> went to was a girls only home so it was a total female environment: the
> staff were female the kids were female and they were from two to
> eighteen. It was a very large place. I suppose there were about thirty
> five kids there. I think my memory is that I was the first Black child
> there, and when I went there I was obviously the youngest child. I was
> much petted to the extent that my first bedroom was to share the
> Deputy Matron's room. I had my cot in her room and she was a sort of
> subsitute Mum person. That was until I was nearly four.
>
> I stayed in her bedroom until as it happened two other children came
> who were also Black. They were Nigerian. They were full Nigerian.
> They weren't mixed race, and they were there because both of their
> parents were studying. In fact, eventually they left. One was two, one
> was four. I was very, very cross with them. They usurped me. I was

quickly out of the matron's bedroom and into the usual dormitory, and the younger of these two children took my place in the cot in the matron's room. They were much darker than me, much tighter hair and people thought they were much more authentic than I was.

Ruby's description of the two Nigerian girls who are placed in the home because their parents are studying is a good example of the different kinds of mirroring that take place when *métis(se)* people are describing themselves in relation to other people. Ruby refers to herself as Black. However, over the years, she has internalized many of the racist stereotypes about Black people. For example, in describing the two Nigerian girls, one of whom 'usurped' her place in the coveted Deputy Matron's bedroom, she points to their 'darker' skin and their 'tighter' hair as markers of their more than her 'authenticity'. Given that the two girls are Nigerian, Ruby has collapsed notions of Blackness and Africanness. Authentic, meaning they are much closer to racialist and essentialist notions of what Black/African people should look like. Hence, she perceives them as being more acceptable and appropriate in a conditional and objectified sense. By internalizing the narrow possibilities for Africanness/Blackness, she has also cancelled herself out. She has then forced herself into the corners of marginality and difference. Ruby continues:

So, I won't say that I hated them, but I certainly looked askance at them. Of course, the three of us were still the only Black people in the place and it was around that time I do remember thinking I would rather be White. I'd had enough of being Black. I certainly didn't get into the disturbed scrubbing my skin in the bath with bleach or soap behavior, but I used to to go to my bedroom at night and pray the Lord to turn me White. In the morning, I used to look and see and I wasn't. So, I don't know, that didn't last for very long, but I can remember it so it must have gone on at some point around that time.

When these other little kids came and usurped me, after some time I decided, well I've had enough of being Black. The White kids seem to have a much nicer time. Us Black ones are always singled out. I went through that little period and then came to the realization very quickly that my skin was black. There was no point praying to the bloody Lord to take it away. 'Cause there was nothing to be done, that was the way it was. I think that was my first lesson in racial awareness. From that time, there was a sense in which I always accepted that I was Black.

With the same results as *métis(se)* children who rub themselves raw in the bath hoping to turn White, Ruby prayed before going to bed each night that she would become White. She would wake up the next morning only to discover that her prayers had not been answered. Both 'White-washing' attempts stem from the same destructive source. Circulating in a *métis(se)* child's mind from a very early age are public negative messages about Blackness and implicitly and explicitly positive ones about elusive Whiteness. These all often shame the child or adolescent into self-destruction – a psychologist colleague recounted her experience working with a young *métis* man who had literally painted himself white with rage – one of the *métis griot* participants attacked all the White nurses in the psychiatric hospital where he was involuntarily detained.

Over time, these forces eat away at the psyche. Without ample space for (self) intervention, self-reclamation or redemption, these wounds cannot heal. The number of *métis(se)* project participants who at some point have attempted suicide, battled with alcohol or substance abuse, been admitted involuntarily or voluntarily to psychiatric facilities, or who have simply been in crisis tells me that the seeds of self-hate and confusion planted in childhood bear bountiful fruits of despair and anger in adulthood.

SIMILOLA: DRESSING 'THE PART'

Black Tanzanian and White German Similola grew up in a Welsh children's home wherein she was made to feel that being White and Whiteness itself were the ideal standards by which she should measure her self worth. In the long run, she knew she could never be completely White and being White-identified always seemed to lead to disappointment and rejection for her. Here she describes a strategy she devised for coping with her ambivalence associated with Blackness and Whiteness:

> I decided, I'm going to have a Black day or a White day. My White day I was ... I'd dress differently for starters. I'd usually wear jeans on my White days. I used to wear jeans because I thought it's more acceptable amongst White students to wear jeans. It seemed like kind of a White uniform in a way and you didn't see many Black girls wearing jeans at that time. So, I'd wear jeans, and whatever else – the bits and pieces that go with it – tee shirts, whatever. Then, on my Black days,

I'd wear flowery skirts and very bright clothes and people used to say, 'God' and I actually got to quite enjoy it. It sounds very silly at that time. I'm not sure if it affected my behaviour in any way. At that phase, I was more outgoing and I tended to be a bit more – to let more of myself show, and not be so self-conscious. Because it was my Black day and I'd think: Oh, I can get away with these things in front of White people because they don't expect Black people to act like them so I can be a bit more outrageous than I normally would. In the end, I couldn't cope with both of these identities. I'd decide the night before. Not necessarily one day ... sometimes it would be like, I'd enjoy my Black day so much on one Monday and I'd think ... it must have been all psychological, I don't think so totally, but I used to notice people treated me differently as well and they reacted towards me in a different way.

To me it was something to do with acknowledging my Blackness. To me, I thought, I can't be Black if I don't wear bright coloured clothes. I had this period of going round dressed all in black clothes and I thought if I wore black clothes all the time, I wouldn't be noticed. It wasn't like now where people wear black clothes all the time. It was the time when black wasn't even vaguely fashionable. It was only worn for funerals and that was it. I got into this wearing black clothes thing thinking I'd be totally unnoticed. My whole wardrobe was full of black clothes. To me, it was an even greater step to suddenly switch into really bright – 'cause I'd got so comfortable with black. Even though people do notice you it's what you yourself feel. I used to feel that when I wore black I was totally insignificant and totally unnoticed. It suited me at that time to be like that and to just fade into the background and not be noticed for any reason.

The giant leap into brightness for me was so huge that I used to dare myself. I'd go into shops and buy very, very bright coloured clothing and then dare myself in the evening to put it on the next day. I'd say, 'God, are you gonna wear that tomorrow or not?' Sometimes I would sometimes I wouldn't. Now, I don't even, I don't want to try and dress in a Black way, just because I want to identify with being Black. 'Cause to me now that's so superficial anyway, there is so much more to it than that and I don't feel the need for that kind of thing anymore. People have to accept me for what I am and if they don't it's just tough.

The way Similola describes her 'Black days/White days' scheme is similar to the ways in which *métis(se)* people who are 'trying-on' being

Black for the first time oscillate uncomfortably between the two. Clothes supposedly being an extension or reflection of one's inner self this binary dress scheme points to the notion that one's appearances determine the way one is categorized and there are essentialized 'Black' and 'White' ways of dressing/being.

YEMI: RE-DEFINING 'THE ISSUES'

A popular assumption and one that is reinforced in much of the primarily American psychological and sociological literature on identity formation is that being *métis(se)* is a tragic condition requiring lots of sympathy and pathologizing.[9] Much of the content of the *griottes'* testimonies does support the notion that being *métis(se)* in a racially polarized society is a painful, challenging, and frequently contradictory existence. Yemi, whose mother is White English and father Black Yoruba from Nigeria grew up in Ibadan, Nigeria in a middle class family where both her White English and Black Nigerian relations accepted her. What Yemi has to say about her family of origin does not really differ from family dynamics which play themselves out in contexts which are not *métis(se)*. As such, Yemi succeeds in normalizing *métis(se)* family life and strife. However, her narratives are also in keeping with a prevailing theme which is the impress of the White mother or the White mother surrogate in the transmission of White English culture, in all its variations. Even if the Black father is physically present, as was the case in Yemi's family, White English cultural codes are frequently reified at the expense of Black continental African or African Caribbean referents in all their complex manifestations. From linguistic silences to dietary omissions, more often than not it is Black/African/Caribbean cultures which are subverted. Back to my Additive Blackness model, if *métis(se)* individuals have been denied access to this aspect of their heritage they may compensate by going through a 'super-Black', 'super-continental African' or 'super-African Caribbean' phase. Until they can effectively merge these disparate identities, their performances of self may simply be caricatures of racialized externally imposed, essentialized and media manufactured representations of Black/continental African/African Caribbean people.

In Yemi's case, as an adolescent a serious argument with her mother made Yemi attempt suicide. At that point, her Nigerian father intervened and took over the exclusive parenting role. Consequently, Yemi was now in a position wherein she had access to her father's Yoruba culture which had previously been perceived as male and from which she had been excluded. In fact, in kinship terms, Yemi refers to herself as 'her father's son'. Nevertheless, one cannot always assume that as *métis(se)* individuals pass through various life stages their only significant issues relate to racial, ethnic and cultural identity. Here, Yemi's expressed discomfort with the size of her breasts serves as a powerful critique of one-dimensional approaches to very complex sociocultural phenomena – identities politics:

The only thing I wished for was my bust to be smaller. That was all I ever worried about. If I could just have a smaller bust, I'd be fine. But that never happened so I guess it's not going to. That was my terrible thing as a teenager. I was like everybody else. My breasts started to grow at eleven. They just didn't stop. Everybody else's breasts stopped growing at eleven and a half. Mine went on growing. When I was thirteen, I was thirty eight inches in a D cup. I didn't know anyone with a bust this big that was a grown-up. It was really really terrible. My mother didn't understand. She would say things like: 'When you get older it will settle down.' Settle down to what? My mother wasn't large-breasted; not as big as I was. She's a fatter person and I was thin with this bust. Just a bust and some glasses. You'd see me coming. You'd see the boobs, the glasses on top. Finish. That's me. The only good thing was that the hips were wide. So that thirty eight was thirty eight also in hips.

All the things you can't imagine that I couldn't wear. You cannot go without a bra on. The funny little skimpy tops with just a little strap that every teenager had on. I couldn't wear them because I'd have this massive bra strap. The fact that my older sister Kemi had a large bust didn't really help because hers wasn't as big as mine. She was thirty six, which is still human. I was thirty eight. This could have been the reason why I got a lot of unwelcome attention. At least that what my friends, my really catty friends at university used to say to me: 'It's the boobs'.

BISI: RACISM IN OUR FAMILIES OF ORIGIN OR NOWHERE TO HIDE

Racism is most difficult to swallow when it is dished out by members of one's own family. Here, Bisi, who is Yemi's younger sister, talks about how she coped with her own White English mother's racism:

A lot of the modern consciousness I have of being African and being Black, which is not the same thing, is probably in spite of my mother. Being Black in the sense that I feel now, that would be in spite of her. It's not something she agrees with. But you must remember that when she went to Nigeria she was in her twenties. She spent her formative years there, not here. She has very little knowledge of how racism operates and how it affects people – American, Caribbean, and African. The sort of feeling that there is the unity there, consciousness. One can get something from it and one owes something to it. She would say things like, 'Why do you want to put yourself on the side of those who are feeling victimized? Put yourself on the winning side.' She would stress this to us very much that we have an English family and English roots, and some heritage from them as well which is bannered. It's funny though, when I started relaxing about it and owning that there is quite a lot of English in me basically. When I could come up with that admission, then that's almost when I started making Mbari.[10] And really finding that, yes, there is a lot of English, but there is also a lot of African.

BEGINNINGS BY WAY OF CONCLUDING REMARKS

Overall, the six *métisse griottes'* rememberances, located in both colonial and postcolonial contexts, shed light on the complexities of African and African Caribbean Diasporic social and cultural life too often distorted by historians. They also successfully re-frame much of the racially polarized and essentialized negativity which usually dominates most depictions of our lived experiences. Their transnational identities represent both their family constellations as well as their individual experiences. These transnationalities challenge the very notion of the English-African Diaspora as a static and unitary formation, one which obviates cultural, national ethnic, regional, and class differences, among others and, of course, ignores inter-racial collaborations.

By naming their gendered, class-bound, regionally specific and generation-centred experiences as those of *métisse* women, the *griottes'* personal stories become political testimonies. They re-insert themselves as active subjects, creating their own place in the re-telling of English-African Diaspora histories. A mosaic of cultures and histories is emblematic of their multiple reference points. This multicultural and diachronic scheme reflects and cannot be separated from the complex realities of all postcolonial, transnational people in the English-African Diaspora.

Akousa, Sarah, Ruby, Similola, Yemi and Bisi are all products of history, the by-products of colonialism and imperialism. Their Black fathers are from Nigeria, and Barbados formerly under British colonial rule, as well as Tanzania, formerly under the auspices of Germany. Their White mothers are Irish, English, and German. The unresolved postcolonial struggles between Africa and Europe, Blackness and Whiteness, Black man and White woman are all permanently inscribed on the faces of these *métisse* daughters.

ACKNOWLEDGEMENTS

Eternal gratitude to Akousa, Sarah, Ruby, Similola, Yemi and Bisi without whose powerful testimonies my ideas would have existed as mere theoretical abstractions. My thanks also to the other sixteen women and men who participated in the original research project. Thank you also to Rohit Barot, Steve Fenton and Harriet Bradley who provided useful editorial assistance on earlier drafts of this chapter.

NOTES

1. The irrational principle underpinning racial classification in England wherein one is subjectively codified as either 'Black' or 'White' and never the twain shall meet.
2. Using 'ethnic' categories, the 1991 government census attempted to quantify the number of 'non-White' people in Britain. According to 1991 figures from the Office of Population Censuses and Surveys, in Bristol, out of a total population of 376, 146 'ethnic minorities' constitute 3.6 per cent and the 'Other' category, which may include *métis(se)* people, comprises 1.6 per cent. However, the categorization scheme was flawed in its conflation of race, ethnicity, and nationality and discriminatory in its homogenization of peoples from continental Africa and the Caribbean. This classification system is even more problematic and thus inaccurate in its attempt to quantify multiple generations of *métis(se)* people in Britain. With specific reference to *métis(se)* individuals, see Ifekwunigwe (1997a) for a full discussion of the 1991 census's failed attempts to make objective what is ostensibly a subjective signifier. Also, see Phoenix and Owen (1996) and Owen (1996) for additional critiques of the 1991 census in relation to the *métis(se)* community. Incidentally, as a postcript, the year 2001 census is said to include two new categories 'Black British' and 'Mixed Ethnic'. In the United

States, *métis(se)* individuals are lobbying for a 'Multiethnic' category on their year 2000 census.

3.   A textual strategy which enables me to acknowledge and work with inherent tensions in ethnography between the spoken and the written word. *Griot(te) – griot* (m) and *griotte* (f) is a West African term which describes someone who functions as a tribal poet, storyteller, historian or genealogist. Their role is to recount culturally specific and provocative parables of daily life. In traditional society, these individuals were part of a caste and learned their craft on an apprenticeship basis. Social change has impacted this institution.

4.   The English-African Diaspora conventionally comprises post-Columbian African constituents from the Caribbean, North and Latin America, and continental Africa who find themselves in England for labour, schooling, political asylum and frequently by birth. See Jones, L. (1994) *Bulletproof Diva*, New York: Doubleday; Camper, C. (ed.) (1994) *Miscegenation Blues*, Toronto: Sister Vision; No Collective (1992) *Voices of Rage, Identity and Deliverance*, Berkeley, California: No Press; Maja-Pearce, A. (1990) *How Many Miles to Babylon*, London: Heinemann; Opitz, M. (1991) *Showing Our Colours*, Amherst: Univ. of Mass. Press for examples of *métis(se)* narratives of identities as cultural critique and sociopolitical commentary.

5.   In keeping with Gates (1985) among others, I have placed 'race' in quotations to acknowledge the fact that it is a fictional and problematic social and cultural construction and not a biological concept.

6.   This signals the complex cultural identities of *métis(se)* people, myself – Nigerian-Irish-English-Guyanese – included, whose parentage provides us with access to multiple and over-lapping ethnic affiliations.

7.   A Rastafarian – members of a religious group (often referred to as a 'cult') which originated in Jamaica and who reject western ideas and values ('Babylon') and regard Haile Selassie the former emperor of Ethiopia as divine.

8.   That is coming to terms with one's Blackness in a way that the *métis(se)* person starts with her or his cultural foundations and builds forward without having to sever ties with their often White English roots.

9.   For the British context, see Tizard and Phoenix (1993) *Black White, or Mixed Race?*, London: Routledge; Alibhai-Brown and Montague (1992) *The Colour of Love*, London: Virago; Wilson, A. (1987) *Mixed Race Children*, London: Allen and Unwin; Benson, S. (1981) *Ambiguous Ethnicity*, Cambridge: Cambridge Univ. Press. For comparative American examples, see Root, M. (ed.) (1992) *Racially Mixed People in America*, Newbury Park, CA: Sage; Spickard, P. (1989) *Mixed Blood*, Madison, WI, Univ. of Wisconsin; Zack, N. (1993) *Race and Mixed Race*, Philadelphia: Temple Univ; Funderburg, L. (1994) *Black, White, Other*, New York: William and Morrow.

10. An Ibo art form primarily practiced in Eastern Nigeria. The artist erects shrines to placate the Earth goddess.

Bibliography

Abrahamd, R. D. and Szwed, J. F. (1975) *Discovering Afro-America*, Leiden: Brill.

Afshar, H. (1994) 'Muslim Women in West Yorkshire', in H. Afshar and M. Maynard (eds), *The Dynamics of 'Race' and Gender: Some Feminist Interventions*.

Afshar, H. and Maynard, M. (eds), (1994) *The Dynamics of 'Race' and Gender: Some Feminist Interventions*, London: Taylor and Francis.

Ahmed, L. (1992) *Women and Gender in Islam – Historical Roots of a Modern Debate*, New Haven: Yale University Press.

Alibhai-Brown, Y. and Montague, A. (1992) *The Colour of Love: Mixed Race Relationships*, London: Virago.

Allen, S. (1994) 'Race, Ethnicity and Nationality: Some Questions of Identity', in H. Afshar and M. Maynard, (eds) *The Dynamics of 'Race' and Gender: Some Feminist Interventions*.

Altekar, A. S. (1956) *The Position of Women in Hindu Civilization From Prehistoric Times to the Present Day*, Delhi: Motilal Banarsidass.

Anderson, B. (1992) *Imagined Communities. Reflections on the Origin and Spread of Nationalism*, London and New York: Verso.

Anderson, B. (1993) *Britain's Secret Slaves*, Anti-Slavery International.

Anderson, B. and Phizacklea, A. (1997) *Migrant Domestic Workers: A European Perspective, Final Report Submitted to Equal Opportunities Unit*, European Commission: DGV.

Andrups, J. and Kalve, V. (1954) *Latvian Literature: Essays*, Stockholm: Golden Apple Tree Press.

Ang-Lygate, M. (1996) 'Women who Move: Experiences of Diaspora', in M. Maynard and J. Purvis (eds), *New Frontiers in Women's Studies: Knowledge, Ethnicity and Nationalism*.

Anthias, F. and Yuval-Davis, N. (1992) *Racialized Boundaries: Race, Nation, Gender, Colour and Class and the Anti-Racist Struggle*, London: Routledge.

Anwar, M. (1979) *The Myth of Return – Pakistanis in Britain*, London: Heinemann.

Anwar, M. (1981) *Between Two Cultures*, London: CRE.

Anwar, M. (1982) *Young Muslims in a Multi-cultural Society: Their Educational and Policy Implications: The British Case*, Leicester: The Islamic Foundation.

Anzaldua, G. (1987) *Borderlands/La Frontera: The New Mestiza*, San Francisco: Spinsters, Aunt Lute.

Appiah, K. A. (1992) 'In My Father's House: Africa', in *The Philosophy of Culture*, New York: Oxford University Press.

Archer, M. (1995) *Realist Social Theory: the Morphogenetic Approach*, Cambridge: Cambridge University Press.

Ardener, S. (1995) 'Women Making Money Go Round: Roscas Revisited', in S. Ardener and S. Burman (eds), *Money-Go-Rounds*.

Ardener, S. and Burman, S. (eds) (1995) *Money-Go-Rounds: The Importance of Rotating Savings and Credit Associations for Women*, Oxford: Berg.

223

Athavale, P. (1986) *Hindu Widow: An Autobiography*, New Delhi: Reliance Publishing House.

Avan, G. (1995) *Perceived Health Needs of Black and Ethnic Minority Women: An Exploratory Study*, Glasgow Healthy City Project.

Back, L. (1996) *New Ethnicities and Urban Culture*, London: UCL Press.

Bailey, F. G. (1971) 'The Management of Reputations and the Process of Change', in F. G. Bailey (ed.), *Gifts and Poisons: the Politics of Reputation*.

Bailey, F. G. (ed.) (1971) *Gifts and Poisons: the Politics of Reputation*, Oxford: Blackwell.

Ballard, C. (1979) 'Conflict, Continuity and Change: Second-Generation South Asians', in V. Saifullah-Khan (ed.) *Minority Families in Britain: Support and Stress*.

Ballard, R. (1990) 'Migration and Kinship: the Differential Effect of Marriage Rules on the Processes of Migration to Britain', in C. Clarke *et al.* (eds), *South Asians Overseas*, Cambridge: Cambridge University Press.

Ballard, R. (1993) 'The Politicisation of Religion in Punjab: 1849–1991', in R. Barot (ed), *Religion and Ethnicity: Minorities and Social Change in the Metropolis*.

Ballard, R. (ed.) (1994) *Desh Pardesh: The South Asian Presence in Britain*, London: Hurst and Company.

Banerji, B. N. (1979) *Hindu Culture, Custom and Ceremony*, Delhi: Agam, Kala Prakasham.

Banton, M. (1967) *Race Relations*, New York: Basic Books.

Banton, M. (1983) *Racial and Ethnic Competition*, Cambridge: Cambridge University Press.

Barot, R. (ed.) (1993) *Religion and Ethnicity: Minorities and Social Change in the Metropolis*, Kampen: Kok Pharos Publishing House.

Barot, R. (ed.) (1996) *The Racism Problematic: Contemporary Sociological Debates on Race and Ethnicity*, Lampeter: Edwin Mellen Press.

Barth, F. (1969) *Ethnic Groups and Boundaries: The Social Organization of Culture Difference*, Boston: Little Brown and Co.

Barton, R. (1987) *The Scarlet Thread: An Indian Woman Speaks*, London: Virago.

Bayly, C. A. (1981) 'From Ritual to Ceremony: Death, Ritual and Society in Hindu North India since 1600', in J. Whalley (ed.), *Mirrors of Mortality: Studies in the Social History of Death*.

Benson, S. (1981) *Ambiguous Ethnicity. Interracial Families in London*, Cambridge: Cambridge University Press.

Benstock, S. (ed.) (1986) *The Private Self. Theory and Practice of Women's Autobiographical Writings*, Chapel Hill and London: North Carolina Press.

Bernstein, B. and Brannen, J. (eds) (1996) *Children, Research and Policy*, London: Taylor and Francis.

Besson, J. (1993) 'Religion as Resistance in Jamaican Peasant Life: The Baptist Church, Revival Worldview and Rastafari Movement,' in B. Chevannes (ed.), *Rastafari and Other Caribbean Worldviews*.

Besson, J. (1995) 'Women's use of Roscas in the Caribbean: Reassessing the Literature' in, S. Ardener and S. Burman (eds), *Money-Go-Rounds: the Importance of Rotating Savings and Credit Associations for Women*.

Bhabha, H. (1990) 'The Third Space', in J. Rutherford (ed.), *Identity, Community, Culture and Difference*.

Bhabha, H. (1994) *The Location of Culture*, London: Routledge.

Bhabha, H. K. (1996) 'Culture's In-Between', in S. Hall and P. du Gay (eds), *Questions of Cultural Identity*.

Bhabha, J. and Shutter, S. (1994) *Women's Movement: Women Under Immigration Nationality and Refugee Law*, Stoke-on-Trent: Trentham Books.

Bhabha, J., Klug, F. and Shutter, S. (eds) (1985) *Worlds Apart: Women Under Immigration and Nationality Law*, London: Pluto Press.

Bhachu, P. (1985) *Twice Migrants – East African Settlers in Britain*, London: Tavistock.

Bhopal, K. (1996) *The Position of South Asian Women in Households in the UK*, Unpublished PhD Thesis, Department of Sociology, University of Bristol.

Bijnaar, A. (1996) *Broko anu n'e gi: Surinaamse Onderlinges*, research report, Amsterdam School for Social Science Research.

Borjas, G. (1990) *Friends or Strangers: The Impact of Immigrants on the US Economy*, New York: Basic Books.

Bourne, J. (1980) 'Cheerleaders and Ombudsmen: The Sociology of Race Relations in Britain', *Race and Class*, vol. 8, no. 4: 331–51.

Boyce-Davies, C. (1994) *Black Women, Writing and Identity*, London: Routledge.

Boyd, M. (1989) 'Family and Personal Networks in International Migration: Recent Developments and New Agendas', *International Migration Review*, vol. 23, no. 3: 638–70.

Bradby, H. (1993), 'Mums, marriage and misery: what do social support and the family mean to young women of South Asian background in Glasgow? Paper presented at Ethnicity, the Family and Social Change, conference of the Centre for the Study of Minorities and Social Change, University of Bristol, September.

Bradley, H. (1996) *Fractured Identities*, Cambridge: Polity.

Bradley, H. (1997) 'Gender and Change in Employment: Feminization and its Effects', in R. Brown (ed.), *The Changing Shape of Work*.

Bradley, H. and Fenton, S. (1999) 'Reconciling Culture and Economy: Ways Forward in the Analysis of Ethnicity and Gender', in L. Ray and A. Sayer (eds), *Culture and Economy*, London: Sage.

Brah, A. (1978) 'South Asian Teenagers in Southall: Their Perceptions of Marriage, Family and Ethnic Identity', *New Community*, vol. 6, no. 3: 197–209.

Brana-Shute, R. (1978) 'Women, Clubs and Politics: The Case of a Lower- class Neighbourhood in Paramaribo', *Urban Anthropology*, vol. 5, no 2: 157–85.

Brown, J. (1970) *The Un-melting Pot*, London: Macmillan.

Brown, P., MacIntyre, M., Morpeth, R. and Prendergast, S. (1981) 'A daughter: A Thing to be Given Away', in Cambridge Women's Studies Goup, *Women in Society*.

Brown, R. (ed.) (1997) *The Changing Shape of Work*, London: Macmillan.

Buck, E. (1993) *Paradise Remade*, Philadelphia: Temple University Press.

Buiks, P. E. J. (1983) *Surinaamse jongeren op de Kruiskade: overleven in een etnische rand groep*, Deventer: Van Loghum Slaterus.

Buschkens, W. F. L. (1974) *The Family System of the Paramaribo Creoles*, Verhandelingen van het Koninklijk Instituut voor Taal-, Land-en Volkenkunde's Gravenhage.

Cambridge Women's Studies Goup, (1981) *Women in Society*, London: Virago.

Campbell, J. K. (1964) *Honour, Family and Patronage. A Study of Institutions and Moral Values in a Greek Mountain Community*, Oxford: Clarendon Press.

Camper, C. (ed.) (1994) *Miscegenation Blues: Voices of Mixed Race Women*, Toronto: Sister Vision.

Carby, H. (1982) 'White Women Listen: Black Feminism and the Boundaries of Sisterhood', in *The Empire Strikes Back: Race and Racism in 70s Britain*, Centre for Contemporary Cultural Studies.

Castells, M. (1975) 'Immigrant Workers and Class Struggles in Advanced Capitalism: the Western European Experience', *Politics and Society*, vol. 5, no. 1: 33–66.

Castles, S. and Kosack, G. (1973) *Immigrant Workers and Class Structure in Western Europe*, London: Institute of Race Relations.

Castles, S. and Miller, M. (1993) *The Age of Migration*, London: Macmillan.

Cave, T. (1988) *Recognitions: A Study in Poetics*, Oxford: Clarendon Press.

Centre for Contemporary Cultural Studies, (1982) *The Empire Strikes Back: Race and Racism in 70s Britain*, London: Hutchinson.

Chadha, P. N. (1978 [1974]) *Hindu Law*, 4th edn, Lucknow: Eastern Book Co.

Chant, S and McIlwaine, C. (1995) *Women of a Lesser Cost*, Pluto: London.

Chen, M. and Dreze, J. (1992) *Widows and Well-Being in Rural North India*, No. 40, The Development Economics Research Programme, London School of Economics.

Chevannes, B. (ed.) (1993) *Rastafari and Other Caribbean Worldviews*, London: Macmillan.

Clancy, K. (1997) 'Academic as Anarchist: Working-Class Lives into Middle-Class Culture', in P. Mahony and C. Zmroczek (eds), *Class Matters: Working-Class Women's Perspectives on Class*.

Cleaver, E. (1970) *Soul on Ice*, London: Panther.

Clifford, J. and Marcus, G. F. (1986) *Writing Culture*, Berkeley/ Los Angeles/ London: University of California Press.

Cohen, A. (1969) *Custom and Politics in Urban Africa*, London: Routledge.

Cohen, A. (ed.) (1974) *Urban Ethnicity*, London: Tavistock Publications.

Cohen, A. P. (1996) 'Anthropology is a Generalising Science. Against the Motion' in T. Ingold, *Key Debates in Anthropology*.

Cohen, R. (1995) 'Fuzzy Frontiers of Identity: The British Case', *Social Identities*, vol. 1, no. 1: 35–62.

Cohen, R. (ed.) (1996) *Theories of Migration*, Cheltenham: Edward Elgar.

Collins French Dictionary, 2nd edn, (1987) London: Collins.

Collins, S. (1957) *Coloured Minorities in Britain*, Guildford: Lutterworth Press.

Collinson D., Collinson M. and Knights, D. (1990) *Managing to Discriminate*, London: Routledge.

Community Relations Commission (1978) *Five Views of Multi-Racial Britain*, London: CRE.

Connerton, P. (1989) *How Societies Remember*, Cambridge: Cambridge University Press.

Cornwall, A. and Lindisfarne, N. (eds) (1994) *Dislocating Masculinity*, London: Routledge.

Coupland, N. and Nussbaum, J. F. (1993) *Discourse and Life-Span Identity*, Newbury Park: Sage.

Crompton, R. and Sanderson, K. (1990) *Gendered Jobs and Social Change*, London: Unwin Hyman.

Crook, N. (ed.) (1996) *The Transmission of Knowledge in South Asia*, Delhi: Oxford University Press.

Cross, M. and Entzinger, H. (1988) *Lost Illusions: Caribbean Minorities in Britain and the Netherlands*, London: Routledge.

Crummell, A. (1862) *The Future of Africa*, Detroit: Negro Press.

Dandavate, P. and Verguese, J. (eds) (1989) *Widows, Abandoned and Destitute Women in India*, New Delhi: Radiant Publishers.

Das, V. and Ashis, N. (1987) 'Violence, Victimhood and the Language of Silence' in V. Das *The Word and the World. Fantasy, Symbol and Record*.

Das, V. (1987) *The Word and the World. Fantasy, Symbol and Record*, New Delhi: Sage.

Datta, V. N. (1988) *Sati: A Historical, Social and Philosophical Enquiry into the Hindu Rite of Widow Burning*, New Delhi: Manohar Publications.

Day, B. (1974) *Sexual Life Between Blacks and Whites*, London: Collins.

Dent, G. (1992) *Black Popular Culture*, New York: Dia Center for the Arts.

Derrett, C. A. (1970) *Critique of Modern Hindu Law*, Bombay: N.H. Tripathi.

Diwan, P. (1984), *Hindu Customary Law*, 2nd edn, Chandigarh: Punjab University Publication Bureau.

Dhingra, L. (1988) *Amritvela*, London: Women's Press.

Diop, C. (1991) *Civilisation or Barbarism*, Chicago: Lawrence Hill.

Diop, S. (1992) Personal communication.

Diop, S. (1995) 'The Oral History and Literature of the Wolof People of Waalo, Northern Senegal: The Master of the Work (Griot)' in *The Wolof Tradition*, Lampeter: Edwin Mellen Press.

Donald, J. and Rattansi, A. (eds) (1992) *'Race', Culture and Difference*, London: Sage.

Dreze, J, (1990) *Widows in Rural India*, No. 26, The Development Economics Programme, London School of Economics.

Dubois, Abbe J. A. (1906) *Hindu Manners, Customs and Ceremonies*, translated by H. K. Beauchamp, Oxford: Clarendon Press, 3rd edn.

Du Gay, P. (1996) *Consumption and Identity at Work*, London: Sage.

Dunlop, A. and Miles, R. (1990) 'Recovering the History of Asian Migration to Scotland', *Immigrants and Minorities*, vol. 9, no. 2: 145–67.

Eagleton, T. (1996) *The Illusions of Post-Modernism*, Oxford: Blackwell.

Eck, D. L. (1983) *Banaras: City of Light*, London: Routledge and Kegan Paul.

Ellison, R. (1953) *Shadow and Act*, New York: Vintage.

Equal Opportunities Commission, (1991) *Equality Management*.

Eriksen, T. (1993) *Ethnicity and Nationalism*. London: Pluto.

Evans, D. (1988) *International Families and the Law*, Bristol: Jordan and Sons.

Evans, P. (1971) *The Attitudes of Young Immigrants*, London: The Runnymede Trust.

Evison, G. (1989) *Indian Death Rituals: The Enactment of Ambivalence*, unpublished DPhil thesis, Oxford.

Ezergailis, A. (1974) *The 1917 Revolution in Latvia*, Boulder, CO: East European Monographs, No. 8.

Fanon, F. (1967) *Black Skin, White Masks*, New York: Grove.

Featherstone, M., Lash S. and Robertson R. (eds) (1995) *Global Modernities*, London: Sage.

Feher, M., Naddaff, R. and Tazi, N. (eds) (1989) *Fragments for a History of the Human Body*, Part 2, New York: Urzone Inc.

Fenton, S. (1996) 'The Subject is Ethnicity', in R. Barot (ed.), *The Racism Problematic: Contemporary Sociological Debates on Race and Ethnicity*.

Fenton, S. (1999) *Ethnicity: Racism, Modernity, Culture, Structure*, London: Macmillan.

Fentress, J. and Wickham, C. (1992) *Social Memory*, Oxford: Blackwell.

Ferrier, J. (1985) *De Surinamers*, Muiderberg: Coutinho.

Firth, S. (1988) 'Asian women and Changing Marriage Patterns', in *World Religions in Education: Women in Religion*, London: Shap.

Firth, S. (1994) *Death, Dying and Bereavement in a British Hindu Community*, unpublished PhD thesis, School of Oriental and African Studies, London.

Firth, S. (1996) 'The Good Death: Attitudes of British Hindus', in P. Jupp and G. Howard, (eds), *Contemporary Issues in the Sociology of Death, Dying and Disposal*.

Firth, S. (1997) *Death, Dying and Bereavement in a British Hindu Community*, Leuven: Peeters.

Fryer, P. (1984) *Staying Power: The History of Black People in Britain*, London: Pluto Press.

Funderberg, L. (1994) *Black, White, Other*, New York: William and Morrow.

Gandhi, M. (1958) *Women*, Ahmedabad: Navjivan Publishing House.

Gates, H. L. (ed.) (1985) *'Race', Writing and Difference*, Chicago: University of Chicago Press.

Geertz, C. (1993) *The Interpretation of Cultures*, London: Fontana Press, first published New York: Basic Books, 1973.

Gergen M. M. and Gergen, K. J. (1993) 'Autobiographies and the Shaping of Gendered Lives' in N. Coupland and J. F. Nussbaum, *Discourse and Life-Span Identity*.

Gibbs, J. (1989) 'Biracial Adolescence', in J. Gibbs, (ed.), *Children of Color*.

Gibbs, J. (ed.) (1989) *Children of Color*, San Francisco: Jossey Bass.

Giddens, A. (1984) *The Constitution of Society*, Cambridge: Polity Press.

Gikandi, S. (1987) *Reading the African Novel*, London: James Currey.

Giles, W. and Arat-Koc, S. (1994) *Maid in the Market*, Halifax, Canada: Fernwood Publishing.

Gillespie, J. (1992) 'Maintenance and Accommodation and the Immigration Rules: Recent Developments', *Immigration and Nationality Law and Practice*, vol. 6, no. 3: 97–100.

Gilroy, P. (1987) *There Ain't no Black in the Union Jack*, London: Routledge.

Gilroy, P. (1992) 'Cultural Studies and Ethnic Absolutism', in L. Grossberg *et al.*, (eds), *Cultural Studies*.

Gilroy, P. (1993a) *Small Acts: Thoughts on the Politics of Black Culture*, London: Serpent's Tail.

Gilroy, P. (1993b) *The Black Atlantic: Modernity and Double Consciousness*, London: Verso.

Glazer, N. and Moynihan, D. P. (1975) *Ethnicity: Theory and Experience*. London: Harvard University Press.

Goffman, E. (1959) *The Presentation of Self in Everyday Life*, New York: Doubleday.

Gordon, L. R. (1995) 'Critical Mixed Race?', *Social Identities*, vol. 1, no. 2: 381–95.

Goss, J. and Lindquist, B. (1995) 'Conceptualising International Labor Migration: A Structuration Perspective', *International Migration Review*, vol. 29, no. 2: 317–51.

Gossett, T. (1965) *Race: The History of An Idea In America*, New York: Schocken Books.

Gowricharn, R. S. (1990) *Economische Transformatie en de Staat*, Den Haag: Ruward.

Grasmuck, S. and Pessar, P. (1991) *Between Two Islands: Dominican International Migration*, University of California Press.

Gray, B. (1996) "The Home of our Mothers and Our Birthright for Ages"? Nation, Diaspora and Irish Women', in M. Maynard and J. Purvis (eds), *New Frontiers in Women's Studies*.

Gregson, N. and Lowe, M. (1994) *Servicing the Middle Classes: Class, Gender and Waged Domestic Labour in Contemporary Britain*, London: Routledge.

Grossberg, L. *et al.*, (eds) (1992) *Cultural Studies*, London: Routledge.

Grove, K. (1990) *Burning Flesh*, New Delhi: Vikas Publications.

Gunew, S. and Yeatman, A. (eds) (1993) *Feminism and the Politics of Difference*, St Leonards, Australia: Allen and Unwin.

Gupta, A. R. (1982) *Women in Hindu Society: A Study of Tradition and Transition*, New Delhi: Jyotsna Prakashan.

Gusdorf, G. (1980) 'Conditions and Limits of Autobiography:' in G. Gusdorf (ed.), *Essays Theoretical and Critical*.

Gusdorf, G. (ed.) (1980) *Essays Theoretical and Critical*, Princeton University Press.

Haizlip, S. (1994) *The Sweeter the Juice: A Family Memoir in Black and White*, New York: Simon and Schuster.

Halbwachs, M. (1981 [1950]) *The Collective Memory*, New York and Cambridge: Harper Row.

Hall, B. (1996) 'Black Skin, Blue Eyes and Muslin', *Soundings*, vol. 1, no. 3: 161–4.

Hall, S. (1990) 'Cultural Identity and Diaspora', in J. Rutherford (ed.), *Identity, Community, Culture and Difference*.

Hall, S. (1992) 'New Ethnicities', in J. Donald and A. Rattansi (eds), *'Race', Culture and Difference*.

Hall, S. and du Gay, P. (eds) (1996) *Questions of Cultural Identity*, London: Sage.

Hann, C. (ed.) (1994) *When History Accelerates*, London: Athlone Press.

Hannerz, U. (1975) 'Research in the Black Ghetto' in R. D. Abrahamd and J. F. Szwed, *Discovering Afro-America*.

Hawley, J. S. (ed.) (1984) *The Burning of Wives in India*, Oxford: Oxford University Press.

Hawley, J. S. (ed.) (1994) *Sati, The Blessing and the Curse: the Burning of Wives in India*, Oxford: Oxford University Press.

Helman, A. (1978) *Facetten van de Surinaamse Samenleving*, Zutphen: Walburg Pers.

Henriques, F. (1975) *Children of Conflict: A Study of Interacial Sex and Marriage*, New York: Dutton.

Herskovits, M. (1958) *The Myth of the Negro Past*, Boston: Beacon Press.

Herskovits, M. J. and Herskovits, F. S. (1969 [1936]) *Suriname Folklore*, New York: AMS Press.

Hiden, J. and Salmon, P. (1991) *The Baltic Nations and Europe. Estonia, Latvia and Lithuania in the Twentieth Century*, London and New York: Longman.

Hiro, D. (1991) *Black British White British: A History of Race Relations in Britain*, London: Grafton Books.

Hondagneu-Sotelo, P. (1994) *Gendered Transitions*, Berkeley: University of California Press.

hooks, b. (1992) *Black Looks: Race and Representation*, London: Turnaround.

Hoolt, J. (1988) *De Amsterdammers in Zeven Bevolkingscategorieën*, Amsterdam: Administrative Information.

Hope, N. (1994) 'Interwar Statehood: Symbol and Reality' in G. Smith (ed.), *The Baltic States. The National Self-determination of Estonia, Latvia and Lithuania*.

Husband, C. (ed.) (1982) *Race in Britain: Continuity and Change*, London: Hutchinson.

Ifekwunigwe, J. (1997a) 'Diaspora's Daughters, Africa's Orphans? On Lineage, Authenticity, and Mixed Race Identity', in H. Mirza, (ed.), *Black British Feminism*.

Ifekwunigwe, J. (1997b) 'Metisse Narratives', *Soundings*, vol. 1, no. 5: 95–110.

Ifekwunigwe, J. (forthcoming) *Scattered Belongings: Cultural Paradoxes of 'Race', Nation and Gender*, London: Routledge.

Ingold, T. (1996) *Key Debates in Anthropology*, London: Routledge.

Jacobson, J. (1997) 'Religion and Ethnicity: Dual and Alternative Sources of Identity Among Young British Pakistanis', *Ethnic and Racial Studies*, vol. 20, no. 2: 238–56.

James, A. (1974) *Sikh Children in Britain*, London: Oxford University Press.

Jeffery, P. (1976) *Migrants and Refugees – Muslim and Christian Pakistani Families in Bristol*, Cambridge: Cambridge University Press.

Jeffery, P., Jeffery, R. *et al.*, (1988) *Labour Pains and Labour Power*, London: Zed Books.

Jegede, T. (1994) *African Classical Music and the Griot Tradition*, London: Goodwin Press.

Jenkins, R. (1986) *Racism and Recruitment: Managers, Organisations and Equal Opportunities in the Labour Market*, Cambridge: Cambridge University Press.

Jenkins, R. (1997) *Rethinking Ethnicity, Arguments and Explorations*, Sage: London.

Jewson, N. and Mason. D. (1986) 'Modes of Discrimination in the Recruitment Process: Formalisation, Fairness and Efficiency', *Sociology*, vol. 19, no. 1: 43–59.

Jones, J. P., Nast, H. and Roberts, S. (1997) *Thresholds in Feminist Geography*, Lanham, MD: Rowman and Littlefield.

Jones, L. (1994) *Bulletproof Diva: Tales of Race, Sex and Hair*, New York: Doubleday.

Jupp, P. and Howard, G. (eds) (1996) *Contemporary Issues in the Sociology of Death, Dying and Disposal*, London: Macmillan.

Justice (1993) *The Primary Purpose Rule: A Rule with No Purpose*, London: Justice.

Kagie, R. (1980) *Een gewezen wingewest: Suriname voor en na de staatsgreep*, Baarn: Het Wereldvenster.

Kakar, S. (1981) *The Inner World: A Psycho-Analytic Study of Childhood and Society in India*, Delhi: Oxford University Press.

Kalra, S. (1980) *Daughters of Tradition*, Birmingham: Third World Publications.

Kane, P. V. (1973) *History of the Dharmashastra*, 2nd edn, vol. 4, Poona Bhandarkar Oriental Research Institute.

Kanitkar, H. (1991) 'Heaven Lies Beneath her Feet?: Mother Figures in Selected Indo-Anglian Novels', in S. Nasta (ed.), *Motherlands*.

Kanitkar, H. (1994) 'Real True Boys: Moulding the Cadets of Imperialism', in A. Cornwall and N. Lindisfarne (eds), *Dislocating Masculinity*.

Kanitkar, H. (1996) 'Imaging the Self at the Expense of the Other: Stereotypes in Juvenile Imperialist Fiction on India', in N. Crook (ed.), *The Transmission of Knowledge in South Asia*.

Kay, D. and Miles, R. (1992) *Refugees or Migrant Workers? European Workers in Britain 1946–1951*, London: Routledge and Kegan Paul.

Khan, V. S. (1979) 'Perceptions of a Population: Pakistanis in Britain', *New Community*, vol. 5: 222–9.

Kilis, R. (1996) 'Social Memory as a Constituent of Collective Identity in Latvia: the Case of Deportations', unpublished paper given at the European Institute, LSE, 5th March.

Killingley, D., Menski, W. and Firth, S. (1991) *Hindu Ritual and Society*, Newcastle: S. Y. Killingley.

Killingray, D. (ed.) (1994) *Africans in Britain*, Ilford, Essex: Frank Cass.

King, A. (ed.) (1991) *Culture, Globalization and the World System*, London: Macmillan.

Kings Fund, (1990) *Racial Equality: The Nursing Profession*, London.

Kligman, G. (1988) *The Wedding of the Dead. Ritual Poetics and Popular Culture in Transsylvania*, Berkeley: University of California Press.

Knott, K. (1996) 'Hindu Women, Destiny and Stridharma', *Religion*, vol. 26: 15–35.

Koubaka, H. (1993) Personal communication.

Krishnakumari, N. S. (1988) *Status of Single Women in India (A Study of Spinsters, Widows and Divorcees)*, New Delhi: Uppal Publishing House.

Kruyer, G. J. (1973) *Suriname: Neokolonie in Rijksverband*, Meppel: Boom and Zn.

Kumari, R. (1989) *Brides are Not for Burning: Dowry Victims in India*, New Delhi: Radiant Press.

Kuper, L. (ed.) (1975) *Race, Science and Society*, London: The UNESCO Press/ George Allen and Unwin.

Lagerberg, C. S. I. J. (1974) *Profiel van een Hoofdstad: Paramaribo*. Tilburg: Werkdocument van het Instituut voor Ontwikkelingsvraagstukken, No. 8.

Lal, S. and Wilson, A. (1986) *'But my Cows Aren't Going to England.' A Study in How Families are Divided*, Manchester: Manchester Law Centre.

Langer, L. L. (1991) *Holocaust Testimonies. The Ruins of Memory*, New Haven and London: Yale University Press.

Lawrence, E. (1982) 'In the Abundance of Water the Fool is Thirsty: Sociology and Black "Pathology"', in Centre for Contemporary Cultural Studies, *The Empire Strikes Back: Race and Racism in 70s Britain*.

Layder, D. (1997) *Modern Social Theory*, London: UCL Press.

Lemelle, S. and Kelley, R. (eds) (1994) *Imagining Home: Class, Culture and Nationalism in the African Diaspora*, London: Verso.

Lenders, M. (1984) Van de Rhoer, M. *Mijn God hoe ga ik doen? De positie van Creoolse alleenstaande moeders in Amsterdam*, Amsterdam: SUA.

Leslie, J. (1987/88) 'Suttee or Sati: Victim or Victor?', *Bulletin of the Center for the Study of World Religions*, Harvard University, vol. 14, no. 2: 5–24.

Leslie, J. (1989) *The Perfect Wife: The Orthodox Hindu Woman According to the Stridharmapaddhati of Tryambakayajvan*, Delhi: Oxford University Press.

Leslie, J. (1991a) 'Suttee or Sati: Victim or Victor' in J. Leslie (ed.), *Roles and Rituals for Hindu Women*.

Leslie, J. (ed.) (1991a) *Roles and Rituals for Hindu Women*, London: Pinter.

Leslie, J. (1991b) 'Religion, Gender and Dharma: the Case of the Widow-Ascetic', British Association for the Study of Religion, *Occasional Papers*, No. 4.

Lice, A. (ed.) (1991) *Via Dolorosa*, Riga: Liesma.

LIFE, (1991) *Filipina Migrant Women in Domestic Work in Italy*, Geneva: ILO.

Lionnet, F. (1989) *Anthropological Voices: Race, Gender and Self-Portraiture*, Ithaca, NY: Cornell University Press.

Lison-Tolosana, C. (1966) *Belmonte de los Caballeros: A Sociological Study of a Spanish Town*, Oxford: Clarendon Press.

Little, K. (1972) *Negroes in Britain: Racial Relations in English Society*, London: Routledge.

Lyon, M. (1972) 'Race and Ethnicity in Pluralist Societies: A Comparison of Minorities in the UK and USA', *New Community*, vol. 1, no. 4: 256–62.

Lyon, M. (1972–3) 'Ethnicity in Britain: The Gujarati Tradition', *New Community*, vol. 2, no. 1: 1–11.

Lyon, M. (1973) 'Ethnic Minority Problems: an Overview of Some Recent Research', *New Community*, vol. 2, no. 4, pp. 329–52.

Maan, B. (1992) *The New Scots: The Story of Asians in Scotland*, Edinburgh: John Donald.

Mac an Ghaill, M. (1988) *Young, Gifted and Black*, Milton Keynes: Open University Press.

Macdonald, I. A. and Blake, N. J. (1991) *Immigration Law and Practice in Britain*, 3rd edn, London: Butterworths.

Macdonald, I. A. and Blake, N. J. (1995) *Immigration Law and Practice in Britain*, 4th edn, London: Butterworths.

MacDonald, S. (ed.) (1993) *Inside European Identities*, Oxford: Berg.

Macklin, A. (1994) 'On the Outside Looking In: Foreign Domestic Workers in Canada' in W. Giles and S. Arat-Koc, *Maid in the Market*.

Macleod, W. (1976) *The Evolution of the Sikh Community*, Oxford: Clarendon Press.

Madan, P. N. (1987) *Non-Renunciation: Themes and Interpretations of Hindu Culture*, Oxford: Oxford University Press.

Mainwaring, T. (1984) 'The Extended Internal Labour Market', *Cambridge Journal of Economics*, vol. 8: 161–87.

Mahony, P. and Zmroczek, C. (eds) (1997) *Class Matters: Working-Class Women's Perspectives on Class*, London: Taylor and Francis.

Maja-Pearce, A. (1990) *How Many Miles to Babylon*, London: Heinemann.

Malik, K. (1996) *The Meaning of Race*, London: Macmillan.

Mandelbaum, D. G. (1988) *Women's Seclusion and Men's Honor – Sex Roles in North India, Bangladesh, and Pakistan*, Tucson: University of Arizona Press.

Marcus, G. and Fischer, M. (1986) *Anthropology as Cultural Critique*, Chicago: University of Chicago Press.

Marquet, M. (1983) *Le Métissage Dans La Poesie de Leopold Desor Senghor*, Dakar: Nouvelle Editions Africaines.

Martin, D. (1995) 'The Choices of Identity', *Social Identities*, vol. 1 no. 1: 5–20.

Mason, D. (1995) *'Race' and Ethnicity in Modern Britain*, London and Oxford: Oxford University Press.

Mason, D. and Rex, J. (eds) (1986) *Theories of Race and Ethnic Relations*, Cambridge: Cambridge University Press.

Massey, D. S. *et al.* (1993) 'Theories of International Migration: A Review and Appraisal', *Population and Development Review*, vol. 19, no. 3: 432–66.

McKee, R. (1995) 'A Burden on the Taxpayer? Some Development in the Role of "Public Funds" in Immigration Law', *Immigration and Nationality Law and Practice*, vol. 9, no. 1: 29–31.

Maynard, M. and Purvis, J. (eds) (1996) *New Frontiers in Women's Studies: Knowledge, Ethnicity and Nationalism*, London: Taylor and Francis.

Menon, R. (1984) 'Widows of Varanasi', *India Today*, 15th February.

Menski, W. (1984) *Role and Ritual in the Hindu Marriage*, unpublished PhD thesis, London University (SOAS).

Menski, W. (1987) 'Is there a Customary Form of Widow-Remarriage for Hindus?', *Kerala Law Times*, 69–71.

Menski, W. (1993) 'The Primary Purpose Rule in British Immigration Law and its Impact on Minority Families', paper presented at Ethnicity, the Family and Social Change, Conference of the Centre for the Study of Minorities and Social Change, University of Bristol, September.

Menski, W. (1994) 'Family Migration and the New Immigration Rules', *Immigration and Nationality Law and Practice*, vol. 8, no. 4: 112–24.

Menski, W. (1995a) 'Widow's Right to Property: Prejudices against Remarried Women', in *Manushi*, V.I. 89, July, August.

Menski, W. (ed.) (1995b) *Coping with 1997. The Reaction of the Hong Kong People to the Transfer of Power*, Stoke-on-Trent: Trentham Books and SOAS.

Mercer, K. (1994) *Welcome to the Jungle*, London: Routlege.

Mernissi, F. (1985) *Beyond the Veil: Male-Female Dynamics in Muslim Society*, London: Al Saqi Books.

Mernissi, F. (1991) *The Veil and the Male Elite. A Feminist Interpretation of Women's Rights in Islam*, Addison-Wesley Publishing.

Merridale, C. (1996) 'Death in Twentieth Century Russia', *History Workshop Journal*, vol. 42: 1–18.

Migration News Sheet, (1996/1997), Brussels Migration Policy Group.

Miles, R. (1982) *Racism and Migrant Labour*, London: Routledge and Kegan Paul.

Miles, R. (1993) *Racism after 'Race Relations'*, London: Routledge.

Miles, R. and Phizacklea, A. (1979) *Racism and Political Action in Britain*, London: Routledge.

Minh-Ha, T. (1989) *Women, Native, Other*, Bloomington, IN: University of Indiana Press.

Mintz, S. (1971) 'The Caribbean as a Socio-cultural Area' in M. Horowitz (ed.), *Peoples and Cultures of the Caribbean*, New York: Garden City.

Mirza, H. (1992) *Young, Female and Black*, London: Routledge.

Mirza, H. (ed.) (1997) *Black British Feminism*, London: Routledge.

Mishra, N. (1989) 'The Murder of Roop Kanwar', in P. Dandavate and J. Verguese (eds), *Widows, Abandoned and Destitute Women in India*.

Misiunas, R. and Taagepera, T. (1993) *Baltic States. The Years of Dependence 1940–1980*, revised edn, London: Hurst.

Modood T, (1988) 'Black Racial Equality and Asian Identity', *New Community*, vol. 14, no. 3: 397–404.

Modood, T. (1992) *Not Easy Being British*. Stoke-on Trent: Trentham Books.

Modood, T. *et al.* (eds) (1997) *Ethnic Minorities in Britain; Diversity and Disadvantage*, London: PSI.

Mole, N. (1987) *Immigration: Family Entry and Settlement*, Bristol: Jordan and Sons.

Momsen, J. and Kinnaird, V. (eds) (1993) *Different Places, Different Voices*, London: Routledge.

Morokvasic, M. (1983) 'Women and Migration: Beyond the Reductionist Outlook' in A. Phizacklea (ed.), *One Way Ticket: Migration and Female Labour*.

Morokvasic, M. (1991) 'Fortress Europe and Migrant Women', *Feminist Review*, no. 39, Winter: 69–84.

Morris, L. (1994) *Dangerous Classes*, London: Routledge.

Morrison, T. (1987) *Beloved*, New York: Alfred A. Knopf, Inc.

Morrison, T. (1998) *Paradise*, London: Chatto.

Mosse, G. L. (1996) *The Image of Man. The Creation of Modern Masculinity*, New York and Oxford: Oxford University Press.

Mouzelis, N. (1995) *Sociological Theory: What Went Wrong?*, London: Routledge.

Mudimbe, V. (1988) *The Invention of Africa*, Bloomington, Indiana: Indiana University Press.

Mumford, D. (1993) 'Family Therapy, Ethnic Minority Families and Cultural Transition' a paper presented at the Family, Minorities and Social Change, Conference of the Centre for the Study of Minorities and Social Change, University of Bristol, September.

Nadel-Klein, J. (1995) 'Occidentalism as a Cottage Industry: Representing the Autochthonous "Other" in British and Irish Rural Studies' in J. Carrier (ed.), *Occidentalism: Images of the West*, Oxford: Clarendon Press

Nasta, S. (ed.) (1991) *Motherlands*, London: Women's Press.

National Ethnic Minority Data Archive (1991) *Ethnic Minorities in Great Britain*, Coventry: University of Warwick.

Nesbitt, E. (1993), 'Children and the World to Come: the Views of Children aged 8 to 14 years on Life after Death', *Religion Today*, 3: 10–14.

Nikolinakos, M. (1975) 'Draft of a General Theory of Migration in Late Capitalism', *Proceedings of International Conference on Migrant Workers*, ICSS, Berlin.

No Collective, (1992) *Voices of Identity, Rage and Deliverance: An Anthology of Writings by People of Mixed Descent*, Berkeley, California: No Press.

O'Brien, O. (1993) 'Good to be French? Conflicts of Identity in North Catalonia' in S. MacDonald (ed.), *Inside European Identities*, Oxford: Berg.

OECD (1995) *SOPEMI, Trends in International Migration*, Paris: OECD.

Office of National Statistics (1996) *Social Focus on Ethnic Minorities*, London: HMSO.

Oguibe, O. (ed.) (1994) *Sojourners: New Writings by Africans in Britain*, London: African Refugee Publishing Collective.

Ojha, C. (1981) 'Feminism Asceticism in Hinduism: Its Tradition and Present Condition', *Man in India*, September: 245–85.

Okamura, J. (1981) 'Situational Ethnicity', *Ethnic and Racial Studies*, vol. 4, no. 4: 452–65.

Opitz, M. *et al.* (eds) (1991) *Showing Our Colors: Afro-German Women Speak Out*, Amherst: University of Massachussetts Press.

Ortner, S. (1995) 'Resistance and the Problem of Ethnographic Refusal', *Comparative Studies of Society and History*, vol. 27: 173–93.

Owen, C. (1996) 'Mixed Parentage and the Census', unpublished paper presented at the Race into the Future Conference, Centre for Research in Ethnic Relations, University of Warwick, 25th June.

Padfield, J. (1908) *The Hindu at Home*, London: Simkin, Marshall, Hamilton, Kent and Co.

Pahl, R. and Thompson, P. (1994) 'Meanings, Myths and Mystifications: The Social Construction of Life Stories in Russia', in C. Hann (ed.), *When History Accelerates*.

Palmié, S. (ed.) (1995) *Slave Cultures and the Cultures of Slavery*, Knoxville: Tennessee University Press.

Pandey, R. B. (1969) *The Hindu Samskaras: Socio-religious Study of the Hindu Sacraments*, Delhi and Varanasi: Motilal Banarsidass.

Parry, J. (1989) 'The End of the Body', in M. Feher, R. Naddaff and N. Tazi (eds), *Fragments for a History of the Human Body*.

Parry, J. (1991) 'On the Inauspiciousness and Impurity of Death', unpublished paper.

Parry, J. (1994) *Death in Banares*, Cambridge: Cambridge University Press.

Parry, J. and Bloch, M. (1989) *Money and the Morality of Exchange*, Cambridge University Press.

Patterson, S. (1963) *Dark Strangers*, Bloomington, IN: Indiana University Press.

Pearl, D. (1986) *Family Law and the Immigrant Communities*, Bristol: Jordan and Sons.

Phizacklea, A. (1982) 'Migrant Women and Wage Labour: The Case of West Indian Women in Britain', in J. West (ed.), *Work, Women and the Labour Market*.

Phizacklea, A. (ed.) (1983) *One Way Ticket: Migration and Female Labour*, Routledge: London.

Phizacklea, A. (1984) 'A Sociology of Migration or "Race Relations"? A View from Britain', *Current Sociology*, vol. 32, no. 3: 199–217.

Phizacklea, A. (1990) *Unpacking the Fashion Industry: Gender, Racism and Class in Production*, London: Routledge.

Phizacklea, A. (1997) 'Sex, Marriage and Maids: Gender and Migration in Southern Europe', paper presented to the Conference on Migration in Southern Europe, Santorini, September.

Phizacklea, A. and Miles, R. (1980) *Labour and Racism*, Routledge: London.

Phizacklea, A. and Wolkowitz, C. (1995) *Homeworking Women*, London: Sage.

Phoenix, A. (1988) 'Narrow Definitions of Culture: The Case of Early Motherhood', in S. Westwood and P. Bachu, *Enterprising Women*.

Phoenix, A. and Owen, C. (1996) 'From Miscegenation to Hybridity: Mixed Relationships and Mixed Parentage in Profile', in B. Bernstein and J. Brannen, (eds), *Children, Research and Policy*.

Pocock, D. (1972) *Kanbi and Patidar: A Study of the Patidar Community of Gujerat*, Oxford: Clarendon Press.

Portes, A. and Bach, R. (1985) *Latin Journey: Cuban and Mexican Immigrants in the US*, Berkeley: University of California Press

Potts, L. (1990) *The World Labour Market*, London: Zed Press.

Pryce, K. (1974) *Endless Pressure*, Bristol: Classical Press.

Puar, J. (1996) 'Resituating Discourses of "Whiteness" and "Asianness" in Northern England: Second-generation Sikh Women and Constructions of Identity', in M. Maynard and J. Purvis (eds), *New Frontiers in Women's Studies*.

Quarles van Ufford, P. and Schoffeleers, M. (eds) (1988) *Religion and Development: Towards an Integrated Approach*, Amsterdam: Free University Press.

Quigley, D. (1993) *The Interpretation of Caste*, Oxford: Clarendon Press.

Radcliffe, S. (1993) 'The Role of Gender in Peasant Migration: Conceptual issues from the Peruvian Andes' in J. Momsen and V. Kinnaird (eds), *Different Places, Different Voices*.

Rao, V. P. and Rao, V. N. (eds) (1982) *Marriage, the Family and Women in India*, New Delhi: Heritage.

Rattray, R. S. (1979 [1929]) *Religion and Art in Ashanti*, New York: AMS Press.

Ray, L. and Sayer, A. (eds) (1999) *Culture and Economy*, London: Sage.

Raza, M. (1991) *Islam in Britain: Past, Present and Future*, Leicester: Volcano Press.

Rex, J. (1993) 'Religion and Ethnicity in the Metropolis', in R. Barot, *Religion and Ethnicity: Minorities and Social Change in the Metropolis*.

Rex, J. (1995) 'Ethnic Identity and the Nation State: the Political Sociology of Multicultural Societies', *Social Identities*, vol. 1, no. 1: 21–34.

Rich, P. (1986) *Race and Empire in British Politics*, Cambridge: Cambridge University Press.

Richmond, A. (1973) *Migration and Race Relations in an English City*, Oxford: Oxford University Press.

Riley, J. (1987) *Waiting in the Twilight*, London: Women's Press.

Roberts, D. (1994) *The Myth of Aunt Jemima: Representations of Race and Region*, New York: Routledge.

Robinson, V. (1980) *Transients, Settlers and Refugees*, Oxford: Clarendon Press.

Root, M. (ed.) (1992) *Racially Mixed People in America*, Newbury Park, CA: Sage.

Ross, A. D. (1961) *The Hindu Family in its Urban Setting*, University of Toronto Press.

Rowlands, M. (1995) 'Looking at Financial Landscapes: a Contextual Analysis of Roscas in Cameroon', in S. Ardener and S. Burman (eds), *Money-Go-Rounds: The Importance of Rotating Savings and Credit Associations for Women*.

Russell, K. *et al.* (1992) *The Color Complex: The Politics of Skin Color Among African Americans*, New York: Anchor.

Rutherford, J. (ed.) (1990) *Identity. Community, Culture and Difference*, London: Lawrence and Wishart.

Sachdeva, S. (1993) *The Primary Purpose Rule in British Immigration Law*, Stoke-on-Trent: Trentham Books.

Said, E. (1994) *Culture and Imperialism*, New York: Vintage.

Saifullah-Khan V. (ed.) (1979) *Minority Families: Support and Stress*, London: Macmillan.

Saifullah-Khan, V. (1982) 'The Role of the Culture of Dominance in Structuring the Experience of Ethnic Minorities', in C. Husband (ed.), *Race in Britain: Continuity and Change*.

Sansone, L. (1992) *Schitteren in de Schaduw: Overlevingsstrategieën, Subcultuur en Etniciteit van Creoolse Jongeren uit de Lagere Klasse in Amsterdam 1981–1990*, Amsterdam: Het Spinhuis.

Saraswati, P. R. (1975) *The High-Caste Hindu Woman*, New Delhi: Sarvadeshik Arya Pratimidhi Sabha.

Saraswati, S. D. (1988) *The Light of Truth*, New Delhi: Sarvadeshik Arya Pratimidhi Sabha.

Sassen-Koob, S. (1984) 'Notes on the Incorporation of Third World Women into Wage-Labour Through Immigration and Off-Shore Production', *International Migration Review*, vol. 18, no. 4: 1144–67.

Scannell, R. (1991) 'Recent Developments in Immigration Law', *Legal Action*, November: 22–3.

Scannell, R. (1992) 'Primary Purpose: The End of Judicial Sympathy', *Immigration and Nationality Law and Practice*, vol. 6, no. 1: 3–6.

Schwarz, B. (ed.) (1996) *The Expansion of England: Race, Ethnicity and Cultural History*, London: Routledge.

Scotland, G. R. O. F. (1993) *1991 Census*, Edinburgh: HMSO.

Scott, J. (1985) *Weapons of the Weak; The Everyday Forms of Peasant Resistance*, New Haven and London: Yale University Press.

Scott, J. (1990) *Domination and the Arts of Resistance: Hidden Transcripts*, New Haven and London: Yale University Press.

Scott, J. (1976) *The Moral Economy of the Peasant: Subsistence and Rebellion in Southeast Asia*, New Haven and London: Yale University Press.

Segal, R. (1995) *The Black Diaspora*, London: Faber and Faber.

Selby, H. and Murphy, A. (1982) 'The Mexican Urban Household and the Decision to Migrate to the US', I.S.H.I. Occasional Papers in Social Change, No. 4, The Institute for the Study of Human Issues, Philadelphia.

Sharma, A. *et al.* (eds) (1988) *Sati: Historical and Phenomenological Essays*, New Delhi: Motilal Banarsidas.

Shaw, A. (1988) *A Pakistani Community in Britain*, Oxford: Blackwell.

Shekhewat, P. S. (1989) 'Sati in Rajasthan', in P. Dandavate and J. Verguese (eds), *Widows, Abandoned and Destitute Women in India*.

Shils, E. (1957) 'Primordial, Personal Sacred and Civil Ties', *British Journal of Sociology*, vol. 8: 130–45.

Shyllon, F. (1977) *Black People in Britain*, Oxford: Oxford University Press.

Singh, I. P. and Singh, R. (1989) 'Sate: its pari-politics', in Dandavate, P. *et. al.*, pp. 54–62.

Skultans, V. (1995) 'Neurasthenia and Political Resistance in Latvia', *Anthropology Today*, vol. 11: 14–18.

Small, S. (1994) *Racialised Barriers*, London: Routledge.

Smith, B. H. (1979) *On the Margins of Discourse: The Relation of Literature to Language*, Chicago and London: University of Chicago Press.

Smith, G. (ed.) (1994) *The Baltic States. The National Self-Determination of Estonia, Latvia and Lithuania*, London: Macmillan.

Speckmann, J. D. (1963) 'De Houding van de Hindostaanse Bevolkingsgroep in Suriname ten Opzichte van de Creolen', *Bijdragen tot de Taal-, Land-en Volkenkunde*, vol. 119: 76–92.

Spencer, S. (ed.) (1994a) *Immigration as an Economic Asset: The German Experience*, Stoke-on-Trent: Trentham Books, and SOAS.

Spencer, S. (ed.) (1994b) *Strangers and Citizens. A Positive Approach to Migrants and Refugees*, London: IPPR and Rivers Oram Press.

Spickard, P. (1989) *Mixed Blood*, University of Wisconsin Press.

Stanford-Friedman, S. (1986) 'Women's Autobiographical Selves', in S. Benstock (ed.), *The Private Self. Theory and Practice of Women's Autobiographical Writings*.

Stark, O. (1984) 'Migration Decision-Making: A Review Article', *Journal of Development Economics*, vol. 14: 251–9.

Stevenson, S. M. (1920) *Rites of the Twice-born*, Oxford: Oxford University Press.

Stevenson, S. M. (1930) *Without the Pale: The Life Story of an Outcaste*, London: Oxford University Press.

Stopes-Roe, M. and Cochrane, R. (1988) 'Marriage in Two Cultures', *British Journal of Social Psychology* vol. 27: 159–69.

Stopes-Roe, M. and Cochrane, R. (1990) *Citizens of this Country: The Asian British*, Clevedon: Multilingual Matters Ltd.

Studelis, E. (1952) 'The Resettlement of Displaced Persons in the United Kingdom', *Population Studies*, vol. 5: 207–37.

Tannahill, J. A. (1958) *European Workers in Britain*, Manchester: Manchester University Press.

Tannen, D. (1991) *You Just Don't Understand: Women and Men in Conversation*, London: Virago.

Taylor, J. (1976) *The Half-Way Generation*, National Foundation for Education Research, Windsor: Nelson.

Thoden van Velzen, H. U. E. and van Wetering, W. (1988) *The Great Father and The Danger: Religious Cults, Material Forces and Collective Fantasies in the World of the Surinamese Maroons*, Leiden: Koninklijk Instituut voor Taal-, Land-en Volkenkunde.

Thompson, M. (1974) 'The Second Generation – Punjabi or English?', *New Community*, vol. 3: 242–8.

Tiano, S. (1994) *Patriarchy on the Line*, Philadelphia: Temple University Press.

Tishkov, V. (1997) *Ethnicity, Nationalism and Conflict in and after the Soviet Union: the Mind Aflame*, London: Sage.

Tizard, B. and Phoenix, A. (1993) *Black, White or Mixed Race*, London: Routledge.

Todaro, M. (1969) 'A Model of Labour Migration and Urban Unemployment in Less Developed Countries', *American Economic Review*, vol. 59: 138–48.

Truong, T. and del Rosario, V. (1994) 'Captive Outsiders: Trafficked Sex Workers and Mail-Order Brides in the European Union' in J. Wiersma (ed.), *Insiders and Outsiders: On the Making of Europe II*.

Tully, M. (1992) *No Full Stops in India*, New Delhi: Penguin Books.

UNESCO (1975) 'Appendix : Four Statements on the Race Question', in L. Kuper (ed.), *Race, Science and Society*, London, the UNESCO Press, George Allen and Unwin, 343–64.

Van Lier, R. A. J. (1971) *Frontier Society; A Social Analysis of the History of Suriname*, The Hague: Martinus Nijhoff.

Van Lier, R. A. J. (1986) *Tropische Tribaden: een Verhandeling over Homosexualiteit en Homosexuele Vrouwen in Suriname*, Dordrecht: Foris.

Van Renselaar, H. C. (1963) 'De Houding van de Creoolse Bevolkingsgroep in Suriname ten Opzichte van Andere Bevolkingsgroepen', *Bijdragen tot de Taal-, Land-en Volkenkunde*, vol. 119: 93–105.

Van Sertima, I. (1976) *They Came Before Columbus*, New York: Random House.

Van Wetering, W. (1987) 'Informal Supportive Networks: Quasi-Kin Groups, Religion and Social Order among Suriname Creoles in the Netherlands, *Sociologia Neerlandica*, vol. 23, no. 2: 92–101.

Van Wetering, W. (1988) 'The Ritual Laundering of Black Money among Suriname Creoles in the Netherlands', in P. Quarles van Ufford and M. Schoffeleers (eds), *Religion and Development: Towards an Integrated Approach*.

Van Wetering, W. (1992) 'Popular Culture and Anthropological Debate: A Case Study in Globalization and Ethnicity', in J. Verrips (ed.), *Transactions: Essays in Honor of Jeremy Boissevain*, Amsterdam: Het Spinhuis.

Van Wetering, W. (1995) 'Transformations of Slave Experience: Self and Danger in the Rituals of Creole Migrant Women in the Netherlands', in S. Palmié (ed.), *Slave Cultures and the Cultures of Slavery*.

Wallman, S. (ed.) (1979) *Ethnicity at Work*, London: Macmillan.

Wallman, S. (1986) 'Ethnicity and the boundary process in context' in D. Mason and J. Rex (eds), *Theories of Race and Ethnic Relations*.

Walsh, V. (1997) 'Interpreting Class: Auto/Biographical Imaginations and Social Change', in P. Mahony and C. Zmroczek (eds), *Class Matters: 'Working-Class' Women's Perspectives on Class*.

Walter, B. (1997) 'Gender, "Race" and Diaspora: Racialized Identities of Emigrant Irish Women', in J. P. Jones, H. Nast and S. Roberts *Thresholds in Feminist Geography*, Lanham, MD: Rowman and Littlefield.

Walvin, J. (1973) *Black and White: The Negro and English Society*, London: Allen Lane.

Watson, J. (ed.) (1977) *Between Two Cultures: Migrants and Minorities in Britain*, Oxford: Blackwell.

Wekker, G. (1994) *Ik ben een Gouden Munt; ik ga door vele handen maar verlies mijn waarde niet: subjectiviteit en seksualiteit van Creoolse volksklasse vrouwen in Paramaribo*, Amsterdam: Vita.

Welsing, F. (1991) *The Isis Papers*, Chicago: Third World Press.

Werbner, P. (1990) *The Migration Process: Capital, Gifts and Offerings Among British Pakistanis*, New York: Berg.

West, J. (ed.) (1982) *Work, Women and the Labour Market*, London: Routledge.

Westwood, S. and Bachu, P. (eds) (1988) *Enterprising Women*, London: Routledge.

Whalley, J. (ed.) (1981) *Mirrors of Mortality: Studies in the Social History of Death*, London: Europa.

White, H. (1987) *The Content of the Form. Narrative Discourse and Historical Representation*, Baltimore and London: Johns Hopkins University Press.

Wiersma, J. (ed.) (1994) *Insiders and Outsiders: On the Making of Europe II*, Kampen: Kok Pharos.

Williams, R., Bhopal, R. *et al.* (1993) 'Health of a Punjabi Ethnic Minority in Glasgow: a Comparison with the General Population', *Journal of Epidemiology and Community Health*, vol. 47: 96–102.

Wilson, A. (1978) *Finding a Voice: Asian Women in Britain*, London: Virago.

Wilson, A. (1987) *Mixed Race Children: A Study of Identity*, London: Allen and Unwin.

Wilson, P. (1973) *Crab Antics: The Social Anthropology of English-Speaking Negro Societies of the Caribbean*, New Haven: Yale University Press.

Wilson, W. J. (ed.) (1993) *The Ghetto Underclass*, London: Sage.

Wolf, E. R. (1882) *Europe and the People Without History*, Berkeley: University of California Press.

Wood, C. H. (1982) 'Equilibrium and Historical Structural Perspectives on Migration', *International Migration Review*, vol. 16, no. 2: 298–319.

Wooding, C. J. (1981) *Evolving Culture: A Cross-Cultural Study of Suriname, West Africa and the Caribbean*, Washington, DC: University Press of America.

Yinger, M. (1981) 'Toward a Theory of Assimilation and Dissimilation', *Ethnic and Racial Studies*, vol. 4, no. 3: 249–64.

Young J. E. (1988) *Writing and Rewriting the Holocaust. Narrative and the Consequences of Interpretation*, Bloomington and Indianapolis: Indiana University Press.

Young, R. (1995) *Colonial Desire: Hybridity in Theory, Culture and Race*, London: Routledge.

Yuval-Davis, N. (1997) *Gender and Nation*. London: Sage.

Zack, N. (1993) *Race and Mixed Race*, Philadelphia: Temple University Press.

Zlotnik, H., (1995) 'The South-to-North Migration of Women', *International Migration Review* vol. 29, no. 1: 229–54.

Index